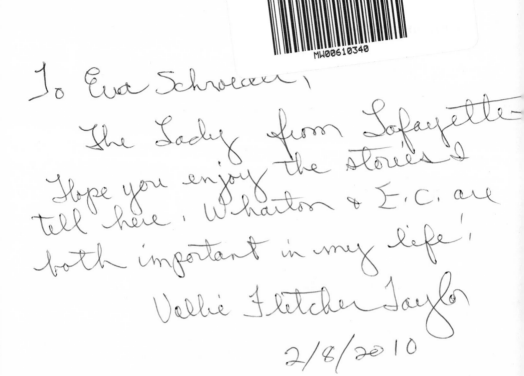

To Eva Schroeder,

The Lady from Lafayette—

Hope you enjoy the stories I tell here. Wharton & E.C. are both important in my life!

Vallie Fletcher Taylor

2/8/2010

EYES

IN THE

ALLEY

Memories of San Antonio

The Great Depression

Vallie Fletcher Taylor

ZUMAYA PUBLICATIONS   AUSTIN TX

2008

EYES IN THE ALLEY

© 2008 by Vallie Fletcher Taylor

ISBN 13: 978-1-934135-34-1

Cover art © François Thisdale

Cover design © Chris Cartwright

The Zumaya Publications colophon is a trademark of Zumaya Publications LLC, 3209 S. Interstate 35, Austin TX.

Look for us online at http://www.zumayapublications.com

Library of Congress Control Number: 2008937635

CONTENTS

DEDICATION

This book is in memory of
my mother

SALLIE ALEEN HAYNES FLETCHER

who believed *lie* and *liar*
were the dirtiest of words and must never be spoken aloud.
Thanks for giving me the courage to write "the truth and nothing but..."
and
of my father

WILLIAM ANDREW FLETCHER II

Generous and loving, with a dry sense of humor,
he taught the meaning of kindness and integrity
with his every word and action.

ACKNOWLEDGMENTS

Special thanks to my friend

JAN WILLIFORD

a former English teacher who bravely read this manuscript
and wrote "What?" in the margin when I got carried away.

To my Revere/Reviere/Riviere cousin in Florida

DONNA OWEN

a skilled genealogist who throws her internet lasso
and catches generations of missing ancestors.

To good friend

MERLENE PARKER WILSON

who took me on a guided tour of my old San Antonio neighborhood
and helped me fill in some empty heart-spaces.

To childhood friends

MARY GWENDOLYN ECHTERHOFF DUGAT
and
BETTY BRENT SCHAEFFLER DUGAL

who listened to my memories and added a few more.

To Beaumont historians and true friends

ELLEN WALKER RIENSTRA, JUDITH WALKER LINSLEY
and
ROBERT ROBERTSON

whose East Texas ancestors kept tripping over mine.

Generations: William Andrew "Bill" Fletcher (top, left), the "Rebel Private," my great-grandfather; WA's daughter Vallie Fletcher I; William Andrew "Bill" Fletcher II, my father; my graduation photo from El Campo High School. People often said they hoped I grew up to look like my mother, but I think it's clear the resemblance is on the other side of the family.

INTRODUCTION

Today, as I walk past any mirror I happen to encounter, I expect to see reflected the image of a young blond girl wearing a giant hair bow held in place by a golden barrette. Instead, an almost perfect replica of my great-aunt Vallie gazes back at me. Most assuredly, it is Aunt Vallie as she was in her elder years and not the glamorous socialite of the late nineteenth century.

I check the back of my hairdo with a hand mirror and realize that every swirl and wave of my swiftly graying hair has emulated the growth patterns of that first Vallie Fletcher's crowning glory.

Yet, I also realize that, somewhere beneath the surface of today's reflection, the little girl whose mother secured taffeta mega hair bows to silky blond hair still lurks. This child loved stories that began with "Once upon a time..."

So...

Once upon a time in south Houston, I found myself surrounded by twelve-year-old history students with inquisitive natures. Their young minds were best served by placing boring textbooks, written by college professors to impress other college professors, on a dusty shelf inside a sizable dark closet. Then, I began telling stories in the manner of ancient tribal wisdom-keepers, who passed along the history and customs of their people. Oral history was the brush I used as I painted portraits of courageous, and often impetuous, characters who once populated our state.

Focusing on the actions of individuals instead of mass political movements or terms of treaties, we proceeded to revisit dreams, fears and eccentricities of early Texans. As novice sleuths, my students acquired investigative skill as they attempted to track and relate to these wilderness pioneers.

Certainly, they came to realize that some who designed the heritage of our state were flawed and misguided, while others operated as true visionaries. Each displayed a combination of human characteristics and frailties which caused him or her to be truly unique.

As we viewed what was going on in the world through the eyes of powerful personalities who had escaped the confines of textbook covers, we discovered new lands, left behind loved ones and comfortable homes and initiated treacherous and physically draining journeys into the unknown. When stories bogged down because of sketchiness, and threatened to sink into a murky void, we turned to research and discovered facts that would float them back to the surface.

Those same pupils taught me an important and long-remembered lesson as we were involved in re-creating their favorite segment of Texas history. That lesson is: "People view what they read through the lens, and in the context, of their everyday life."

The first log cabins built and occupied by early Texas settlers held precious little in the way of furniture and personal belongings. These cabins, along with their meager contents, inspired a great deal of fascination and comment among my students. I was of the opinion that I had done a worthy job of transmitting details and concepts concerning the lives of these courageous individuals.

At the end of days of discussion pertaining to the lives of 1830s settlers, I tested student comprehension by passing out copies of a simple cabin floor plan and asking these seventh graders to draw the cabin's contents. As I checked the drawings of several students, I viewed some extremely puzzling pieces of furniture.

"What is this mysterious piece in the corner with three circles in front of it?"

"Oh, that's their TV with the stools the children sat on while they were watching."

Another student was asked, "What is this large object outside the cabin?"

"That's their car. I wasn't sure if they had a garage."

So, I was confronted with the sudden realization that, regardless of the time devoted to discussions of journeys by horseback, wagons or on foot, despite the fact that we had listed and re-listed the few pieces of furniture and personal belongings they built or brought with them, regardless of heaping a large measure of attention upon items we now take for granted but they did not have, my generous students greeted the settlers' arrival with gifts of modern technology.

As we advanced through numerous decades within the school year, we eventually came upon one that occurred a century later. Television historians of today refer to it as "the dark decade." In the past few days, with precious little time to devote to tube-watching, I have heard this same decade referred to as *brutish*, *gloomy*, *dismal*, *disastrous* and *doomed*.

Teachers searching for visual aids to illustrate classroom tales from this time period come upon the same few pictures reproduced in a variety of sources. Observing a current television documentary, I watch the identical miserable family standing in a cloud of dust that I first saw pictured in a copy of the *San Antonio Express* during the 1930s. A melancholy portrait showing a long line of men awaiting a steaming bowl of charity soup has also been used endlessly to illuminate the era of the Great Depression.

Yet families trying to survive farm life in arid Midwestern dust bowls or somber job seekers hoping for a hot meal in the Northeast neither illustrate nor represent the totality of contrasts embodied in the culture of the 1930s. When history is recorded for the benefit of future generations, it is most valuable when told through the eyes of one who lived it. This individual must stick to recounting firsthand experiences so the world around him or her will eventually fall into place for the reader.

I am either blessed or cursed with a wonderful memory. During the years I cared for my mother, until her death at age 93, I realized the importance of writing a memoir when one's memory is still intact and anxious to be tested.

I honor the writers who have gathered historical data and statistics for the rest of us to access. My strength does not lie in the field of numbers but my mind delights in the ability to revisit a past era at will and re-experience the sights, sounds, tastes, feelings and emotions of a young child.

Some terms used in the 1930s and '40s, especially those with relation to racial issues, sound crude and insensitive today. Yet those same words were not meant to be derogatory at the time they were spoken. In attempting to become more informed and sensitive, our culture has changed its vocabulary in a number of situations. In being true to the events and the era when these experiences occurred, and at the same time writing for today's readers, I tend to use terms from several different generations in my descriptions.

Lynda Powell, who works as a "land man" in the gas and oil industry, has become aware of numerous Depression-era sagas as she labors in courthouse basements tracing the ownership of mineral rights.

"I'm very sensitive to that era," she explains, "because my grandfather was a poor tenant farmer and my father a Depression baby. I remember my grandmother telling me that she once had nothing but a sugar cookie to give my dad to eat.

"My father, L.B. Billingsley, began delivering milk twice a day at age ten. He earned a dime for each shift and that helped feed his family.

"Now, as I search through old records, I learn so many facts that bring tears to my eyes. Land deeds tell of families who lost everything they had—their homes, their food, vegetable crops they grew and animals they raised, their income—all because they didn't have the money to pay taxes.

"I read where the lack of cash caused one woman to sell her prized milk cow in order to raise money to bury her husband. The owners of mercantile stores, where these poor farmers 'traded on account,' sometimes ended up owning their land as debt payment.

"On the other hand, records show where individuals with cash sometimes were able to accumulate great wealth and large land holdings during the Depression era. They were in a position to purchase prime farms and ranches that had been confiscated by a sheriff, simply by paying back taxes. Selling off timber, raising cattle or profiting from the minerals that were transferred with theses lands created a new wealthy class."

Lynda's insights into the Great Depression come from tedious research, turning the pages of dusty ledgers to which few people seek access. They bring to mind situations, both enviable and pitiful, of families I knew as a child.

This book was written in a manner opposite to the manner in which non-fiction works are normally executed. Rather than doing copious research and then sitting down at a computer with note-filled legal pads, I enjoyed working hind-part-before. I let my memory flow nonstop on each particular subject or category; and when I came to a stopping point, only then did I look up family notebooks, old newspaper articles or do research on the computer to check my facts. It was a painless procedure, and I was able to easily transport myself into early childhood surroundings.

Sometimes even Google does not have a memory that stretches back as far as mine. When I typed in "Comic strip character Tillie the Toiler," it shot back the question, "Do you mean Tillie the Toilet?"

My true ace in the hole, as far as memory goes, is having been born in the first half of the 20th century, living surrounded by elders who lived in the 19th century and being able to enjoy a happy and healthy 21st-century life. It helped that my elders and ancestors were fond of writing memoirs. Those who didn't record events were wonderful tellers of tales.

I invite you to explore a time that was very different from the one in which you now live. Visit my neighborhood, which none of the residents considered "gloomy" or "dismal." Share a delicious meal with my family, who set a fine table despite "dark" and "disastrous" events occurring elsewhere in our nation. Ride a bus into downtown San Antonio where surroundings were tranquil rather than "brutish." Play games with me and my childhood friends. We were all too naive to realize we were "doomed."

I have attempted to sketch vignettes that will both elucidate and polish some of the many facets cut into that heavy and symbolic stone called the Great Depression.

CHAPTER ONE

NEIGHBORHOOD REFLECTIONS

My toddler bed, with low railings on both sides, was considered a step up, or rite of passage, from one's baby crib. The railings were designed to insure a small child's safety. I proved this to be a fallacy numerous times by using a rare talent that enabled me to roll up and over railings, plop on the floor and never wake up.

What did wake me, however, was the lion that invaded the bedroom, where he crouched in the corner poised to attack. I quickly pulled the covers over my head so I couldn't see him but still heard the terrifying sound of his snarls and growls.

Hoping he wouldn't notice, I furtively reached for my mother's hand somewhere in the nearby double bed. When I located it, I felt assured that as long as I held onto it the lion would be held at bay.

In later years, I realized our lion was actually a hulking shadow thrown from a dresser with attached mirror. Those ferocious growls that awakened me to shudder at the sight of our nightly predator were generated by my father, a world-class snorer.

Once the lion had awakened me, I became aware of the incessant tick-tock of our ancient bedroom clock. This small home did not contain any of the massive grandfather clocks owned by our ancestors. However, sitting on mantels and dressing tables were numerous gently curved wooden clocks, each with its own distinctive voice.

These timepieces also interrupted the night's ebony silence in a manner totally out of synch with the lion's growls. Our bedroom minute-counter chimed at the same time bongs reverberated from my grandmother's bedroom. Chimes and bongs with slightly different inflections answered from the more distant front bedroom and living room.

My mother absolutely loved, and felt soothed by, all of these talking timepieces. Even as a toddler, I found their ticks most irritating. Their rhythm and mine dueled like conflicting metronomes. We each had been assigned a different time signature by our Maker.

This disharmony left me with the problem of daring to let go of that reassuring maternal hand in order to place both hands over my ears. Silence was something I needed more than pillows or blankets.

Mother's hearing was perfectly normal, so I assume her cocoon of contentment so insulated her from the noises emanating from the one who lay next to her that she was not in the least disturbed. Unfortunately, this talent was not genetically transferred. I was never able to tranquilly share space with a clock that ticked or a person who snored.

The homes that lined both sides of Kayton Avenue in San Antonio,

My parents on the steps of their home at 736 Kayton Ave. My mother's dress and the newly planted shrubbery put the date in the early 1920s

Texas, in 1932, the year of my birth, had been built a decade earlier. These 20s-style bungalows were located close to the street side of narrow, slightly sloping and deep lots. Detached one-car garages were placed at the far back of the lot adjacent to a wide alley. The single-story frame dwellings were surrounded by trees and shrubs that had been cleverly placed by landscape artists to fool the eye of observers and visually enhance the size of the structures.

Two notable exceptions to the houses on our block were built on corner lots just east of our home. A large white two-story dwarfed all of the nearby homes. The neighbors directly across the street from this house planted tall-growing shrubbery so thickly that it created a high and dense barrier around the perimeter of their lot. This family became "the mystery people" to neighborhood children. Since their garage opened onto a side street, no one ever saw them enter or leave their property. For that reason alone, the family contributed greatly to currents of curiosity and flights of fantasy among others who lived in the 700 block of Kayton Avenue.

Number 736, our home, and a few others were blessed with large Southern-style front and side porches. Square brick pillars topped with white-painted extensions provided both eye appeal and roof support.

On the 1930 census form, my father estimated our house to be worth $5,750. Other Kayton Avenue dwellers listed values ranging from $3,500 to $10,000. The average rent, recorded by people who did not own the homes in which they lived, was $35 to $45 per month. Census pages reported that adults living in this area could read and write and most spoke English in their home. German, reflecting the heritage of a large number of southwest Texans, was still spoken within many of these residences.

Three generations shared the limited space within a large percent of these gracious cottages. As parents grew older, it was taken for granted that they would live with a son or daughter rather than be ushered to the nearest retirement center or nursing home. The era of elders who were considered both inconvenient and disposable had not yet arrived.

Since radio was the primary source for news and entertainment within a home, one column on the 1930 census form asked if the home had a "radio set." A little over half of the homes were still without that luxury.

Most heads of households were in their thirties or forties. The column that asks for age at the time of marriage showed that many of these couples had married while still in their teens.

Servant's quarters were attached to garages, and since indoor bathrooms were considered optional at the time of the homes' design, baths intended for family servants were placed in a separate structure next to, but outside of, the quarters.

These small, square rooms contained an older-style toilet than the one found in the main house. A water tank was suspended from the wall high above the seat. One flushed these antiques by pulling a brass chain with a wooden handle.

I recall that the Franz sisters, who lived next door, owned the only place on our block where the quarters actually housed a household employee. "Uncle Bill," an English immigrant who worked as gardener and handyman, occupied their room-out-back. In addition to working there, he also helped our family by doing yard work.

We used our quarters to store a number of antique humpback trunks and their unique historical contents. That left a good deal of room for Josephine, our "washwoman," to keep the large galvanized steel tubs as well as her ironing paraphernalia.

Kayton Avenue homes were designed to have two or three bedrooms, a living room, dining room and kitchen. In a search through my mother's cedar chest, I once found a copy of the original brochure for this neighborhood development. It proclaimed proudly, "A bathroom inside of every house!"

These homes did, indeed, have indoor baths. However, they seemed to be intended more for display than privacy. As a feature attraction of the twenties, the one bathroom was placed in the very center of the house.

Most bathrooms of that time had at least two doors, and I have seen some that had three. The idea behind this placement seemed to be that the facilities could be easily reached from the maximum number of rooms. Our bath, as those in many other houses, was situated where a hallway would have been far more efficient to accommodate the flow of traffic. In fact, it was used as a pass-through quite frequently.

The only logical access to my parent's bedroom was by using the hall door into the bathroom, walking through and then entering the connecting door into the master bedroom. When the bathroom was occupied, this path was blocked.

There were two other circuitous routes that allowed detours. One option was to enter the other back bedroom and then go through another door connecting to my parents' room. This bedroom was occupied by my grandmother during most of my childhood, and she did not like having her privacy disturbed.

The other detour meant exiting the house through the living room door onto the covered front porch, turning the corner where it continued on to become a side porch, then once more entering the house through a door into the master bedroom. This was hardly a convenient path, yet it was often the route used.

I assume the original builders of these homes must have regarded indoor baths, with their pedestal lavatories and deep claw-foot tubs, as precious jewels. They sought to protect them by surrounding them with all of the other rooms.

The front and side porches of these homes were used almost as much as the rooms. San Antonio was known as "the city where the sunshine spends the winter." Not only did we have mild winters, but the sun was a major factor in our summer activities as well. So, porches offered an opportunity to sit in a prevailing breeze and enjoy a certain amount of relief from the heat.

Porches also provided a natural location for neighborhood social life. Our comfortably furnished porch was a frequent gathering spot. During daytime hours, housewives usually arrived carrying something to keep their hands busy. Sitting in the porch swing or one of the rockers, women shelled black-eyed peas, mended garments, darned cotton socks and silk stockings or crocheted an afghan as they chatted. My mother served coffee, iced tea or freshly squeezed lemonade during these gatherings. Aunt Julia Franz often carried a plate filled with my favorite "Ju-Ju's Cookies" when she attended what she called by the Cajun term a *tour nay*. She was well-known on our block for her cooking ability and especially for seafood gumbo and those marvelous sugar cookies.

Today, the only recognizable vestige of my childhood home is the 736 painted on the front curb. The front lawn, where my friends and I played ball games and chased one another, is now a small forest filled with trees and shrubs. Most of the families on this block have enclosed the elegant old verandas to create more interior floor space. Altering original designs resulted in losing the integrity of shape and created homes that most resemble boxes.

I understand the need for more room for a family, but I shall never forget the fun of playing with my friends while listening to stories told by our elders on those shady and elegant porches of the past.

Census forms filled out during my childhood never mentioned two unseen presences who shared our home. I was never burdened by rigid beliefs of any organized religion, so was privileged to create God's countenance from my own imagination. The God who shared my home was clean-shaven and looked a great deal like my father. He also shared Daddy's penchant for wearing the type clothes my father wore on his days off or when driving to Jackson County to tend to his herd of Hereford cattle. Western-cut khaki pants, a khaki shirt with the sleeves rolled up and cowboy boots suited both God and my father. Evidently, God had as much disdain for the long robes I had seen him wearing in Sunday school book illustrations as my father had for business suits, ties and starched white dress shirts.

God smiled all of the time and often winked at me when we shared a joke.

Emily Post, on the other hand, frowned constantly. Whereas God was perceived as laid-back and enjoying himself, Emily remained ever-stern and deadly serious.

I knew that she and God were both writers of big, important best-sellers. My elders indicated that God's book was called The Bible, and it dealt with treating others with kindness and consideration and always telling the truth. Emily's books dealt with all facets of behavior called "etiquette."

My mother could quote chapter and verse from Emily's books, though she sounded rather vague when answering my questions about what God had in mind. I much preferred sharing our residence with God to hanging out with Emily. God was lots of fun, and he wasn't persnickety as long as I remembered my nightly prayers. Emily was sneaky and often lurked in the hall with her beady-eyed stare fixed on the dining table. She hoped to catch one of us forgetting to keep our non-dominant hand in our lap during a meal.

During those years, prior to air-conditioning and central heat, the temperature was adjusted by simply opening or closing windows and doors. Every family owned oscillating fans, which were moved around often during summer months.

Fan blades were not encased behind the type of safety grills used today. People often sustained damage to hands or fingers by inadvertent carelessness. Someone with a finger missing might report trying to move a fan while it was still in motion. At times, people simply made the mistake of gesturing with their hands while standing too close to a fan.

Heavy iron doorstops were used to prop doors open as breezes blew through the house. Our doorstops were cast in the shape of women wearing hoop skirts and sunbonnets. They looked intriguing, so I tried to play with them; but their weight would not allow me to pick them up. Every door had a keyhole lock and a removable key.

During the late fall, natural gas-burning heaters were taken out of storage and attached to gas jets to prepare for winter. People who lived in the country used wood, butane or kerosene stoves for heat. Friends up north heated with coal.

Most of the homes on our street had fireplaces, used for heat and not just atmosphere. Gas logs or push-a-button instant flames would not appear for many decades, so everyone kept a woodpile and a stash of kindling in their back yards. Match-holders containing large kitchen matches could be found sitting on end tables and matchboxes hung in a painted tin holder on kitchen walls.

Newspapers ran frequent articles telling of people whose clothing caught fire from standing too close to gas stoves. It was a temptation to hover around these small heaters during the process of changing clothes because the heat they generated did not reach very far. Concerned with keeping me safe, my parents purchased sturdy iron screens they placed around our household heaters and the fireplace. "Don't stand so close to that stove" was a warning I received repeatedly during winter months.

Other news stories dealt with explosions of butane stoves and heaters. The tragic aftermath of one of these events was brought into our family consciousness when my parents and I drove to the little East Texas town of Woodville in the piney woods.

We made the trip to visit a couple of old family friends. Both my parents and I found it extremely difficult to look directly at the woman who was undergoing treatment for serious burns on her face and most of her body. Our friend had managed to live through an explosion caused by escaping butane gas that ignited as she tried to light their cookstove. I tried hard to keep my dismay from showing as I realized this formerly beautiful woman had been left covered with deforming scars.

"Couldn't you smell the gas escaping before you lit the match?" Mother blurted out as she sat on a black Victorian sofa. She was told that, unlike natural gas, butane had no odor. She quickly replied, "Well, there ought to be a law that some sort of scent must be added so people can realize when there's a danger."

It happened that the state representative from that area was also visiting in the home of our friends. He responded, "That's a wonderful idea!"

We never knew if it was due to his subsequent efforts in Austin, based upon my mother's suggestion, but our state soon had such a law.

Butane stoves did not quit exploding, but leaking gas began to give olfactory warnings to those who remained attentive.

Because the narrow lots on Kayton Avenue meant houses were just a single driveway apart from one another, we were lucky to live between two quiet households. We often heard the words spoken by M— family members as they sat at their kitchen table drinking coffee and engaging in conversation.

The spinster Franz sisters, on the other side of our home, used to say, "We know it's time for breakfast when we hear Mother Fletcher scraping [the burned spots off] the toast." Since conversational noises traveled, one had to be careful in what room, and how close to which window, he or she stood while speaking.

Heavy paper roll-type window shades could offer visual privacy when they were pulled down, but they did not create a sound barrier. Country curtains made of sheer organdy and trimmed with ruffles crossed over our windows and were held back on the sides by ruffled swags. Anything hanging in front of the windows would have contributed to a lack of cross ventilation so important at that time.

Various small farm animals inhabited some of the yards on our block. Many of our neighbors had previously lived self-sufficient rural lives, so they clung to previous habits. The Wallace family on the far side of the Franz home kept goats. The Yeager family, in the two-story home on the corner, provided neighborhood cock-a-doodle-doos courtesy of their back yard filled with chickens.

Soon after Christmas Day of my seventh year, I tried to ride my new bicycle and fell into a hedge of rose bushes at the side of this corner home. I soon forgot about painful scratches when I heard a terrible racket and saw a woman wringing a chicken's neck. A moment later, I saw the same headless chicken running around in circles on the ground. Totally horrified, I pulled my bike from the rose hedge and pedaled home as fast as I could.

Most homes had a small room between the kitchen and back porch. This great-grandfather of current day utility rooms contained the ancestor of today's crop of refrigerators: an icebox.

An icehouse in almost every neighborhood sold heavy chunks of ice, priced by weight. Many families also used the services of an iceman, who delivered a large, square chunk of ice each day. He carried this block of ice in a heavy canvas bag and lifted it into the top compartment of the icebox with a pair of huge tongs.

Kitchens contained a dangerous tool called an icepick—sacks of crushed ice and refrigerators able to spit out crushed or cubed ice at the push of a lever had not yet been envisioned. So, someone in each household had to repeatedly chop the ice blocks to obtain enough small pieces of ice for several glasses of that perennial Southern favorite, iced tea.

Icemen used gates leading into fenced back yards to deliver their product through back doors. Milkmen normally left fresh bottles of milk, cream and containers of butter on the steps of front porches. They also picked up the empty quart, pint and half-pint glass bottles that were sterilized at the creamery and used over and over again. If the woman of the house wished to change her daily order, she left a note, rolled up and inserted into one of the empty bottles.

The use of glass containers for all liquid dairy products as well as cold drinks meant that bottles were constantly in use and did not jam our garbage trucks or landfills.

Due to the high rate of unemployment during the Depression years, men who delivered milk, ice or the mail valued their jobs and held them for years. So, they became almost like a member of the extended family. Our family knew the names of our delivery men and many details about their personal lives. Their services were appreciated, counted upon, and the men were always remembered with cards and gifts at Christmas.

Though none of the Kayton Avenue homes would have particularly impressed a passerby from the exterior, our home was known for its interior beauty. Antique beveled-glass French doors between the living and dining rooms created visual elegance as one entered the front door. Another pair opened out from the front bedroom and reflected the glass cutter's artistry. As sunrays connected with prisms of glass, sparkles of myriad colors were projected onto walls, floors and ceilings.

Trained in Europe, my great-aunt Vallie Fletcher was a well-known Texas artist. Her landscapes, still-life scenes and portraits, all beautifully framed, filled the walls of our home. Though she often held shows in New York City and other centers of culture, she gave most of her paintings to family and friends. A massive painted tapestry dominated the east wall of our dining room and hypnotized diners with its peaceful motif.

Mother was blessed with amazing skills as a decorator, though this talent was instinctive rather than learned in any formal setting. Aunt Vallie, educated in the intricacies of artistic flower arranging while living in Paris, never failed to marvel at the arrangements Mother created from flowers grown in our garden. Cut glass vases were placed in each room so we could enjoy both the beauty and aroma of fresh flowers daily.

Our feet connected with hardwood floors, partially covered by area rugs, in each room of the house. Plush woolen rugs allowed bare toes to feel pampered in the living and dining rooms. Crocheted multicolored cotton rag rugs, created by my mother and grandmother, covered floors in the bedrooms. Smaller versions of these rag rugs lay in the bathroom and kitchen.

Our entire house changed its interior look along with the seasons. Furniture reflected autumnal hues during late fall and winter. When spring arrived, custom-made slipcovers in pastel colors miraculously appeared on each piece of furniture as well as every pillow and cushion. Rainbow shades painted the chenille bedspreads that replaced heavy quilts, afghans and woolen blankets needed to keep winter sleepers cozy.

Wallpaper did not change every season, though it was also replaced with great regularity. Mother impressed us with her ability to blend shades and values of color as well as textures and an assortment of patterns.

Antique furniture, first used by our ancestors, filled this small home. Such lovely and unique pieces could not have been acquired on my father's salary. Both sets of paternal great-grandparents left these valued items behind.

Great-grandfather A.N. Vaughan educated his four children with private tutors and art teachers. When his daughter Florence became engaged to Bill Fletcher's son Harvey, sets of fine Limoges porcelain and Havilland china were ordered from Europe. These sets were solid white so that my grandmother could paint rims of gold and an ornate monogram—FVF—on each piece. Every size and shape of serving piece was included. I still marvel at the extreme patience, and firm grip on the paint brush, she must have exhibited. Even the tiny individual salt cellars were exquisite in their perfection.

A curved-front glass china cabinet in our dining room held this wedding china while a similar corner cabinet encased other decorative pieces painted by my grandmother and her two loony, but artistically talented, sisters. All of these items, though fragile museum pieces in appearance, were used on a regular basis.

The triangular corner cabinet, filled with crystal and cut glass, sat close to a giant console radio. This prized possession was placed next to the French doors opening into the living room so it could be heard by listeners in either room. A tall, hand-cranked Victrola also shared the dining room with our formal table, chairs and buffet.

I have some very early and specific memories of the two china cabinets, and their priceless contents, which stood next to our dining room windows.

After supper one spring evening, Daddy took me out into the back yard to play. Looking at the western sky, he reached down, picked me up and set me on his shoulders.

"Look at the funny-looking sky," he said. "It's yellow." In the next sentence, he remarked, "Boy, that really must be a big freight train we are hearing!"

We lived several miles from a railroad track, and when the wind blew from the right direction, the soulful sound of passing freight trains could be heard.

My father had barely finished speaking when our yellow sky became totally black and our freight train, in the form of a mighty hailstorm, was upon us. Daddy raced up the back steps with me still on his shoulders. By the time we got inside, huge hailstones were crashing through all of the windows on the west side of the house.

Daddy ran into the living room, grabbed a large overstuffed chair and put it in our central hall. I was quickly plopped into it and told to stay by both parents, who were yelling in order to be heard over the roar of the wind. Mother and Daddy yanked mattresses off of two double beds, dragged them into the dining room and placed them up against the windows. My parents, grandmother and uncle Nick leaned into these mattresses with every ounce of their weight, trying to keep them in place to protect the china cabinets.

Hailstones still poured through other windows and rolled across the floor to join bits of broken glass that littered the floors. In the eyes of a child who was twenty days short of her third birthday, this March 5, 1935, storm was high adventure. My only concern was for Stormy, my aptly named wire-haired terrier. In an agitated state, Stormy raced back and forth barking at the unknown invader. His path could be easily traced by a series of bloody pawprints running into, and out of, each room.

The storm (later considered to be a series of tornadoes) lifted as quickly as it had arrived. The rooftops of many homes across San Antonio were either gone or seriously damaged. Most every home had lost windows. There were estimates of more than a million dollars of property damage across the city. In 1935, people seldom spoke in terms

Me and my faithful fox terrier Stormy. I have no idea why I'm dressed as an Indian.

of that amount of money.

The closest we came to a casualty was when my father tried to substitute as a handyman, a job for which he was not at all suited. In the wake of this destructive storm, roofers were in heavy demand throughout the city, so people were urged to get on a waiting list and do temporary patch work themselves. The day after the storm, my dad climbed a ladder with roofing nails and patching material to do his best.

After he finished and surveyed his work, Dad climbed down and folded up the ladder. It was then that his hammer, which he had left on top of the ladder, fell, hit the top of his head and knocked him out.

Leaving storm memories behind and continuing our house tour, a Victorian loveseat, marble-top tables that held reading lamps, several upholstered chairs and my great-grandfather Fletcher's wicker rocking chair were arranged to create an extremely comfortable living room. Floor-to-ceiling bookshelves with glass doors framed the brick fireplace.

Steinway piano #51250, one of the first few made in the United States and originally sold in 1883, was a gift to our home from Aunt Vallie. She learned as a child to play on this small spinet, which had only eighty-five keys.

During the Christmas season, our living room became a place I never wanted to leave. The fireplace created a magical atmosphere as its dancing flames were reflected by every glass ornament that hung from the tree. Cut-glass French doors and glass book-case doors beamed even more images-in-motion around the room.

When strings of Christmas tree lights became available, a few of the families we knew began to use them. My father banned them after reading newspaper articles that told of house fires caused by problems with these new, and sometimes dangerous, decorative items. So, silver icicles and garlands of shiny materials wrapped around the tree substituted for electric tree lights in our home.

The rearrangement of furniture to accommodate a Christmas tree resulted in a fresh, unique and sometimes peculiar assemblage of shadows. These shadows invited me to watch in enchantment as they bent to chase rays that glittered, glistened and gleamed from glass ornaments.

Each bedroom in our home held a double bed, a chiffonier, a mirrored vanity with upholstered stool as well as the traditional rocking chair. A New Home treadle sewing machine, constructed with decorative ironwork, was an additional piece in Grandmother's room.

The only room that was a close replica of those in nearby homes was our kitchen. Each kitchen on our block included a breakfast nook, like the booths used in many restaurants today. Except for weekends when my father was able to stay at home, we ate our breakfasts there. Any meal served when Daddy was around was eaten in the formal dining room. Our table was set with monogrammed table linens, sterling silver place settings and napkin rings, crystal goblets and bouquets of fresh flowers. Each time my mother rang a tiny sterling silver dinner bell, our cook popped through the swinging door between the kitchen and dining room to see how she could serve us.

The only time my father had ever spoken crossly to my mother, or so the story was told, was when she handed him a stainless steel fork with which to eat a piece of pie. He informed her not to ever serve him with anything but sterling silver.

This bit of information would astound people who knew my father because he was in no way a snob. He had been raised in a home surrounded with elegant furnishings. Though his tastes were usually quite simple, he had definite ideas about how a family should dine. Thus, we were a linen-and-fine-lace family living in an oilcloth neighborhood.

Our kitchen was equipped with a tall stove supported by four narrow legs. There were no electric stoves, and gas stoves did not have automatic controls, so in the center of the waist-high natural gas burners was a pilot light.

Pilot lights were supposed to remain lighted at all times, but they could be tricky. A gentle breeze coming through a nearby window could extinguish the flame. Cooks were cautioned to always check the pilot prior to lighting a match and turning on a gas burner or the oven. An explosion caused by escaping gas was an ever-present danger, so we had to consider many safety precautions when we used these stoves.

A large pantry dominated the east side of our kitchen while a single porcelain sink beneath a window facing south served for washing the cast iron skillets and farmhouse classic enamelware.

Bottles of liquid detergent were an item devised in future years, so the lather created from a bar of Ivory soap was our cleaner of choice. Dishes, silverware and glasses were carefully washed separately in a dishpan then rinsed with boiling water heated in a teakettle.

Families with small children and pets almost always had fenced back yards. Because families were not as mobile as they are today, people seldom moved away from our area. Neighbors became close emotionally as well as geographically. Our white picket fence had gates leading into the back yards of both of our next-door neighbors. A larger gate could be opened to allow the car to be driven into the back yard and down to the garage.

A tall black telephone with a rotary dial and an arm that held the receiver rested on a tiny table in our hall. While operating this mode of communication, one hand held the body of the phone, containing the mouthpiece, and the other hand kept the receiver at the user's ear. Residence phones were almost always party lines, meaning that one or more other families used the same line. This situation could be most irritating to everyone involved, and certainly required utmost patience.

14

The best-case scenario called for everyone sharing a line to use consideration and limit the length of their conversations.

Numbers assigned to a household or business contained the name of an exchange plus four numerals. Ours was Kenwood-7275. Area codes would not become necessary for decades.

Many homes still did not have a telephone in the 1930s. Families who owned phones had only one, which was installed with a permanent plug in a central location. A tiny two-shelf phone table and stool were the only pieces of furniture in our hall.

Local numbers could be dialed from one's home, but to reach anyone long distance it was necessary to go through the operator. Long distance calls were not common at that time, so when the operator announced, "I have a long distance call for you," the first thought was "Oh, my gosh, it's an emergency!"

When placing a long distance call, one told the operator to make the call either person-to-person, which meant the call could be accepted by one particular individual only, or station-to-station, designating the caller would talk to anyone at the number dialed. Station-to-station calls were less expensive to place.

This was a time totally devoid of telephone solicitors or recorded commercial calls of any kind. A call received during the night was almost always a death message or news of someone's dangerous physical condition. I remember Mother's anguish after receiving middle-of-the-night news that her younger sister had accidentally shot herself.

Families in rural areas dealt with a different kind of telephone exchange. Even in the 1940s and 1950s, many had to rely on an operator called "Central." When our family moved into a coastal ranch home, we had to learn the intricacies of a wall-mounted wooden phone with a crank.

Cranking the phone put the caller in contact with Central, who was normally a local woman with phone equipment installed in her home. The caller told Central whose residence she or he wanted. Central then used her switchboard plugs and attempted to make a connection.

Many ranch families shared one line, with each household on the line assigned a specific series of short and long rings. Unlike city telephones, which rang only when someone in a particular house was wanted, rural phones rang in all of the homes that shared a line. One home might have two shorts and one long as their phone signal. It was difficult to tell the difference between that ring and three longs. So, it was not unusual for a phone to be answered by individuals at several locations.

No one became perturbed about this. They were most likely long-time friends or close relatives.

A situation that was both funny, and sometimes helpful, was the knowledge that Central frequently listened to conversations. She wasn't alone. A number of the older women might hear an ongoing conversation as they prepared to use the phone and decide it was rather interesting.

I once placed a call to a cousin and was in the midst of informing her about my father's hospitalization with a broken leg. As I related the tale of an attack by a mother cow as Dad was worming her newborn calf, elderly women from several neighboring ranches asked me to "Please speak up and say that again."

Central overheard family plans and invitations all of the time. A relative from Beaumont tried to call us one evening. When she reached Central at La Ward, she was told, "Oh, they're not at home. They're over visiting at Cousin Katie Traylor's house. I'll ring them over there."

So, everyone knew to limit phone conversations to subjects that were innocent enough to be overheard by countless other families. Frankly, I would gladly go back to a friendly, curious and good-hearted Central and dispense with recorded calls where one is asked to punch in a continuous series of numbers and no human is available.

When my parents, grandmother and uncle Nick first moved into our Kayton Avenue home, Aunt (a term of respect) Julia Franz ran a boarding house next door. This solved a problem for my father, who would not allow his wife or mother to act as cooks or housekeepers. Daddy arranged for his family to take all of their meals at the Franz home until a time when suitable household help could be found. During these months, my family became close to Aunt Julie and her sister, Aunt Annie.

These two delightful women were of pure German blood yet spoke with thick Louisiana French accents learned in their home town of St. Martinville, Louisiana. Mealtimes proved to be an excellent opportunity to meet new neighbors, who had been unable to resist the fine food, often Cajun dishes, served at the Franz residence.

It was an undisputed fact that both my mother and grandmother were wonderful cooks. Each had mastered culinary skills at some point in

16

their lives and was able to prepare an endless list of succulent dishes. Both were patient teachers as they instructed women hired to cook for our family.

My father was a Southern gentleman of the old school who truly believed it was his duty to take care of his womenfolk in every way, including providing them with household servants. Though he lacked personal wealth, somehow he managed to do this during our years in San Antonio.

Garbage was carried outside and through a double gate in a high picket fence. Large covered galvanized cans sat on a stand in the wide alley and awaited garbage trucks, which rattled through daily as crews collected refuse. No one would have dreamed of placing a sack filled with garbage on their front curb.

Our family saw the desperate families who prowled these alleys constantly, digging through garbage cans in a quest for something to eat. So, our throwaway edibles, such as crusts trimmed off bread, peelings cut from fruit, half-eaten sandwiches and leftovers of all sorts, were carefully wrapped in waxed paper, put into small paper sacks then placed on top of garbage can lids. This was to keep any item that might possibly be needed for bare sustenance from being polluted by coffee grounds and other messy refuse.

Families who prowled our alley daily knew the approximate time the garbage truck would arrive. They showed up before the truck was due so they would have ample time to scavenge the large cans. If Mother was a little late gathering edible food items, those who knew her routine would pause in the midst of their pitiful journey and look through the fence. Eyes staring between the pickets always looked troubled. *Did she forget us? Isn't she coming today?*

As soon as Mother opened the back door, descended the back porch steps and crossed the yard to the fence, those who waited backed up and pretended they had not noticed her delayed delivery.

My mother once described me by saying "She never met a stranger." In later years, my eldest daughter observed, "Mother would talk to rocks!"

Somewhere between these two vivid depictions was a small child who ran to the back fence in order to visit with frail children in the alley. I once hurried to the fence when I spied a girl who looked to be about my

17

own age. She had large brown eyes and long blonde hair. If it had been clean, it would have probably been the same shade as mine.

Our eyes locked as we stood separated by tall white pickets. She probably read the curiosity reflected in my eyes as I felt the despair in the gaze of the woman who stood behind her. Wordlessly, the little girl and I made a strong connection. Our palms and fingers touched as our spirits entwined.

We would soon have been talking, but my father walked over, took my hand and turned me around to face him. He then led me away from the back fence and spoke softly as we approached the back of our home.

My father's words of wisdom still ring in my ears.

"Honey, the only kind thing to do is to pretend you don't see them."

In answer to the familiar query "Why?", he explained that those families who searched through garbage felt terrible about their plight.

"They know that they are ragged and dirty. They are ashamed that they have to do this to feed their children. We must try to keep them from feeling humiliated by looking in the other direction."

Daddy reminded me of the many men who rang our front doorbell daily.

"These people are not ashamed to ask for help. The families who roam the alleys and dig through garbage have a fierce sort of pride. We need to respect that."

Along with small sacks of food, Mother often placed boxes of clothing I had outgrown on garbage can lids. She also gave clothing items that the adults in our family did not need. So, "looking in the other direction" was taken literally and never meant that we turned away from these sad families if we had means to help.

As my father requested, I showed respect for the condition of these families by not running out to greet them or even seeming to notice they were there. However, I never forgot the emptiness and desperation I saw in those eyes in the alley. That little girl I had been close to for just a few minutes stayed with me throughout my childhood. I even gave her a name since I had not had the opportunity to ask what she was called.

Names like Shirley, Dorothy, Virginia, Patricia, Barbara and Marjorie were common at that time. I didn't choose any of those for my almost-friend who became my secret sister. Vivian Jean shared my initials and all of my future experiences. Vivian and I never got close enough to meet again, yet the strong bond we had formed during those eventful few minutes decreed that everywhere I went she accompanied me. Eyes in the alley continued to view my world and interpret it in their unique fashion.

CHAPTER TWO

CHILDHOOD PLEASURES

My father ambled into the front yard wearing large pearl earrings, lipstick, rouge, thick blobs of face powder and a golden barrette which anchored a gigantic pink hair-bow. Passengers in the few Model-As, Model-Ts and Ford V-8s making their way down San Antonio's Kayton Avenue appeared to be awestruck when they first spied him.

As Dad moved a garden hose and adjusted the sprinkler, neighbors simply grinned and waved to acknowledge his presence. They realized that Lucillio was once again visiting our house.

Children of the Great Depression were extremely inventive when it came to games and pastimes. Multi-colored plastic toys, electronic games and television belonged to the unimaginable future, yet, I cannot remember ever feeling bored or hearing friends claim they had nothing to do.

As an only child surrounded by adults, I created an imaginary friend who lived only in my head until certain conditions occurred that allowed him to manifest.

I was blessed with a father who was an avid reader. His ability to totally tune out the rest of the world as he sat in his grandfather's wicker rocker and picked up his current book or magazine set the stage for Lucillio's entrance. It allowed me ample time to bedeck him and select dialogue for his character.

I'm not at all sure where I came up with the name Lucillio. The second part indicates that Lu was about to act "silly-o" by wearing strange attire. As long as Daddy sat still, like a mannequin in a window display, and remained completely immersed in his reading material, he never seemed to be aware of what I was doing. I had total access to the top portion of his torso and took great delight in transforming him into my most unusual friend.

Lucillio loved to wear outfits I collected by searching through my mother's and grandmother's closets and cedar chests. His makeup and jewelry came from drawers and china receptacles found in, and on top of, their dressing tables. His millinery, purchased at San Antonio's Frost Brothers, Wolff and Marx or Joskee's of Texas, was always the latest style, and usually sported jaunty veils and assorted adornments.

Mother wore bright red lipstick, pink powder-type rouge and loose face powder, as did most of the younger women of that time. Grandmother wore no makeup, which was typical of older women. However, what she lacked in makeup to contribute to Lucillio's persona she made up for with a plethora of fine jewelry and fur stoles to add to his wardrobe.

Though I always referred to Lucillio as "he," my friend was really envisioned as being genderless. Certainly, as we chattered away while I applied his decorative attire, he expressed great admiration for the finery I offered.

Once he had made discerning comments and indicated his selections, I began applying ornamentation in the manner of one in the process of decorating a freshly cut Christmas tree. My father seldom moved or made any sounds as various accouterments found their way onto Lucillio's head and shoulders. Once in a while he would emit a slight cough as face powder was being applied.

Only when Lucillio and I agreed that his toilette was complete did I invite others within the household to enter our space.

My mother, grandmother, Uncle Nick, the housekeeper and any visiting neighbors or great-aunts would slowly and quietly make their way into the living room for the viewing. They walked single file, as if approaching a body during the "laying out" prior to a funeral.

Trying hard to keep straight faces as they greeted Lucillio and voiced appreciation for his latest get-up, they wandered past the rocker one at a time. Daddy was normally as unaware of this parade of admirers as he was of Lucillio and me. Thus, when he finished a chapter, or closed a book for the last time, he would often go outside for a smoke or to take care of some chore.

This was how our neighbors first met Lucillio, wearing large pearl earrings, heavy pink rouge and an ivory feather boa. Unless some member of my immediate family saw him heading for the door and relieved him of hat, fur, ribbons, jewelry and makeup before he went outside, he was a totally oblivious cross-dresser.

Like most small children, my attention span lasted only a short time. After Lucillio had been suitably bedecked and admired, I would become bored with that activity and wander off to find, or create, other means of amusement.

One Saturday, Daddy finished a book and walked to a mirror to carefully check his image for any vestiges of Lucillio before he headed for the barber shop. Short hair, kept in place with hair oil, was the style. On Saturdays, there were long lines at barber shops as heads of families, along with their sons, awaited their turn to sit in one of the ornate barber chairs.

My father patiently waited, flipping through the shop's collection of well-worn *Saturday Evening Post* magazines. Finally seated in one of the barber chairs, he watched in the mirror as the barber picked up a comb and proceeded to begin his usual routine.

The comb stopped, and the barber suddenly yelled, "My God, man! What's in your head?"

The men and boys who filled the shop were treated to the sight of the barber extracting an entire box of my grandmother's hairpins, one by one. When Daddy stalked into our house, his face was still beet-red as he told of the snickers and whispers at his expense that made the rounds of that tonsorial palace.

After this experience, Lucillio's visits became fewer and farther between.

I'm not sure that my over-protective mother and grandmother would have ever allowed me to leave the house and play with neighborhood children had it not been for an event that caused both of them to become totally mortified.

A friend of my father's, who was one of the highest ranking officers stationed at Fort Sam Houston, came to our home for a visit. He was handsome and immaculate in his dress uniform and, no doubt, greatly impressed his two hostesses. Wanting him to meet the resident toddler, Mother brought me into the living room for an introduction.

I began the visit standing near Mother's chair, but suddenly dropped to the floor and crawled on all-fours across the room to where our visitor sat. Once I reached his chair, I began sniffing his feet and legs. I kept up this mysterious form of behavior until, in an advanced state of embarrassment, my mother abandoned her chair and grabbed me up off the floor.

After our guest departed, my perplexed parent asked Dad, "What on earth could have caused Vallie to act that way?" Laughing and using his perpetual common sense, he responded, "Who does she play with all day?"

The answer to his question was easy—Stormy, our wire-haired terrier. All guests who entered our home were immediately and thoroughly sniffed by Stormy. Since he had been banished to the back yard during our guest's visit, I evidently felt a need to fulfill his obligations.

My mother was suddenly confronted with the same dilemma many parents eventually face, "Is she running with the wrong crowd?" This incident offered sudden insight into the wisdom of allowing other children into my life.

Thus, unlike Victor, the Wolf Boy of Aveyron, south Texas was spared Vallie, the Wire-Haired Girl of San Antonio.

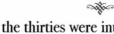

Young children of the thirties were inundated with rhymes and lyrics of ancient historic origin, stemming from the time adults first began using games to interact with their infants. Starting with "This Little Piggy Went to Market" as we lay in a crib, we progressed to our toddler versions of "Pease Porridge Hot," "London Bridge is Falling Down" and "Ring Around the Rosey." Our elders failed to teach us that as we sang, clapped and danced in circles while singing these rhymes, we were actually perpetuating tales of a cereal popular long before oatmeal and, allegedly, British scandal and political intrigue and outbreaks of bubonic plague in the UK. So, with smiles on our faces, we happily hit the dirt while singing "all fall down" and never dreamed we were supposedly imitating a ghastly form of death from an historic epidemic disease.

When a child of the 1930s received a toy as a gift, it was for a special and specific occasion. Superstores, where children accompany parents and point to assorted colorful displays recognized from advertisements, were half a century into the future. Scattered pieces of cheaply made toys did not litter homes of that time.

My father built a long, wooden three-shelf piece of furniture for my collection of dolls, games and assorted paraphernalia. When I was not actively playing with one of these, it was expected to be placed neatly in its proper location on the toyshelf. Dolls occupied the top shelf, books were relegated to the second and boxes of games or puzzles were kept on the bottom.

When I finished playing, it was my duty to see that nothing was left behind on the floor, the porch or out in the yard. I took this responsibility seriously, so my toys always looked as if they were brand-new.

Because I was an only child, related to a number of wealthy and well traveled individuals, I received many lovely gifts throughout the year. Acutely aware of this, several times a year my mother reminded me that there were many children who had no toys because they had lost their parents. I was asked to select some favorite dolls and games to keep then help her pack everything else in cardboard boxes.

"You have been given more toys than any one child needs. The kind thing for you to do is share with boys and girls who may not have any."

The filled boxes were placed in our two-door gray Ford V-8, which Mother drove to the "Orphan Asylum." In those days, one huge brown-brick building housed the children rather than the cluster of smaller cottages normally used today.

In route to the children's home, Mother talked about the importance of recognizing the needs of others and acting to fill those needs when we have the opportunity. She kept the conversation casual, encouraged my remarks and never preached.

Staff members at the home always acted overjoyed at the contents of our boxes. Sometimes, I watched as older children set tables for a meal. They usually invited us to stay and eat, but we never did.

During our visits to the orphans' home, I learned more by seeing how the children looked at my mother than I ever could have from a series of lectures on sharing. A small child easily connects with another's broken heart and yearning for missing parents. Watching young children gather around my mother and look at her with such longing never failed to touch me deeply. I yearned to take everyone home with us. In fact, I was so overwhelmed with emotion during these visits that I retreated into silence on the drive home and remained unusually quiet for several days.

Toys available for purchase were well made as were the many toys made at home. Fathers carved wooden guns and slingshots for their sons while mothers worked on sewing and stuffing rag dolls. When a girl received a purchased doll, there was a good chance that it had been made in the likeness of Shirley Temple, the famous child star and Hollywood's darling. In later years, Princess Elizabeth dolls, patterned after the little

This photo of me with my "Princess Elizabeth" doll was likely taken shortly after the abdication of Edward VIII. Dollmakers went crazy making dolls in the image of the little girl who would one day be queen.

girl who grew up to become queen of England, became popular.

Teddy bears were favorites and came in all sizes. My teddy was black, wore a red collar and squeaked when pressed on his upper back. Teddy always accompanied our family during out-of-town trips. My father often joked about a specific return trip to San Antonio after a weekend journey to Junction. I became so upset when I realized Teddy had been left behind at our hotel Daddy turned the car around and rescued my constant companion.

Red Radio Flyer wagons, in which we could be pulled or used to pull our toys around, were toys valued by most children. The Highland Park Community Center once sponsored a children's parade for which participants were asked to come pulling their decorated wagons. To encourage participants, they offered a prize for the prettiest wagon. I was too young to understand what was going on, but Mother purchased pink and blue crepe paper and decorated my Radio Flyer so beautifully that I won the prize.

Toys received by Depression-era children were gender-specific. The dreams and expectations of adult family members, when it came to their children's future, were sharply divided between male and female-oriented occupations. Little girls were expected to grow up to become wives and mothers. Those who were encouraged to consider higher education as a possibility could choose between being a nurse, a teacher, someone's secretary or some form of the arts. It was expected that most of these means of gainful employment would be dropped immediately when a young woman married.

Since adults never considered that their daughter might grow up to become a doctor, or their son might decide to become a nurse, boys received doctor kits while their sisters enjoyed nurse kits. It was on this same premise that bats and balls, toy guns, dolls and all variety of playthings were selected, purchased and presented to a child of the proper gender.

Once these toys were in the possession of the children, however, both sexes managed to enjoy them unless a grown-up intervened. I often recruited male neighbors to play jacks with me and reciprocated when they needed an extra thumb to shoot marbles.

Jumping rope, with all of its assorted rhythms, chants and speeds was a favorite pastime of little girls. The truth was that many a young boy loved to show off his skill by jumping in when the girls sang out, "Hot Pepper!" This was the signal for the two rope-turners to switch over to the fastest turning-speed they could manage. They were obliged to keep up this speed until the jumper tripped and was "out."

Probably the most obvious difference between young children's games of the 1930s and our current-day children's activities is the fact that there were no organized teams or practice sessions scheduled for children to attend.

Families who owned cars usually had only one vehicle, and this automobile's primary purpose was to transport the man of the house to his job and back. San Antonio had a marvelous public bus system, so a large segment of the population did not own a car.

When Mother needed the car, she drove my father to work or he walked over one block to a Rigsby Avenue bus stop. There, he caught a bus that delivered him to the Frost National Bank building in the heart of the city. As Dad and fellow workers reached their office building, small crowds of the faithful entered the historic San Fernando Cathedral next door for the celebration of morning mass.

As part of the laid-back attitude prevalent toward all team sports, children of the 30s played softball by what was called the "work in, work out" method. There was no competition except for doing the best one could on an individual basis. No grown ups were involved. No player was yelled at unless he carelessly ran into the street to retrieve a ball or batted one through someone's window. No one was expected to work hard at the game and win a college scholarship in later years.

Climbing trees with my girlfriends—brown-haired, green-eyed Georgia Lee, redheaded, freckle-faced Betty Jo and platinum-blonde Myrna—was one of my favorite pastimes. This colorful trio of girls were four, six and eight years older than I but graciously included me in their activities. Myrna's corner lot held several of the best and tallest climbing trees on our block.

Now, none of us had ever seen an apartment other than those pictured in movies. We thought that this lifestyle looked sophisticated and glamorous, so we created our idea of living in an apartment building by climbing up to various levels, or "floors," in tall pecan trees. Since I was the youngest and smallest, thus lightest in weight of the group, I always got the penthouse at the very top. Mother frequently received phone calls from nervous neighbors who worried about the heights to which I climbed. Mercifully, during all of my pre-school climbing, I never had a fall. This was probably because I intuited the weight-bearing potential of limbs in frequently climbed neighborhood trees.

When I was eight, I learned a good safety lesson while visiting a classmate named Mickey in another neighborhood. As I climbed up into an unfamiliar "apartment building," my choice of domains turned out to be a dead limb. As soon as I entered my new residence, the penthouse and I both came crashing down. It took what seemed like forever for me to catch my breath and start breathing normally again. Fortunately, nothing but my climber's dignity was injured.

When Myrna's family left San Antonio and moved to New England, their house was sold to a family whose last name was Tom. Jimmy Tom, several years younger than I, soon became one of my most unique friends.

I have read about churches where glossolalia is practiced. Is seems that whenever a member begins to speak in tongues, there is another member of the congregation who receives the interpretation. Jimmy spoke his own special language, which usually left both family and friends in the dark. For some reason, I had no trouble understanding him when he expressed himself. Mrs. Tom was delighted to discover that her son had acquired a new friend who was bilingual as far as her son's verbal hieroglyphics were concerned. There were many occasions over the years when she called our house and put him on the phone to tell me what he was saying. She then took the phone back so I could relay the translation.

Jimmy scowled all of the time, so some of our neighbors decided he must be an unpleasant child. He was actually extremely witty and a most pleasant companion. His scowl had probably become permanent due to frustration over not being understood.

The first time I took Jimmy home to meet my parents, Mother had just taken a sheet of cookies out of the oven. She and Dad were sitting in the breakfast nook enjoying coffee and warm cookies. Dad offered cookies to Jimmy, who put his hands on his hips, scowled and answered, "Doh wahn no tootie!"

This amused my parents so much that they interrogated him each time he came over to play. They enjoyed listening to his strange lingo, and since he was a young man of few words, the only way they could manage this was by asking him questions.

I don't think Jimmy was ever fooled by what was going on. He was extremely intelligent, and probably answered all of their questions simply to get that part of his visit over with.

Hide-and-seek was a game favored by children in my neighborhood. Ample shrubbery in various shades of green provided more than adequate places to secret ourselves. The child who was designated It chose a base, covered his eyes and counted to an agreed-upon number. Once his eyes were open, he called out, "Ready or not, here I come!"

As he began the hunt, we each watched for a moment when he turned away from us so that we could seize the opportunity to venture forth from our place of concealment, run to the base and get home free. If we were caught in this act prior to reaching the base, we were "out."

This was a very adaptable game, which we played inside some

houses. If the home was not suitable for hiding ourselves, we used a variation of the game and hid an inanimate object instead.

After Stormy's death, I often played hide-and-seek with his replacement, a Boston terrier named Rusty. Daddy would hold on to Rusty's collar while I hid in another room. Then he would instruct, "Go find Vallie." In this version of the game, Rusty was always It. He never failed to find me or to demonstrate his excitement by hopping up and down. Of course, he was always praised and petted and sometimes rewarded with a doggy treat.

Stiff-Starch was a popular pastime when only two children were in the mood for play. We straightened and stiffened our arms as much as possible as we held them out in front of us. Then we locked just the ends of our bent fingers. Standing on tiptoe, and leaning back, we whirled around and around as fast as possible. The object was to be the last to get dizzy, let go and fall down on the grass.

Swinging Statues was another game where combating dizziness and remaining upright was the goal. The swinger held onto one hand of a player and swung him around and around, building up speed, then finally releasing him. The other player tried not to fall and to remain totally motionless once he stopped flying across the yard. He was required to keep the pose in which he landed as other players took their turns at being launched in different directions. The end result was a yard filled with statue-like children each trying to suppress their giggles. The swinger then chose the best human statue, and that child replaced him as the next swinger.

If we found ourselves temporarily without playmates to swing us, we were likely to simply go into the yard and whirl in a series of Sufi-like circles until we eventually became dizzy and collapsed laughing.

A favorite game played both in and out of trees was Tarzan. The Tarzan films, starring Johnny Weissmuller, were extremely popular; and we all loved to pierce the neighborhood tranquility with our version of the famed Tarzan yell.

Naturally, we had to take turns playing the Tarzan role. Though my middle name is Jane, I did not like playing the part of Tarzan's rather passive mate. I did, however, greatly relish turning myself into Cheetah the Chimp. This role allowed one free rein to do extemporaneous acrobatics on the lawn or to swing from a rope or limb while vocalizing an amazing variety of sounds.

Often, extra children were assigned the roles of explorers who ventured into Tarzan's wilderness. They, of course, created danger and conflict and took our jungle-based imaginations and egos thousands of miles away from Kayton Avenue.

When enough children were gathered in one spot, the game Red Rover was often requested. In this game, two teams were formed. The children on each side held hands with strong grips, which they hoped could not be broken. Members on each side agreed upon a person on the other team to call over. They choose a person whom they believed was least likely to be able to break through the grip of any of their players.

After a choice was made, they sang out, "Red Rover, Red Rover. Let Mary come over." Mary then left her team and ran as fast as she could in order to break through the opposite side. If she managed to break someone's grip, she selected a member of that team to return home with her. The child thought to be the strongest was normally selected. If Mary failed to break through, she became a captive member of the other team.

This game was usually played until one side ended up with most of the players.

By the time we reached the upper elementary school grades, popularity replaced strength as the criterion for choosing people during this game. However, before we started school, and in early elementary school, an ability to run fast and a willingness to hurl oneself into a human barrier allowed Red Rover to be played in its pure form.

Guessing games, such as I Spy, could be played anywhere, so were often started during a lull between more active pursuits. I played this with my family members frequently when no other young folks were around. The object a player selected had to be located in a pre-designated area. Normally, the first clue given had to do with its color. "I spy something green," a player might say. Others responded with questions like "Is it up high?"

If guesses were not connecting, the player who chose the object eventually started giving clues as to its location: "You're getting warm." If the children guessing looked farther and farther away from the object, they were "getting cold." The person who guessed the correct object got to select the next one.

Many times a parent transporting a carload of squirming young children started a game of "I Spy" in order to occupy minds and settle down an energetic cargo. A variation of this game played in cars used cloud formations as objects.

Sometimes clouds resemble animals or inanimate objects if one's imagination is allowed free rein. So, a child might say, "I spy a lion." Fellow passengers scanned the sky until they located a cloud that fit that description.

Wearing roller skates made us feel taller and more grown-up. These steel skates were not mounted on shoes but were adjustable and attached to the bottom of our own shoes using a tool called a skate key. One had to wear a shoe with a sole that protruded enough for a skate-grip to fit over and lock onto. Using the skate key, the skates were then locked on as tightly as possible and a leather ankle strap was fastened firmly.

Even with careful precautions and adjustments, it was not unusual for a skate to come off as we rolled rapidly down the sidewalk. Most of us wore an assortment of skinned knees, bruises and scratches on our arms and legs, attesting to our love of speed, the instability of the roller skate mechanism and, sometimes, a cracked and bumpy sidewalk.

Bright-colored steel scooters were also a popular means of using one's energy to propel down a sidewalk. Often, children used wooden scooters that rolled on a set of skate wheels. This unique method of transportation normally meant that a father's elbow-grease had triumphed over a lack of funds.

Exercises people of today are urged to do regularly are the same type of activities children of my generation did on a daily basis as a form of releasing energy and expressing the joy of movement. No one had to tell us to go outside and run. We ran for blocks, sometimes chasing others and sometimes simply enjoying how good it made us feel. We turned cartwheels and somersaults, did backbends, stood on our heads and would try any sort of acrobatic maneuver we had seen demonstrated by a friend or observed when taken to a circus. During my entire childhood, I only knew two people who were overweight, and they were a mother and daughter.

Our connection with the circus, once it arrived in San Antonio, was twofold. In that era, the arrival of the big tent show was a momentous occasion. The circus traveled by train, so there was a parade of all of the performers and animals as they left the railroad station and headed for the arena in which they would later perform. Circus parades were free, so many a family who lacked the money to buy tickets to the big show took their children to view the amazing animals and flamboyant performers as they passed by. Circus people understood this, and played to the crowds along their route, leaving many a happy child behind.

My mother wrote, "Oct. 16, 1933. Vallie saw her first circus parade. Hagen-Beck-Wallace had the first parade that has been given here for thirteen years. Mother Fletcher, Jo Ella (our beloved housekeeper) and I took her. She enjoyed every bit of it, but most of all...the horses."

Most of my friends and I did get taken to the show under the big tent. Our favorite performers were the clowns who drove into the arena in an extremely small car. How they were packed in, we never knew, but we laughed and laughed as one clown after the other opened the door and ran out of the car. Each time the door was closed, we *knew* there could absolutely not be another clown inside of that car. Then, the door would open and another clown would pop out.

Carnivals coming into town were another sure lure for young people. My parents would sometimes take me to a carnival and allow me to ride some of the safer-looking rides and go through the Fun House. However, the carnivals of that day always had a large portion of their area devoted to freak shows. When I asked about this, my father said, "None of us will ever attend a freak show. Carnival promoters are very cruel when they exploit individuals who have some sort of physical deformity.

"The people in these shows cannot help their birth defects. Exhibiting them before an audience is deplorable. They not only have to endure the stares of onlookers, but they have to listen to crude and insulting remarks. People who produce this sort of show ought to be arrested."

No matter how cold or warm the weather, most children preferred outside fun until a parent called them in. Once we reluctantly left pursuits requiring physical energy and went inside, we had to turn to activities more sedentary in nature.

Paper dolls, with a wardrobe of clothes that had to be carefully cut out, were a lot less expensive than regular dolls. Little girls could remain enchanted for a long time by freeing these pretty beings, along with their wardrobes, from the printed page. Then, of course, identities and scenarios had to be created and acted out for each paper doll.

Filling in the pages of coloring books, drawing pictures and using crayons to finish our masterpieces or putting together pieces of a puzzle were all good activities solitary or shared with friends. Mother purchased picture books that displayed each facet of Shirley Temple's life in Hollywood.

Other child celebrities of that day were Canada's Dionne quintuplets. In those years, prior to fertility drugs, the entire world considered the survival of these five children a miracle. Each stage of their development was photographed and turned into a magazine article, children's book or film documentary.

Boys played with metal toy soldiers and built all sorts of things from wooden Tinker Toys—circular blocks with holes in them that were connected using short dowels. Sturdy toys of that day lasted and, if someone had the foresight to pack them away in boxes, could still be enjoyed by the great-grandchildren of the original owners.

In 1934, Charles B. Darrow of Germantown, Pennsylvania, tried to get Parker Brothers to accept a game he invented. The company rejected his idea; but Mr. Darrow thought it would be a big hit, so he produced the game himself and sold it in Philadelphia. Darrow's game caught on so fast that he was unable to keep up with the orders, so he contacted Parker Brothers again. They took a second look, and by 1935 Monopoly was the best-selling game in America.

This game soon found its way into the homes of many of my friends. A heavyweight game board with original artwork, wooden houses and hotels, Chance and Community Chest cards decorated with illustrations which haven't been used since that year combined to keep my friends and me fascinated as we plotted to obtain pieces of real estate.

As far as remaining seated at a card table, I preferred playing Chinese checkers, Old Maid, dominoes or Go Fish. Fortunately, there were always adults ready to indulge me by providing me with opponents. My two unmarried great-aunts, Vallie and Lulu, never seemed to take offense when told "You're the Old Maid!"

After sunset, we often chased, caught and collected fireflies in canning jars with breathing holes punched through the lids. Those tiny, miraculous creatures fascinated small viewers and were always released prior to our bedtime.

We also enjoyed sitting in yards and simply looking up at a star-filled sky. This was a great time in which secrets could be shared and fledgling ideas concerning mysteries of the universe exchanged.

Cool evenings, plus a back yard filled with comfortable lawn chairs, provided the perfect setting for my father and me to play jokes on our very proper female relatives. Together, we hatched many schemes and all sorts of tricks to play on my mother, grandmother and great-aunts. We conspired ahead of time and set up props we might need before it got dark.

One of my favorite deceptions involved putting several sets of reflectors in different locations in the back portion of our lawn. The reflectors were placed just far enough apart to look like the eyes of a large animal when a flashlight beam was turned on them at night.

After dark, when family members had gathered and were enjoying conversation and cool breezes, Dad would ask, "Did you hear on the radio about that panther escaping from the zoo?"

None of the others, of course, had heard it.

I would respond, "Yes, I heard the newscast over at Gwen's house. They said it had been tracked into this area and then they lost it."

Mother, always a patsy and never a conspirator, chimed in, "Well, I hope they find it soon. I don't like to think of something like that wandering around."

The seed was planted. We dropped the subject and initiated other topics.

After about thirty minutes, Dad piped up, "Be quiet, I thought I heard something."

I offered, "I think I heard a noise in the pecan tree."

Dad picked up the flashlight, turned it on the pecan tree and did a limb-by-limb scan. Sure enough, there was a pair of large shiny eyes staring at us.

The women gasped and jumped. Dad cautioned, "Shhh."

He then turned the beam on the wood pile where the creature had obviously jumped. Eyes, fierce and ominous, looked at us from a new location. Another beam from the flashlight showed a move closer to the back fence.

The women were going nuts. "William, call the police immediately!" Aunt Lulu demanded.

Dad and I drew our scenario out with frequent moves of the mountain lion until we became bored and finally confessed. This particular ruse worked so well that we left the reflectors in place in order to pull the same trick on different groups.

One evening, a group of Girl Scouts gathered to spend the night on cots in our back yard. They proved to be the bravest of our victims. Each one accepted my challenge to help capture the creature. As my father muffled his laughter, troop members followed as I ventured forth into the dangerous darkness. We each were armed with a broom or mop.

Our family and friends spent endless daytime hours in the back yard knocking wooden balls through metal wickets with heavy wooden mallets. San Antonio had the perfect climate to leave a croquet game set up for a time when the urge might strike potential players.

After my first trip to the circus, my father purchased heavy steel pipes and constructed a sturdy set of swings, a trapeze and an acting bar so I could enjoy trying some of the stunts I had witnessed being performed by trapeze artists. Hanging by my knees as the trapeze flew in arcs both thrilled and relaxed me.

My first swing and trapeze hung from ropes that were interchangeable. Once, Daddy took down the trapeze and placed it on the ground so the swing could be hung from large metal hooks. Unfortunately, he made the mistake of leaving the trapeze on the ground overnight.

Without anyone realizing it, our dog amused himself by chewing on the trapeze rope sometime that evening. The next day, Mother joined me in the back yard, and I asked if she would like to swing from my trapeze. In a playful mood, she agreed.

As Mother got up speed, hanging by her knees, the rope broke. Fortunately, she did not break her neck, but she did sustain a hard blow to her head. It was not until years later, during a physical examination, that she learned her skull had been fractured.

The egg-sized knot, just above her hairline, never went away. However, the offending ropes did. They were promptly replaced by heavy chains, which did not even tempt our dog.

Organized circle games, such as The Farmer in the Dell, were usually initiated by adults and played at special events like birthday parties. This game was one of the many games of selection we learned.

Children hoped to be chosen from the outer circle to stand in the center as part of the farmer's realm. The original farmer chose his wife, prompted by the song lyrics. As subsequent verses rang out, the wife chose the child who chose the dog who chose the cat who chose the rat who chose the cheese...and so on.

Other circle games used a common formula and were simply a variation of the popular game of tag. Normally, an individual player was tagged by the child who was designated as It. He or she then had to run around the outside of the circle and return to his spot before he was caught, or his space was occupied by the original tagger. If either of these events occurred, he was doomed to go into the "Mush-Pot" in the center of the circle. Quite a few of these circle games included a Mush Pot, which one assiduously tried to avoid.

The San Antonio Mexican culture acquainted children with the excitement of being blindfolded while swinging a stick at a moving piñata packed full of small surprises. Of course, after the elusive piñata finally sustained a hit and spilled all its contents on the ground, we all dropped to our knees and scooped up an assortment of candies, gum and tiny toys.

Dropping wooden clothespins into a milk bottle, throwing bean bags into a container, being blindfolded, whirled in circles and then trying to pin the tail on the donkey were all birthday party games for which one could win a prize purchased for a nickel or dime. We each tried our best to win, and when we did, we cherished the prize.

I probably owe my hand-eye coordination to the hours I spent playing two particular games. Tiddly winks and pick-up sticks could keep a solitary child occupied trying to "beat the system." Though both games were designed for several players, a single child could forget about the scoring system and practice flipping a wink into the small glass cup or picking up a single wooden stick from a stack of sticks without causing any other stick to move.

If forced to stay in one spot for a period of time, a child could spin a colorful tune-playing top or practice batting a small rubber ball attached with a line of stretchy rubber to a wooden paddle.

During games of dress-up, a large portion of our fun was in locating and collecting various articles of adult clothing. Surely, the high-heeled shoes, feathered hats, dress gloves, long skirts and leather purses we ended up with were too large for us. Our pride in searching for, assembling and modeling a make-believe wardrobe inspired such artists as Norman Rockwell, and became the subject of many a magazine cover in the thirties and forties.

As small children, we observed and admired older friends as they left for school. So, we played Rock School, and promoted ourselves from grade to grade. All that was needed for this game was a small rock and a staircase of some sort.

"Teacher" held her hands behind her back, concealing the rock in one hand while the "students" took turns guessing which hand the rock was in. Each correct guess meant a student could move up a step, which represented a promotion to the next grade. Graduation awaited us on the top step, so our goal was to be the first to reach this plateau. Of course, our scholastic careers were extremely dependent upon the integrity of the teacher, as it was simple to switch the rock from hand to hand behind one's back.

"Button, button, who's got the button?" was the name of another popular game of the 1930s. Just as Rock School required only a small rock to keep a group of children guessing, an easily obtained button of any size or color kept us mesmerized and honed our observational skills. Many housewives sewed the clothing worn by family members, and just about every woman mended garments in need of repair. So, buttons were kept in stock and supplied on loan to offspring in the mood for this popular pastime.

Players stood in a circle holding their hands at waist level with palms together as if in prayer. The person who was It secreted the button in his hands as he progressed around the circle placing his hands in between the hands of each player in turn. He withdrew his folded hands slowly and carefully, trying to disguise the moment when he dropped the button into the hands of one player.

Children tried to avoid making any facial expression that would give away if the button was, or was not, dropped into their hands. At the same time, everyone else watched carefully hoping to read the expressions and body language of the other players.

After It finished making the rounds of the circle, he asked, "Button. button, who's got the button?" Each child in the circle was allowed one guess in turn. The child who actually held the button was supposed to keep a straight face and guess the name of another player when it was his turn.

If the child with the button did a good job of concealing his identity, guesses kept making the rounds of the circle. Often, children could not suppress a giggle, which gave them away. If the button-holding participant's name was called, he was required to open his hands and show the button to the group.

When children on Kayton Avenue heard the music of a hand-organ coming near, we ran to our parents and asked for some change. About once a week an organ-grinder brought his monkey around to entertain us.

Monkeys who accompanied these musical masters were always dressed in costumes that included some variety of cap. We knew that as long as we threw pennies down on the sidewalk the monkey would continue to dance. Once we ran out of change, the music stopped playing and the monkey began picking up all of our pennies and placing them into his hat. While still surrounded by fascinated neighborhood children, he handed his hat to the organ-grinder and waved goodbye as they continued their musical stroll, seeking another audience and more precious pennies.

Playing House excited groups of small girls, who were always ready to start their version of this game. I only knew one child who actually owned a playhouse and it was a humdinger!

Judy was a distant cousin whose grandparents lived on a ranch in the Texas Hill Country. Her grandfather built her a stone playhouse that was a duplicate of the large ranch home. Several rooms were furnished with everything a housewife might possibly need, in miniature. I often visited the Armour ranch when Judy was in residence and was in my element sharing this magical domain.

On Kayton Avenue, my friends and I simply staked out an area of a room or front porch, brought along our babies and tiny kitchen equipment and set about running our household. There had to be a mommy and daddy, often grandmothers and grandfathers, and other children. Dolls, of course, were the babies.

Unless a doll was made in the image of a person, real or imaginary, it was a baby doll. There were no sexy, sophisticated Barbie-type dolls on the market.

Our portrayal of parents tended to be bossy if not downright dictatorial. These games of house could be abandoned if one of us was called home to eat a meal, and then taken up later. When we were lucky, the real mother in the home where we played would donate food for us to "cook" on our make-believe stove.

Two games that required players to stay focused and listen carefully to words being spoken were Simon Says and Mother, may I? Each of these games required at least two players but could involve a much larger group.

The ability to give rapid-fire verbal instructions, while keeping a straight face, was a definite asset to the leader of Simon Says. His duty was to issue orders requiring his followers to progress forward in a particular manner. "Simon says, 'Take two baby steps.' Simon says, 'Take four giant steps.'" On and on he would go, each time altering the

38

type and number of steps. As the tempo of the game increased, the leader would try to sneak in an order, omitting the prefix "Simon says."

The correct response by players when "Simon says" was left out was to remain still and not follow the order. However, players were often so focused on the number and type of steps they were supposed to perform that they went ahead and followed the leader's order. Any player who moved without Simon's okay was immediately out of the game.

"Mother, may I?" also gradually increased in tempo, and included a leader who gave his followers a specific number and kind of body movements to perform. The leader might say, "Take three side jumps." A follower was required to ask, "Mother, may I?" prior to moving. He was to listen for the response "Yes, you may" before he moved a muscle. With a number of children involved, and their focus on different types of physical movement, a child often forgot to ask the key question or listen for the leader's response. A clever leader might answer, "No, you may not," countermanding his order. Thus, an alert player, who mastered the art of careful listening and paid constant attention to both verbal and physical responses, was the last child left in the game.

Contrasting games of the 1930s with the unlimited supply of children's manufactured games today, it is obvious that creativity of that era was up to the individual child, or group of children. They had simple toys and games which they expanded on with their own resourcefulness. A wooden gun, hand-carved by a father, in the palm of a young child's hand took on a life of its own when someone suggested, "Play like..." Those were the two words that started most of our adventures. Ideas exploded like popcorn, and soon a group of small children were cowboys protecting a stagecoach loaded with gold. We were our own writers, directors, producers and actors.

The ball of imagination was tossed back and forth with the greatest of ease. When caught by one of the players, it was often altered somewhat by another: "Then, let's play like..." This mighty sphere of creative pretense never touched the ground nor remained static as long as children were allowed free rein.

A sense of fairness, which is built into the persona of each child, made us realize that we could not always be the hero and sometimes had to be the bad guy. We relished playing the part of the one who got shot, and honed our looks of surprise and horror, practiced our cries of pain and perfected our slow drops to the ground where we uttered our whispered last words.

When I was small, my father often drove me to the banks of a tree-lined creek near San Antonio. I was content to sit in the shade of large oak and pecan trees and throw small rocks into the dark green water for long stretches of time. The plopping sounds and expanding circle of ripples that appeared on the creek's smooth surface combined to keep me well entertained. Conversation was unnecessary, yet a strong father-daughter bond developed during this silent and simple activity within an extremely tranquil environment. Those peaceful moments gave me time to remember Vivian Jean, and to pretend she was away from her alley and sitting on the creek bank with us.

Certainly, children of today are endowed with vast amounts of imagination and creativity. They see more of the world on television during their first few years than we encountered, or even dreamed about, when we reached adulthood. Today's child may choose a toy, press a button or flip a switch, and the toy will set about performing whatever function it has been programmed to do. Thus, at times the only creativity involved is that of the original designer and manufacturer.

A toy of today may not need a child to contribute anything of value to its operation. Indeed, the toy can continue to do its own thing if placed on a chair or dropped to the floor.

After the excitement of unwrapping Christmas gifts and admiring new toys, today's child might turn her attention to the cardboard boxes discarded amidst piles of gift wrapping. Just like children of the thirties, they are tempted to enter their own make-believe world and use these boxes to create a train, fort or playhouse while carefully chosen gifts, now forgotten, languish beneath an artificial tree.

CHAPTER THREE

FAMILY ENTERTAINMENT

What on earth did you do?" I've been asked any number of times by young people suddenly confronted by the fact that homes of the 1930s did not have television or electronic games.

"We talked."

"What did you look at?"

"One another."

"You're kidding!"

This was a generation of communicators. Radio was an important addition to homes of that era, but people did not sit and listen for long periods of time nor did they leave their radios turned on except for a specific program. During dreaded afternoon naps, I lay next to my mother and listened to soap operas. These programs were in their infancy, and were called by that name because sponsors were almost all makers of newly introduced "wash powders."

"Have the whitest wash on your block," urged radio announcers as they appealed to housewives during commercial breaks. Large galvanized tubs, a washboard and a bar of lye soap were used to launder clothes and household linens. The wet wash was then carried in woven straw laundry baskets and affixed to backyard clotheslines with wooden clothespins.

It was assumed by New York advertising executives, never known for their connection to reality, that women based their social status upon their neighbor's assessment of their wash as it flapped in the breeze. A typical radio commercial featured two women standing at their back fence and talking.

"Have you ever seen anything like Alma's wash?" one asked.

"No, I haven't," answered her friend. "Her whites are so brilliant, they absolutely sparkle!"

"Compared to hers, both of our washes look dull and dingy! My husband was so embarrassed at work the other day. One of his coworkers made a remark about his shirt collar being tattletale gray!"

At this time, Alma is heard as she carries another basket of wet wash to hang on her clothesline. She is singing, "Rinso white! Rinso white! Happy little washday song."

Those phrases—"dull and dingy" and "tattletale gray"—were 30s-era buzz words used to persuade and coerce housewives into abandoning their bars of lye soap and trying a particular brand of wash powder.

So, we followed the dramatic stories of "Oxydol's Own *Ma Perkins*," *Stella Dallas*, *Our Gal Sunday* and other homespun heroines. As the dramas unfolded, they were about family, with a few innocent romances thrown in. Each tale was quite safe for the ears of small children.

During the commercial breaks, listeners were informed about special items that a box of a specific wash powder contained. If a housewife purchased a certain brand over a period of months, she could collect an entire set of glasses or dinnerware. One only had to check the picture on the box to see if it held the serving piece needed to fill out a set. A cash shortage, plus the idea of a free gift in each box, persuaded many a housewife to give these new wash powders a try.

Many a bride collected silverware by serving her groom cereals made by the Post Product Division of General Foods. By consuming Post's Huskies or Whole Bran Shreds, a couple collected Consumer Coupons which they could redeem for William Rodgers heavy silverplate. Thirty coupons mailed to Battle Creek, Michigan, would buy a teaspoon (valued at $4 per dozen). If the couple felt flush enough to part with fifteen cents, they could mail that in accompanied by only one coupon. With patience and persistent cereal crunching, 30s-era newlyweds could eventually collect an entire set of silverware without parting with any cash.

The radio next to my parents' bed was a small ivory-colored tabletop model. When Daddy came home in the evening, we gathered in the living room and listened to world news on the enormous console in the front of the house. There were only two dials, one for power and volume and the other to search for the few stations available. When the dial ranged between stations, loud static assaulted our ears.

As soon as the news was over, the radio was switched off, and our family entered the dining room to eat supper. (*Dinner* referred to the noon meal.) Radio news reports concerned important local, national and world events. Absolutely no air-time was given to the antics of celebrity entertainers.

Most people ate their last meal of the day early. After that, evenings were quiet and devoted to family togetherness. Bedtimes were usually early, and I never heard anyone complain of insomnia during my entire childhood.

When I was very small, my parents and I often took a stroll after supper. A particular one of these forays away from our block stands out in my memory.

We approached a house with an appealing raised flower bed in the front yard. Its ornate stone holding-wall intrigued me, so I decided to investigate. To pull myself up, I reached out and grabbed hold of something that appeared sturdy and green. This impulsive act served as my introduction to Texas cactus. Both parents spent the next few hours holding tweezers as they tried to extricate numerous tiny spines from my hands.

Back at home, a family member in the mood for comedy might turn the radio dial until he heard the voices of Bob Hope, Fibber McGee and Mollie, Edgar Bergen and Charlie McCarthy (a famous ventriloquist and his dummy), George Burns and Gracie Allen, Lum and Abner or Amos and Andy. Wanting people to leave the radio tuned to their station, announcers would say things like, "Ah, ah, ah! Don't touch that dial!" during a commercial break.

At times, our evening programs were interrupted, or totally blotted out, by Spanish-language broadcasts from Mexico. The Mexican stations were not regulated like those in the United States. Rather than have a certain area assigned in which they could legally broadcast, their air-waves were free to reach out and travel as far as possible. Like pirates, they often captured and scuttled the broadcasts of our local stations.

One Man's Family, a Sunday evening series, featured several generations of one family who lived together. This show was a national favorite, and certainly mirrored the three generations in our own home. Our entire family gathered each Sunday and listened with rapt attention as events in this drama unfolded.

Children loved *Captain Midnight*, *Jack Armstong, the All-American Boy!* and series featuring other heroic males. Females were never the lead character of a children's show.

Many of my friends loved *Let's Pretend*, broadcast on Saturday mornings. I thought those adult-produced shows were overly dramatic, and preferred the pretending my friends and I did on a regular basis. The announcer who read us the Sunday funny papers displayed a similar kind of fake enthusiasm. I much preferred listening to my father's monotone delivery than the pruned voice, polished diction and insincere words of the performer.

Rather than soap, children's series were almost all sponsored by a brand of cereal or Ovaltine, billed as a drink that would make skinny kids beef up with muscles and gain weight. My friends and I sang their sales-jingles and urged our parents to buy Wheaties, Post Toasties, Malt o' Meal, Ralston or any cereal that offered an opportunity to mail in a nickel, along with a coupon cut from the box, and receive such treasures as a secret code ring by return mail.

My favorite radio shows were those broadcast in the evenings with

Gwen

mysterious titles like *Lights Out*, *Inner Sanctum*, *I Love a Mystery* and *Suspense*. The music and content of these programs scared both my mother and one of my best friends, Mary Gwendolyn Echterhoff.

Frightening Gwen was very easy to do, and she traditionally broadcast her fear with ear-splitting screams. I often chased poor Gwen with wiggling earthworms or a jar containing her tonsils and adenoids that was kept prominently displayed on the Echterhoff's living room mantel.

When I tired of this, I plotted to lure her to our house just in time to hear the opening music for one of those supernatural thrillers. I knew from experience when Gwen heard the first bars of the introductory music—loud, dramatic sounds chosen to frighten—she would scream and run.

So, deviously, I would position myself where I could grab hold of her as she bolted. I then held on to her as her feet ran in place, her expression changed to wild-eyed horror and she commenced to release a pitiful, pathetic series of screams. By the time the music stopped, Mother was in the room, and Gwen had been saved from my clutches.

Always sweet and polite, Gwen deserved a friend who was not so entertained by her vulnerability to worms, tonsils and scary music. Today, she claims she does not even remember the times I tormented her in order to watch her run away screaming. In any event, since I've reviewed my memories with great guilt, she forgives me.

Mysterious music was just one of the many sound effects used in early radio to set a mood and to keep the story moving. During the 1920s, when radio changed from being a simple tool of military communication into a method of popular entertainment, all manner of manual sound effects were invented. By the 1930s, the busiest person during a radio show was the sound man.

Most sound men entered the field simply to get into radio, and had neither experience nor training for the job. Some were so eager to say they were in show-biz that they were not even paid.

Mistakes and miscalculations often occurred on these live broadcasts as a sound man raced around a small studio trying to implement all of the script's necessary noises by hand. Hilarious situations often occurred when sound effects went awry but the actors continued reading the original script.

Astute, experienced actors could sometimes ad-lib in an effort to cover a sound man's mistake. Writers began to pre-identify sounds in the script so the radio audience could more easily differentiate between the sounds they would soon be hearing.

The imaginations of both children and adults worked overtime as they formed pictures of characters brought to life by mellow-voiced radio performers. Sometimes, children sat and shared their ideas about a certain character's physical appearance. Arguments often occurred when mental pictures clashed.

A beautiful example of an erroneous opinion formed while listening to a radio broadcast was shared with me by Native American writer Hyemeyohsts Storm in the summer of 2006. An extremely popular 30s era radio series was *The Shadow*. The Shadow was a superhero whose fame equaled that of Superman, Batman, The Green Hornet and the Lone Ranger during my childhood. The back-story involved the Shadow's alter-ego, wealthy playboy Lamont Cranston, making a journey to the Orient, where he learned "the power to cloud men's minds." Since these secret hypnotic powers allowed him to become invisible at will, the Shadow was able to solve all variety of mysterious crimes.

Orson Welles was the voice of the Shadow until 1937. Each segment of this eagerly awaited radio series began with a man's voice, accompanied by spooky background music, asking, "Who knows what evil lurks in the hearts of men?" Then came the answer, "Only the Shadow knows!"

Storm remembers the words of one of his favorite tribal aunties who lived on the Montana Cheyenne reservation of his childhood. Aunt Millie told his mother that she really enjoyed listening to the Indian actor who played on *The Shadow*.

"What Indian actor?" his mother asked.

"You know," responded Millie, "Shadow Nose!"

Orson Welles did not disappear from radio fame after he relinquished his role as the Shadow. One of the most famous radio broadcasts from the 1930s was his October 30, 1938, production of *War of the Worlds*.

Welles used the novel by that name, which tells of a Martian invasion of Earth, and adapted it for radio by writing a script to sound like a series of live news broadcasts. At the beginning of the program, an announcer for the *Mercury Theater of the Air* told the radio audience that they were about to hear a radio play. Unfortunately, many Americans tuned in later when the show was in progress or did not pay attention to the original announcement.

It was a well-written and professionally acted show, and it sent people all over the nation into a panic. Convinced that they were hearing an actual account of an invasion by Mars, rather than a pre-Halloween scary story, many individuals immediately took steps to protect themselves and their families. Law enforcement agencies were inundated with calls.

Radio audiences of that era were extremely naive when it came to the ability to see through deceptive simulations. Listeners terrified by *War of the* Worlds were probably more susceptible to belief because they remembered hearing a well-known newscaster describe a horrible tragedy a year before.

Luxury airships called zeppelins, manufactured in Germany, carried wealthy travelers across the Atlantic prior to that job being taken over by airliners. The largest and most luxurious of these flying hotels ever built was scheduled to land at Lakehurst, New Jersey, on May 6, 1937.

Radio announcer Herb Morrison was awaiting the arrival of the *Hindenburg* at the Lakehurst airstrip accompanied by a small film crew who would capture this illustrious moment by filming a newsreel to be later shown in movie theaters.

As the impressive *Hindenburg* hovered above members of its ground crew, who were preparing to catch and secure ropes dropped from the ship, it suddenly burst into flame. It only took seconds for the flames to envelope the entire ship as newsreel cameramen recorded the awful sight of bodies dropping from the zeppelin onto the landing strip. Morrison, broadcasting live, fought to control his emotions so he could let his radio audience know what was happening.

His smooth description of the ship's approach soon turned into a jumbled sobbing as he reacted to the horror in progress. Those of us who listened on our radios will never forget the anguish with which he relayed the event in progress.

"This is one of the worst catastrophes in the world!...Oh! It's four or five hundred feet into the sky...It's a terrific crash, ladies and gentlemen...Oh, the humanity... and all of the passengers!"

I did not hear Orson Welles' *War of the Worlds* broadcast, but I can imagine how professional actors and sound men could have fooled listeners into thinking another disaster was taking place.

Probably the most important home activity for children of my generation was listening to stories, read or told to us by our elders. It was during this time we not only learned about the lives of our parents and ancestors but in so doing became very clear about who we were and what family influences had helped us become that person. No counselors or prescription drugs were needed for us reach that conclusion.

I would remain totally transfixed when Mother read to me or my father told stories. Dad was a great teller of historic tales as well as my favorite—panther stories. The first panther stories he told were true events from his ranching experience.

I became so addicted to hearing the adventures of these wild creatures, also called cougars or mountain lions, that I begged for more and different accounts. Dad's stash of true tales was soon depleted, so he became most adept in spontaneously inventing new ones. I often tested his ability by requesting plots in a color-specific manner: "Tell me a story about a black panther."

Mother read nursery rhymes and poems to me from the time I was an infant. When I began to talk, my elders insisted I usually spoke in rhyme. I assume it was because I had already heard a lot of rhyming words and I took delight in creating my own. My rhymes were used both to express my feelings and desires—"I have had a very long trip. An ice cream cone I'd like to nip" was one of those Mother recorded as we drove back into San Antonio from a Hill Country journey.

Everyone accepted this, though I supposed they judged my habit to be a little odd. Before my parents knew what was happening, however, our neighbor, Mrs. M., alerted a group of professors who needed a guinea pig to study. Their plan was to follow me, pen and paper in hand, and record what I said. They asked my mother to do the same in their absence.

Having these serious profs in our midst was no fun, so I eventually began to talk like everyone else and they went away. Meanwhile, my mother had an unfinished anecdotal record to which she continued to add. I have found it both hilarious and invaluable when it comes to testing my own memory of events.

Hearing my mother recite "The Raven," memorized when she was a student at Beaumont High School, introduced me to the works of Edgar Allen Poe. I wanted more and more of his stories. Perhaps this was a strange choice for a small child, who may not have understood the subtleties within his plots but loved the magic of his words.

Longfellow's *Evangeline* also affected me strongly, and though it is a long poem, I often asked to have it re-read. Each time I heard the story of these young Acadian lovers, parted by the misfortune of their exile, I wept.

Yet, I was always ready to have my mother start over when the tale ended. She would pour herself a glass of water to drink during the lengthy readings and would provide several linen handkerchiefs for me to use as I shed tears for Evangeline Bellefontaine and Gabriel Lajeunesse.

I was quickly and easily transported into the thatch-roofed village of Grand Pre, home of the Acadian farmers, the minute I heard "This is the forest primeval. The murmuring pines and the hemlocks..."

My emotional connection to this tale was so strong that, when I was a little older, my parents drove me to the legendary home of the individuals who were said to have inspired Longfellow's work. Saint Martinville, Louisiana, with its Evangeline Oak, old Catholic Church and the boat landing where these persecuted exiles finally reached a safe harbor, made the characters in the poem seem even more real.

Because my mother was such a devoted reader, and we often played games with my wooden alphabet blocks, she made it easy to learn the alphabet. Mother wrote, "November 15, 1933. By 19 months, baby Vallie knew every letter in the alphabet. On her blocks...in her books... in the newspaper or anywhere she sees them. I can take a pencil and write the letters and she will call them out as fast as I write them."

This was not a skill that could be attributed to my IQ. It was purely a by-product of my mother's ability and determination to turn anything of an instructional nature into enjoyment for her toddler.

I really don't know what inspired Mother to teach me sign language, but the two of us enjoyed using our secret language around others. The type of sign language she knew differs from that now taught in schools for the hearing impaired.

This came about because Mother's first cousin, writer Norma Patterson, suffered a nervous breakdown while in college. During this stress-related time, she totally lost her hearing, although the doctors could find no physical damage whatsoever to her ears. Whether or not the deafness was psychological, Norma never regained her hearing. Mother was determined to continue a lifetime of close communication with her cousin, so she learned the sign language Norma was being taught. Later, they both became expert lip-readers.

In this atmosphere, I was reading on my own long before entering the pre-primer at Highland Park Elementary. Like many young girls of that time, I devoured Nancy Drew mysteries. *The Secret of the Old Clock*, *The Hidden Staircase*, *The Bungalow Mystery*, *The Mystery at Lilac Inn*, *The Secret at Shadow Ranch* and *The Secret at Red Gate Farm* were the original six classics that hooked a generation of females into this series in which one of their own gender starred. The exploits of super-sleuth Nancy and her "chum, Bess" would sound quite dated if one could obtain copies of the original 1930 edition. Other titles were later added, and in 1959, the books were updated, rewritten and condensed.

The Judy Bolton mystery series, Louisa May Alcott's *Little Women*, the Bobbsey Twin series, *The Secret Garden*, *Peter Pan*, *Just David* and the wonderfully humorous *Ferdinand the Bull* were other favorites of my generation. Young boys collected books about the Hardy Boys instead of Nancy or Judy.

Mother tried on several occasions to read *Alice's Adventures in Wonderland* and *Through the Looking Glass* to me. I absolutely hated those stories and would ask her to please stop. She patiently waited for me to get a little older, then tried again and received the same response. Eventually, she suspended her efforts to acquaint me with those classic tales that I considered irritating and chaotic.

There was a story called "The Fat Little Fairy" within an extraordinary set of children's books my parents purchased. It told of a fat fairy the other fairies made fun of until they learned she was not a fairy at all; she was something called "a baby." I used to wonder why Mother read that tale so often. When I look back over my black-and-white baby pictures, though, I realize I resembled a sumo wrestler, and she was probably trying to reassure herself.

An extension of 30s-era comic strips, which children called "funny papers," were the ever-popular comic books. The exploits of Lil Abner and Daisy Mae in Dogpatch, Blondie and Dagwood trying to deal with his boss Mr. Dithers, Popeye and Olive Oil interacting with an assortment of unusual characters were just a few of the totally nonviolent personalities that held fascination for the young public.

Tillie the Toiler was a comic book character who pre-dated the feminist movement. These stories chronicled the exploits of and pitfalls encountered by a young woman who abandoned her "proper" place at home in order to pursue a job in the work force. As I visualize Tillie's face, as drawn by her creator, her expression mirrored a great deal of stress and anxiety.

Children saved their pennies until they had a dime to purchase one of the desired comic books. Most eventually acquired a collection of which they were proud. The more astute boys and girls learned the skills required to barter: "I'll trade you two copies of Dick Tracy for your new Superman after you've read it."

Few of us could be persuaded to lend a copy of a treasured comic book unless the borrower first provided us with a copy of a comic we judged to be of equal value. We may never have heard the word "collateral," but the business of comic book collecting and swapping taught us how to bargain.

Mother's childhood home housed parents and siblings who were musical and loved to perform. She was used to the sounds of multiple musical instruments, singing and noises of children at play. She also had developed an enthusiasm for cards and board games early in life. She once told me that she had hoped her child would also be a game player. Alas, it became apparent that, like my father and paternal grandmother, I preferred a quiet atmosphere and was happiest when my nose was in a book.

Of course, the rest of us sometimes compromised by taking a break from our fascinating reading material to play Chinese checkers or another parlor game with Mother.

Visiting neighbors, relatives and friends frequently showed up at our door, so we never suffered from the lack of stimulating conversation. Often, we sat on the porch during these visits.

A major drawing card for our particular porch was the almost nightly gathering of neighbors who loved to listen to my Uncle Nick take a bath. This process, I can assure you, created far more honest hilarity than one of today's sit-com simulated laugh tracks.

If this sounds perverted, let me hasten to explain that no one could see him. There was a high bathroom window that opened onto the side porch. The only possible explanation I can offer as to why this was such an entertaining pastime is that Nick must have shifted into an alternate reality the instant he stepped into our deep claw-foot bathtub.

Immediately, he began telling a series of jokes, roaring with laughter after each one. Diving under the water, he blew bubbles and made sea mammal sounds. It seemed at times that he conversed with others whom we could not hear.

Pausing, he would listen and then respond with strange remarks while laughing uproariously. Like a toddler, he slapped the water and laughed at the sound of the splashes. He sang songs and applauded himself. His baths were long in duration and his antics nonstop.

Nick never realized that members of a spellbound audience were trying to stifle their laughter so he would not stop his performance. Out of the bathtub, he was a normal, intelligent and traditionally witty young man. Handsome, and a sharp dresser, he often followed his bathtime routine with a visit to one of his many girlfriends.

That particular bathtub saved my grandmother's modesty when I escorted a parade of young children on a tour of our house. We were playing "tour guide," and the quickest route to my parent's bedroom was from the hall through the bathroom and into the east portion of the house.

My guests were quite short so, added to the depth of the tub, all they were able to see was Grandmother's head and neck as we interrupted her soak. However, none of us had any trouble hearing her shouts and admonitions.

Visiting the home of my friend Georgia Lee, I soon learned that we were required to be totally silent during the broadcast of *The Lone Ranger*. Her father sat with his ear next to the radio speaker in order to catch each word spoken by the Lone Ranger or Tonto. Certainly, this was a harmless habit, but his wife had a hobby that I felt was awful.

One could call a nearby drugstore, order ice cream and it would be delivered by a teenage boy on a bicycle. Our family often did this, and always tipped the boy who had fast-peddled for several miles so the ice cream would not melt. Only the amount of ice cream that could be consumed in one sitting was ordered—iceboxes did not keep things frozen like future electric refrigerators.

Mrs. H. often made bogus phone calls, ordering quarts of ice cream in many different flavors. When she did this, she gave the name and address of a close neighbor across the street. After she hung up the phone, she would sit on her porch in order to be an eyewitness to the delivery.

Of course, when the homeowners answered the doorbell they were astounded at the amount of ice cream the delivery boy carried.

"But we didn't order any ice cream," they would tell the crestfallen young man. He would be forced to remount his bicycle and transport his rapidly melting cargo as he made other deliveries prior to returning to the store. Hard work for a tip he did not receive.

There were times Mrs. H. ordered ice cream herself and served it in a most peculiar manner. She handed her husband, Georgia Lee and me bowls that held a miserly serving. Then she took the carton, a large spoon and sat in a porch glider until the container was empty. What prompted Mrs. H.'s thoughtlessness, I never knew, but my heart went out to a string of delivery boys who were defrauded by her mean-spirited actions.

From time to time, most parents took their children to a place where they could order an ice cream cone. The destination was usually a drugstore with a marble-top soda fountain. This was considered a special event, and something to which children eagerly looked forward. Two big dips of ice cream atop a tasty cone cost a nickel.

My favorite spot to enjoy this delicacy was the outlet for Borden's Creamery, which offered more than the usual flavors of vanilla, chocolate and strawberry. On trips there, I normally ordered a cone of lemon custard.

Being treated to a bottle of soda pop was also a special occasion. Drinks were served in ice-cold bottles and sweetened with pure cane sugar. This was many decades before sugar substitutes began flooding the market. There was no need for them because obesity was extremely rare.

Iceboxes were not kept filled with soft drinks at home. There is absolutely no contest when comparing the taste of the bottled drinks served in that era and today's canned drinks filled with artificial sweeteners. To make a taste test, drive to Dublin, Texas, and visit the original Dr. Pepper plant where this famous product is still made with pure cane sugar and sold in glass bottles.

Empty cold drink bottles were collected and returned to the store, where you could get a few cents for a six- or twelve-bottle carton. The bottles were then reused many times.

There were no fast food chains or convenience stores along the highways, so junk food had not yet been invented. For a snack, children were given an apple, banana or animal crackers along with a glass of milk or fresh-squeezed fruit juice.

Besides Dr. Pepper and Coca-Cola, the favorite cold drinks were Grapette, Delaware Punch and Orange Crush. My pediatrician insisted that I drink only Delaware Punch because it contained no carbonated water.

Our cook's afternoon off was on Thursday, so on that day my family headed downtown for dinner and a picture show. The Guenther Cave, a cafeteria below the lobby level of the historic Guenther Hotel, lured us with a seemingly unlimited selection of marvelous food.

Chicken a la king on toast and cherry pie were my usual selections. An orchestra played on the other side of a large dance floor, though we were usually there too early to witness any dancing. My parents embarrassed me often by repeating tales of the times I walked over and danced solo in front of the musicians. I have no memory of that but do remember that I was not fond of sitting still.

After our meal, we walked a short distance to either the Majestic Theatre or Aztec Theater. The interiors of both these ornate buildings offered most unusual scenery, so moviegoers usually sat and gazed at the walls and ceiling until the lights went out. Every theater employed ushers who helped patrons find a suitable seat. If you were a little late, and the lights had already been dimmed, ushers took your arm and shone a flashlight beam on the floor to guide you.

I always pretended that Vivian Jean had left her alley and was somewhere in that same building getting ready to enjoy a film.

I never dreamed that I would be able to watch the very same movies in my own home in the future. When one of my mother's favorite musicals is on Turner Classic Movies, I understand why my father spent most of his time out in the lobby smoking.

Movies of the 30s had not come very far from 20s-era vaudeville stage productions. Screenwriters assumed that everyone in the United States wanted to be in show business and live in New York City or Hollywood. Musicals tended to contain only the barest notion of a plot and simply featured a series of acts strung together with a minimum of dialogue. Characters who fell in love expressed their feelings by singing to one another or breaking into a wild tap dance routine. I think I must have written my first stories in my head as I sat in these elaborate old theaters and mentally constructed a plot for the actors.

The impact of child star Shirley Temple on the American public during the 1930s cannot be overestimated. She was the dimpled darling who lifted them out of their dismal Depression doldrums and made them believe in happy endings once again. Not just a talented child, Shirley was packaged and sold as an industry. Shirley Temple picture books flew in and out of bookstores with the launch of each new film. Shirley Temple dolls, paper doll books, coloring books and lunch kits were big sellers in department and dime stores. Each facet of Shirley's life was the subject of articles and photos in the nation's top magazines.

Her fame also created a generation of wanna-be stage mothers who could visualize their own child's talents, real or imagined, translated into wealth and fame.

My parents often told me about their abortive attempt to take me to see my first movie. *The Red Haired Alibi*, Shirley's first film, was made the year I was born. When I was two or three, Mother decided I would be entertained by her latest movie, so we drove downtown for this big event.

Mother said, "We were surprised that you didn't pay any attention at all to the screen, but you looked all around and were fascinated by the people and the theater."

Daddy's blunter and more detail specific version was, "You went hopping over the backs of seats like an orangutan! You jumped in and out of people's laps, and I had to run back a bunch of rows so I could trap you.

"Everyone was laughing at this wild little girl who was all dressed up. Some folks in the crowd helped me catch you. Mammy (a name he often called my mother to tease her) was all embarrassed, so we left the movie and went on home."

The popularity of Shirley Temple gave birth to a generation of eager stage mothers, including mine.

I must have been persuasive for my parents to try that again. Actually, children could attend any film from that era. There were no suggestive scenes or profane dialogue. Dramas only inferred romantic involvement between characters by a fade-out and switch to another scene. Passion was relayed to the audience by the musical score.

The bill of fare always contained a newsreel of current events and an animated cartoon. Often, there was also a short documentary or a humorous feature like the original *Little Rascals* or *Our Gang*. My father remained in his seat until these were shown.

During the war years of the early 1940s, theaters in downtown San Antonio stayed packed full, especially on weekends. This was due to the large number of servicemen stationed at Fort Sam Houston or one of the Air Force training fields. During one memorable weekend Nannan, my maternal grandmother, was visiting our family. Both grandmothers and I took the bus downtown to see *Boy's Town* on Sunday afternoon. With theater seats at a premium, we each had to be led by an usher to a separate location. I was to meet them on the stairs when the film was over and the lights came back on.

Spencer Tracy and child star Mickey Rooney gave very convincing performances. To my mind, however, the star of the show was an adorable little dog that played Rooney's pet.

Suddenly, the plot took a terrible turn. The dog was hit by a car and killed. Not only was Mickey crying on the screen, but I started bawling in the balcony. I probably provided comic relief for those who were trying to hold back tears. In any event, I heard a lot of laughter coming from around me.

When the house lights came on and I went to meet my grandmothers, neither one would claim me! I'll admit that people were still snickering and pointing at me saying, "That's the kid." My grandmothers would not look in my direction, and their body language seemed to say, "We've never seen this child before."

Both of them would normally have had a firm grip on one of my hands. That afternoon, I had to try to keep up with them and not get lost in the crowd. I followed them for several blocks with the fervent hope they would allow me to board the same city bus they planned to take home.

Downtown theaters sometimes had stage shows along with the films. Talent was usually local, and the bill included a drawing for prizes. As with manufacturers of wash powder, sets of dishes seemed to be the most favored giveaway of theater managers.

There were times when one or more stars of the film being screened went on a promotional tour and performed on stage during the first day or two of the showing. These appearances were well-publicized in advance and drew large audiences. However, some of these film stars, whose only talent was their good looks, could not connect with a live theater audience. Performers with stage experience prior to making films were the ones to whom audiences could relate.

Hoagy Carmichael—songwriter, pianist, singer and actor who usually portrayed himself in films—was my favorite. He accompanied romantic star John Payne to San Antonio. Payne tried his best to entertain but was noticeably uncomfortable. Carmichael, with his charisma and relaxed style of delivery, made up for it by giving a musical performance that totally captivated his audience.

Movie stars accumulated fans, but people who came to see them perform did not scream or jump up and down while in their presence.

When emaciated-looking crooner Frank Sinatra slunk into a national spotlight in the early 1940s, his singing style supposedly started an epidemic of screaming and swooning among teenage girls. This was actually a press-agent's pre-planned and orchestrated phenomenon.

Watching newsreel scenes of teenage females supposedly overcome with emotion as they fainted at the sight of their idol, teens across the nation began to emulate these audience reactions. Prior to this, singers had been greeted by enthusiastic applause when they walked out upon a stage.

The general public was a great deal more polite and mannerly when approaching a well-known actor to ask for an autograph. There was no paparazzi threat, so being famous in this era was a great deal easier than it is for singers, musicians and actors today.

Prior to tabloid magazines, movie studios invented names and background stories for a large number of their featured actors. The movie-going public was more naive and far less inquisitive, so for the most part, they got by with their imaginative fabrications.

News media of the 30s did not pander to celebrities. Their names were not heard in news broadcasts, and their private lives were not a constant source of speculation. Teenage girls could purchase a movie magazine for a dime if they wanted to learn more about the lives of film stars. Fiction manufactured by major Hollywood film studios, and presented as fact, was regularly cranked out for young female fans.

My pre-teen girlfriends and I began to invest a portion of our allowances in these fan magazines. We would pore over the pictures together and speculate upon the stories of this or that star's "perfect marriage." Often, before the ink was dry on an issue, we would note a terse paragraph in our local newspaper telling of this same star's divorce. Nevertheless, these magazines were collected and, like comic books when we were younger, traded back and forth.

On Saturdays, most children were attracted to the double feature at a smaller neighborhood theater. The price of admission for these events was a nickel, dime or fifteen cents depending upon the location of the theater. A western, usually called a "cowboy show" by the young viewers, headed the bill. A low-budget second feature and several cartoons were also included. Though most of my friends begged to attend these lengthy shows, I disliked them intensely.

Quite a few parents used the double features, which lasted all afternoon, as a babysitter. Not knowing how to handle their sudden freedom from parental control, unsupervised children of all ages ran back and forth in the aisles and created a great deal of noise.

Gene Autry, John Wayne, Tex Ritter or Roy Rogers and Dale Evans were often the stars of the western feature. In order to ensure attendance week after week, a shorter third feature, shown in serial form, was included in the format. Each week, as the episode ended, the hero or heroine met with a catastrophic, and obviously fatal, event. They were goners for sure. The next week, the final scene was shown again from a different camera angle. This explained how the hero or heroine had survived certain death and was amazingly hale and hearty. Camera angles and the abilities of stunt men were the only special effects in use at that time.

Photography was not the only thing that remained black-and-white in these low-budget films. They retained the character portrayal of old Victorian melodramas in which an actor was either hero or villain. There were no complicated characters here. Audiences knew that the cowboys were the good guys and the Indians were bad. Historic fact was ignored, and American history rewritten every Saturday afternoon across our nation.

Film editing was in its infancy, which resulted in awkward scene shifts and some moments of crisis being turned into comedy. One suspected that, for budgetary reasons, a scene was shot only once. For instance, it was not uncommon to see a lone cowboy rider turn to face his villainous Indian pursuers. As he fired his gun once, seven mounted warriors fell from their ponies and bit the dust.

⚜

My mother frequently expressed distress over the fact that I had never met most of her kin and had a difficult time keeping their names and family relationships straight. Friends from East Texas often came to visit and greeted me with the remark, "Honey, did you know that your mother was always known as the prettiest girl in Beaumont?" Their second sentence would be, "You sure don't look anything like her." So, there were times when our family went to a neighborhood theater in order to view the work of relatives.

Since I had a normal curiosity about the good-looking Haynes family, and since most of them lived in East Texas or Louisiana, Mother took me to see my first cousin Robert Castaine at the Highland Park Theater. He and his wife Pauline were professional dancers and had even done command performances in London. Handsome enough to land lead and second lead rolls in a number of low-budget and easily forgettable films, Robert tried Hollywood for a while. His most memorable performances were when he and Pauline simply danced on the silver screen.

Daddy's cousin from East Texas did a lot better on the big screen and, later, television. When I first glimpsed Faye Emerson, she wore heavy dark makeup and a long-haired black wig in order to slink around in *Desert Song*.

In 1944, she married Elliot Roosevelt, son of President Franklin D. Roosevelt. My family and I were invited to the wedding and the big reception held later in Beaumont. I did not want to go because I would have to miss school. Peer pressure was enormous in my junior high school mind at the time.

⌘

One of Mother's cousins, Dick Haynes, entered the entertainment field at radio station KRIC in Beaumont in 1937. He soon moved on to KTSA in San Antonio, KMOX in St. Louis and KMPC in Los Angeles. Dick invented and played the parts of a whole gang of comedic characters on his radio shows. During the years he was in San Antonio, we often went to the station and watched his antics as Gum Drop Gus, Wilhelmina Mildew or Sir Chester Drawers through a glass wall. After his move to California, he and his wife Bobbie enjoyed their celebrity-filled lifestyle, so they remained there.

At one point, a pug-nosed young singer named Dick Haymes—with an M—was featured in Hollywood musicals. Richard was asked if he wanted to change his screen name, but he declined. Sure enough, his career lasted for many decades while the singer's was short-lived.

Dick's first movie role was right up his alley. He played the part of a disc jockey in *Make Believe Ballroom* then went on to make three pictures for MGM, including *Red Badge of Courage*. Later, he made westerns *Support Your Local Sheriff* and its sequel *Support Your Local Gunfighter*.

Though Dick lacked the dark, brooding good looks of my cousin Robert, he was a born comedian and character actor. His eyes sparkled with mischief, and the corners of his large mouth were perennially tilted into a grin. In his personal and professional lives, Dick kept everyone around him in a state if laughter.

When television took the place of radio, Dick became the nation's first television disc jockey. His first TV showcase was *Dick Haynes' Joke Shop* and featured Betty White in one of her first appearances. While continuing to run his own shows, Dick later became a regular in the television series *Starsky and Hutch*, *Bionic Woman* and *Fantasy Island*.

Richard Haynes

Probably the series which allowed him to have the most fun was *Hee-Haw*. Later in his career, Dick was invited to this series to make a guest appearance. He arrived wearing overalls as his famous character Gum Drop Gus. Gus made a hit, habitually popping up out of the corn as that comedy series became a favorite with television viewers, so Dick became a weekly regular.

A tradition Dick began in Hollywood still lives on today, but unfortunately, it has been turned over to a group of vapid Barbie Dolls asking insipid questions as they paw celebrities standing on a red carpet. Dick was Hollywood's first official greeter at world premiers and special events. Lacking a silicone bosom spilling out of a low-cut gown, he made up for it by conducting intelligent and witty interviews.

❦

Major Bowes' Amateur Hour was supposedly designed to allow unknown, would-be-performers to have a national audience. Major Bowes sounded kind enough when he interviewed the contestants prior to their performances. However, if their act was deemed awful, they "got the gong."

Local radio stations began running their own amateur hours. I sometimes drove to a local station with my Aunt Norine, who took both of my cousins to perform. Jimmy, six months older than I, was known for his wonderful singing voice. Unfortunately, his audience could not observe his sparkling blue eyes and engaging grin. Grace, his older sister, chose to simultaneously twirl a baton and tap dance. Since these could not be viewed by a radio audience, her choice of talents perplexed me.

The winner was selected by listeners, who called the radio station and placed a vote for their favorite contestant. Thus, if an ambitious mother called a large group of her friends and they responded by calling the station, a child who stood next to the microphone and cracked his knuckles could win the talent contest.

A strange custom of local stage-struck females, which also appealed to mothers of future stars, was an instrument of child-abuse called a Tom Thumb Wedding. Unfortunately, this was my first venture into kinder-show-biz.

Under the guise of community fundraising events, self-made directors advertised in a manner that lured mothers of pre-school children. These proud women were persuaded to gather up their little bundles of talent and present them at a cattle call.

When I was just past the toddler stage, I was cast as the mother of the bride at one of these events. Each of the actors had one line, and mine was "Oh, why do mothers of the bride always cry at weddings?"

After offering this dramatic dilemma to the audience, I was actually expected to break into tears! The boss lady was extremely unhappy that I was not able to cry on cue. She tried all sorts of methods she must have found in a stage director's manual. Nothing worked. I could imitate her and repeat my line using different tonal inflections but was unable to squeeze out even one tear.

At the last minute, she handed me a handkerchief, showed me how to twist it using both hands. She also changed my line. Now, I was to say, "Oh, why do mothers of the bride always get so nervous at the wedding?" Twist. Twist. I was an expert twister, so Madam Director was pleased and the show did go on.

Actually, during rehearsals, the main challenge of this group of one-line thespians was to avoid the little boy who played Grandpa. The word was out that if you got too close to him he would bite. The director was aware of his proclivity, so she kept a pocket full of treats for him. When she noticed him furtively edging close toward another child, she would quickly plunk a candy into his mouth. Her method was similar to the one used by dog-handlers in a ring filled with show dogs.

I soon learned to keep both of my tearless eyes fixed on Grandpa.

It became obvious to one and all that this boy could not only inflict bodily harm with his teeth but would skillfully brandish the cane upon which his character was supposed to rely. Having his mouth stuffed with treats did not deter him from swinging the cane and using it to swat his fellow actors. Being taller than the rest of us allowed him effortless escape from the grasp of volunteer hands lurking behind the curtains and intermittently darting out in a vain effort to grab him.

I don't believe any child involved, including the bride and groom, really cared whether this wedding came off or not. We were all there trying to satisfy a parent's need. Grandpa was the only one of us who had the courage to display his true feelings.

⁂

The arrival on the silver screen of Mickey Rooney, Judy Garland and Elizabeth Taylor added to the roster of child stars and intensified motherly ambitions. In addition to the number of my friends enrolled in dance classes, some parents began to seek out voice teachers.

These voice teachers were always eager to display the talents of future stars, so my parents and I sat dumbfounded through countless recitals as we heard strange and abnormal sounds emitted from the throats of children we knew. Some of these young ones actually had fine voices when they sang in their regular style. The trend, however, was to force a stilted and overly dramatic manner of presentation upon them, which negated any natural sweetness and made them appear replicas of adult performers.

For some unknown reason, a song called "The Green-eyed Dragon with the Thirteen Tales" was a favorite among singing instructors. I sat by helplessly as many of my playmates were bullied into performing this one song. Perhaps because it was belted out in the form of a warning to the audience, it particularly impressed me. Indeed, I tried to avoid any close encounters with dragons after having the lyrics tattooed on my brain.

I was extremely fortunate that my mother never took me to meet a voice teacher. Instead, each week at Woolworth's she purchased song sheets containing the lyrics of popular tunes. She would then teach me the songs so we could enjoy singing them together. One of the songs that stands out in my memory was an extremely popular tune titled "It's a Sin to Tell a Lie."

Mother considered the words "lie" and "liar" to be dirty words, and I was forbidden to use them. Of course, I wanted to know why all of the popular vocalists could sing those words if they were so dirty. Since "It's a Sin to Prevaricate" didn't fit the music, I was allowed to sing the song as written but told not to use the words on any other occasion.

⁂

My grandmother owned stacks of 78 RPM records, which she began collecting as a young woman. I would pull up a chair to stand on, place a record with an Edison, Victor or Columbia label on the turntable then start up her huge and ornate 19th-century Victrola by turning the crank. After playing for awhile, the music would get slower and slower until it eventually stopped, creating the necessity of climbing back on the chair and turning the crank once more.

I played Grandmother's records over and over again, memorizing the lyrics and singing along with them. Many were operatic arias sung in Italian, French or German. The language of the lyrics didn't matter at all because children are born mimics. I could sing every word along with Caruso, though I had no clue what they meant. These songs were quite dramatic, so I cried, moaned or yelled in contempt on cue.

Among Grandmother's collection were Rudy Vallee songs as well as a stack of humorous Cajun productions by "The Mayor of Bayou Pom Pom." On these, a series of silly Cajun jokes and risque stories were told followed by someone laughing like a donkey: *Hee-Haw! Hee-Haw!* Naturally, I committed the Cajun tales, followed by the donkey laugh, to memory.

My mother went to Betty's Beauty Salon each week for a wash, set and manicure. No "nice women" colored their hair in those days. Dye-jobs were used in Hollywood with the invention of Technicolor film. Folks who saw film stars in person often remarked upon their ugly orange hair. If a woman with obviously dyed hair was seen on the streets, it was assumed she was a prostitute.

So, women who were not actresses or ladies of the evening had to make do with whatever hair color God gave them.

Mother began allowing me to accompany her on her weekly visits to the beauty shop. The hair stylists who were not busy would sit me up in a chair and fool with my hair to keep me occupied. There was not a lot they could do with my short bob, so they mainly asked me questions in order to hear my answers.

Beauty shops of that day contained a section that most resembled an execution chamber. Women who endured permanent waves were connected to a head full of electric wires with steel clips that dangled from a tall machine. When their hair was sufficiently fried, it was washed, pulled taut and rolled on steel curlers with round rubber locks. It took a brave woman, totally devoted to fashion, to withstand all of that discomfort.

When the operator who was entertaining me had a customer, she put me under a hairdryer. Now, the hairdryers of the 30s gave off a humongous roar like a wind tunnel. Once a person sat down and the dryer was placed over her head and turned on, that individual was deafened to any other sound.

In my case, I must have assumed that since I could hear no one no one could hear me. Encased within my own particular wind tunnel, I always got the urge to sing. Certainly, I was no longer able to hear my own voice or the dramatic inflections I knew so well.

So, I sang song after song while Betty's customers and employees cracked up. It was obvious to everyone that I was totally unaware of my audience. If Caruso suffered heartbreak and cried during the course of his operatic aria, I wailed my faux emotional pain out to one and all. Over the next few minutes, I might be Rudy Vallee crooning "My Time is Your Time" through a makebelieve megaphone or Bayou Pom Pom's Cajun mayor telling naughty stories.

At times, people walking past the open front door would stop to see what on earth was going on. The hairstylists always urged Mother to bring me back the next week. With a hearty laugh, Betty later told Mother that several customers had called wanting to book an appointment "on the day that little girl performs."

❦

People who spend a great amount of their time dealing with frustrations caused by driving in heavy traffic might judge one of my family's favorite pastimes as somewhat strange. However, taking drives into the Texas Hill Country during the 1930s provided a treat for each of one's senses.

Because automobiles were still a rather new luxury, one could drive for hours without passing a filling station that offered a chance to refill the gas tank and visit the restroom. On these Sunday drives, my grandmother, Aunt Lulu and Aunt Vallie often accompanied my parents and me. Like everyone else undertaking lengthy drives, my father would sometimes have to stop near a wooded area to allow his passengers to leave the confines of the car and locate trees or bushes that would hide them as they answered nature's call.

At times, this meant fences had to be climbed. Sometimes, a helpful rancher would install a stile over his fence to aid travelers who might otherwise get tangled up in barbed wire.

Hill Country water tables had not yet been lowered by an increased population and major industries moving into that area's cities. There were beautiful clear-running streams, creeks and rivers everywhere, as well as a plethora of low water crossings on highways. Most families on such outings prepared picnic lunches and stopped near one of these delightful bodies of water to enjoy their meal. Like filling stations, restaurants were not encountered unless a good-sized Hill Country town was on one's route.

There were times when we made plans to drive to a specific restaurant in Boerne, Comfort, Blanco, Luling, Kerrville or Fredericksburg to enjoy a Sunday meal.

Springtime in the hill country was a visual paradise with roadsides and fields absolutely covered with a display of bluebonnets and myriad other wildflowers. Wildflowers don't make good cut flowers—they need to be enjoyed where they grow. Unfortunately, as the beauty of this area became well known, tourists from other areas began to visit. Ignorance of the nature of these plants caused them to stop their cars by the side of the road and yank up entire patches of flowers by the roots.

All of these plants go through a time of dropping their seeds onto the ground to insure next year's crop. So, little by little, many roadsides and fields were robbed of their inspiring vernal visions. It wasn't until Lady Bird Johnson became First Lady of the United States that this issue was addressed and attempts were made to reseed fields that had once blossomed for the enjoyment of viewers.

In an era when there were no highway billboards, a shaving cream company began advertising by placing a series of small signs along our nation's roads. Drivers found the Burma-Shave signs entertaining, and always looked for their latest rhyme.

Cattle crossing
Means go slow
That old bull
Is some cow's beau.
BURMA SHAVE

Grandpa's Beard
Was stiff and coarse
And that's what caused
His fifth divorce.
BURMA SHAVE

Each line was painted on a separate sign and enough space was allowed between the signs to keep the occupants of a car curious as to what the next would say.

⤞✤⤝

Friends who told of family vacations usually talked about driving to another part of Texas, or another state, to stay with relatives. Hotels and meals on the road were priced above what many family budgets could bear.

Fortunately, my family was able to take vacations where we stayed at tourist courts, dude ranches and small hotels. The tourist court of the 30s was a predecessor to today's motel. Though few in number, this type of hostelry allowed a more informal sort of vacation where people did not need to dress up or walk through a lobby to reach their room. Most tourist courts had cottages that included one or two bedrooms and a kitchenette off the sitting area. My parents and I made repeat visits to Grande Courts, little stucco cottages just a block off a pristine beach and the waters of Corpus Christi Bay.

Women's bathing suits of that day were one-piece and made of wool. They were hot and scratchy until the wearer immersed herself in water. Once they were thoroughly wet, they became comfortable. Men's bathing suits had a top like a heavy woolen undershirt. Just as with the designs for women and children, the bathing suit bottoms covered the top portion of their thighs.

A short distance from our lodging, an open air bingo parlor had been set up. My parents and I often walked over to play and I once had the thrill of winning the top prize of the evening—five dollars.

Another vacation favorite was a stone lodge called Ramble Inn near Bandera. Like most of that area's dude ranches, they kept a string of very mild-mannered horses used for trail rides.

Women did not wear slacks or blue jeans in those days unless they planned to ride. So, Aunt Vallie and I coerced my mother into investing in a pair of slacks so she could go along on trail rides with us.

On one of our visits, Mother allowed herself to be helped into the saddle the first morning of our stay. Just before we were to depart, her horse turned his head to the side.

"Get me off of here," she yelled. "He turned around and looked at me!" She was immediately helped down by a cowboy who could barely suppress his laughter.

Why this head movement frightened my mother so much, I didn't know. Probably because she was about to participate in an activity for which she had no enthusiasm, knew nothing about and had no desire to learn. My father had been an excellent rider since childhood, so for years Mother was teased about the horse that made the mistake of looking at her.

The Fritz Hotel, later called Hotel Las Lomas, offered a genteel vacation more suited to my mother's taste. There was not a heck of a lot for tourists to do in the little town of Junction, though, other than to relax and read on the hotel's shady veranda.

Dining room fare was appetizing and usually delectable, so we took all of our meals there. Enjoying such generous repasts three times a day convinced my Aunt Vallie that we should follow breakfast each day by walking around the courthouse square. Someone in the hotel had passed on the information that three times around the square equaled one mile.

Our morning walks were memorable due to the number of vendors who sat on curbs outside the courthouse selling a variety of items. Most

The Fritz Hotel, later renamed the Las Lomas

sold fruits or vegetables they had grown. Others displayed carved wood or handmade leather goods. Many of these people lived deep in the country and spoke in a manner my mother was unable to understand. She once quizzed a weathered old man for some time, trying to ascertain the variety of fruit displayed in his crates.

"Well," she finally told us, "he insists that these are wall plums, but I've never heard of a wall plum." My aunt and I broke into laughter, realizing that she had been unable to decipher his pronunciation of the word *wild*.

Some years, my father would stay only on weekends and return to his job in San Antonio during the week. This arrangement left Mother, Grandmother, Aunt Vallie and me at our favorite little hotel for the rest of the summer. My elders were pleased by this set-up, but it challenged me to find something to do other than eat, rest and walk around the courthouse.

Two elderly sisters offered quite a diversion one year. They were the first women I had ever seen who wore eye shadow. The type they wore appeared to be greasy blue stage makeup, and was applied all around their eyes rather than on the eyelids.

The sisters were somewhat eccentric, or so it seemed from stories they shared with others relaxing on the hotel's front veranda. Subject matter sometimes verged upon the bizarre. It seemed they often returned to this little Junction hotel because it was an excellent spot to communicate with their dead relatives. Both considered themselves to be Spiritualist mediums and were well pleased at the number of spirit connections they had achieved since arriving. The sisters told us their habit was to hold a seance each afternoon after lunch.

This tidbit inspired an epidemic of eavesdropping among my relatives and me. My mother and I realized that the room shared by the sisters was directly below ours. All of the hotel bedrooms had exposed pipes that served as a conductor of words spoken on one floor up to the room above. So, we inadvertently became privy to some of the conversations between these women.

With this new knowledge of early afternoon seances, we invited Aunt Vallie and Grandmother to put off their usual naps and join us to see what we might hear. Certainly, my well-dressed and sophisticated elders were a strange sight to behold in that bedroom as they each stood with one ear glued to a vertical pipe.

We were able to hear some dramatic entreaties made to people who had crossed over. Chime-ringing and chanting were interspersed with more cajoling of the deceased to venture, once again, onto our plane. However, entertainment provided by the sisters was rather repetitious and devoid of results as far as we could ascertain, so we eventually abandoned our careers as eavesdroppers in favor of naps.

A waitress at our hotel took pity upon me one weekend and asked Mother if I could accompany her to a Saturday night dance. I had just turned twelve, so I'm sure my elders and I all thought that I would be purely an observer. We didn't take Southern hospitality and cowboy manners into consideration.

The dance was held in someone's pasture, and featured a western band playing on an open-air concrete dance floor. Dancers were local cattle men and their cowhands, all washed up and wearing their dancing boots. This rugged and energetic population did not let me sit through a single tune. I felt like the belle of the ball and thoroughly enjoyed swinging out to Cotton-Eyed Joe, Ten Pretty Girls, Herr Schmidt, the Schottische, Put Your Little Foot and all of the country waltzes and polkas popular at the time.

The informality of that special occasion was far different from any event I had experienced before. I fell in love with country dances that night—as well as the individuals who attend them.

At later dances, in and around El Campo, I was introduced to two other forms of dance used as mixers in that era—"Paul Jones" tunes.

In a Paul Jones, the females formed a circle in the middle of the dance floor. The males formed a larger circle outside the girls' ring. When the music began, one circle moved clockwise while members in the other circle danced counter-clockwise. At the sound of a whistle, the circles stopped moving, and each male was required to dance with the female who was standing closest to him. This allowed an informal meeting with a member of the opposite sex with whom one might later want to dance again...or carefully avoid.

Wallflowers—girls who sat in chairs pushed against the wall and were seldom, if ever, asked to dance—were guaranteed a dance partner as long as a Paul Jones was being danced.

Another dance form popular in the 30s and 40s was the broom dance. It was especially popular with band members, and often the only way they were paid.

Every couple in attendance was expected to get out on the floor when a broom dance was announced. One male started out dancing with a broom instead of a live partner. When the music stopped, he grabbed another dancer's partner and handed him the broom. The man tagged had to put a quarter into a specified small bucket and dance around the floor with the broom until the music, once more, came to a stop. Then, he could trade the broom for a live dance partner.

Most orchestras kept this dance going until the bucket filled up with quarters. Really good musical groups could get by with playing quite a few broom dances each evening. Male dancers were expected to good-naturedly part with their quarters until the orchestra collected what they considered adequate pay for that particular gig.

⌘

Downtown San Antonio, at least in the daytime, was considered a safe place for school children to roam about. The parents of my friend Merry Tom owned a printing business in town, and there were times her mother took us along when she had a few hours of work to do. Mrs. Blue named a time for us to return to Sigmund Press, and we were allowed to wander around that area of town in the meantime.

I will never forget one specific adventure I shared with Merry Tom. The thirty-story neo-Gothic Smith Young Tower (later the Transit Tower and now the Tower Life Building) was then the tallest building in town. Merry Tom asked if I had ever been to the observation platform on top of the tower. I told her, "Yes, but not recently." She then suggested that we go up there, and she would show me something she liked to do. That sounded interesting to me.

We walked to the tower building, boarded an elevator and arrived at the totally deserted open-air platform. Looking over the edge of the railing, we had a wonderful view in all directions.

"Watch," I heard Merry Tom say. Turning around, I saw her standing up on one of the railings with her arms extended like a high-wire acrobat. Unlike a circus, there was no safety net below.

She began walking toward me, and I thought I would faint dead away. There was no type of safety device or security personnel, and she was thirty stories above the street! Whereas I had been happily engaged in spotting familiar landmarks from an entirely new vantage point, I found watching my friend's antics dizzying.

"This is fun," she challenged me. "Come on and try it."

Merry Tom and I had enjoyed challenging one another since we first met as tap-dancing toddlers at the Bonner Studio of Dance. We competed in extemporaneous games of all sorts. We engaged in friendly competition for top grades in the classroom. As the fastest-growing, thus tallest, girls among our group of friends, we even tried to outdo one another's growth spurts.

Seeing who was the most fearless by walking the railing of a thirty-story building, however, was one challenge she would win by default. From a vertiginous viewpoint and afraid to startle her, I almost whispered, "Please get down from there."

I realized that I was pressing myself into the brick wall of the tower. My body language was trying to sway her in the right direction as a whirlwind of thoughts swirled through my brain. Obviously, I worried about her suddenly losing her balance and falling to her death. It was extremely breezy on that deck, and I had visions of how a strong gust of wind might affect her precarious stance.

"I do this all of the time. Don't worry," she assured me.

My expression must have given away the extent of my concern. Not knowing what else to say, I suddenly heard the voice of my mother speak clearly inside my mind: "Deprive her of her audience."

Those of us who listen to our inner wisdom often find that, in urgent matters, it uses our mother's voice. Perhaps because that is the first voice a baby hears, the sound forms a strong psychic connection.

"I don't like watching you take chances," I told her. "I'm going back downstairs. I'll wait for you in the lobby."

Still shaking inwardly from the shock of seeing my friend's perilous position above downtown San Antonio, I turned and entered the elevator. I had not been in the lobby more than a few minutes before Merry Tom joined me.

As glad as I was to see her safely walking toward me, I would have enjoyed giving her a good hard pinch for acting so foolhardy and putting herself in such danger. Merry Tom was a valued friend, so I never told anyone about that experience and sincerely hoped her career as a tower rail-walker ended that day.

⚜

San Antonio offered so many fascinating places to visit that my family was never at a loss for places to go. Because we had a constant stream of visitors from East Texas, we continually hosted tours of the old Spanish missions, the Governor's Palace, the Alamo, the Witte Museum, the Brackenridge Park Zoo and the Japanese Tea Garden.

As many times as we revisited mission San Antonio de Valejo (the Alamo) and the other old missions, the weathered stones and sacred images never failed to amaze me. They mystically held my imagination, in which played scenes of the passionate artisans who had created these structures at a time when they were at the isolated edge of the known universe. Spaniards who built the missions and forts to protect frontier friars from the Indians also created our nation's oldest cathedral and the first aqueduct, used to power their grist mill.

When my mother and I drove downtown to pick up my father from work at the Frost National Bank building, I loved to walk next door and go inside the Gothic facade of the San Fernando Cathedral. Creating such beauty in a frontier settlement must have taken enormous dedication.

San Antonio's Sunken Gardens have been known by many names and have lived through numerous incarnations since 1899 when George W. Brackenridge donated 199 acres of rock quarry for a park. This act was followed by the donation, in 1915, of an eleven-acre tract by Emma Koehler, the widow of Pearl Brewery owner Oscar Koehler.

Local stonecutters had leased these lands since the mid-1800s, and supplied limestone used in building numerous San Antonio homes. Prison labor was used in these undertakings and, later on, in the quarry's conversion to a tourist attraction.

Japanese-American designer and artist Kim Eliza Jingo was the force behind turning the abandoned rock quarry into a Japanese cultural adventure. His family moved into the newly built complex and opened the Bamboo Room, which served lunch and tea.

Our East Texas visitors always marveled at the many arched stone bridges overlooking lily ponds populated with giant goldfish. The tiny old Mexican musician who played harp solos on the patio of the Japanese pagoda kept my rapt attention during our visits.

When World War II came along in 1941, the Jingo family was evicted due to a flood of misplaced anti-Japanese sentiment. The name was changed to the Chinese Tea Garden, but most of our San Antonio population simply referred to it as the Sunken Gardens. Later, in a rare wave of political sanity, the original name was restored, and Jingo family descendants honored.

Of course, Brackenridge Park Zoo was a magical spot for a child. I especially loved visiting a large area surrounded by a moat called Monkey Island. Various fascinating and extremely active primates screeched as they leaped from tree to tree entertaining viewers. My birth year was the Chinese Year of the Monkey, so maybe that was why I felt such kinship to the population of that little island.

Because I found the antics of these creatures so intriguing, and spent a lot of time in trees myself, my father teased that I had been born on Monkey Island. This information pertaining to my natal day seemed both logical and satisfactory to me. However, in later years, office workers at Highland Park Elementary refused to accept my word as I assured them that this was my place of birth.

CHAPTER FOUR

THE COLOR OF OUR SKIN

With closed eyes, I feel myself being rocked in a large wicker rocker and hear the voice of an angel. I lie draped across an extraordinarily ample breast, which heaves and bounces to the beat of the song in progress. Lyrics soar *a capella* except for the accompaniment rendered by the ancient rocker itself. There is a squeak-whoosh sound at each backward rock, so the one who sings provides her own musical background by varying the tempo of her pushes.

I enjoy this reverie as I recall Jo Ella, my mother's housekeeper in the early 1930s. Her main job was to take care of me, and I called her "Lella" because my toddler tongue could not quite manage her full name.

Her powerful voice seemed limitless in its range, and her gift to our family was a repertoire of songs that crossed lines from Gospel to folk to popular as well as those classified as "Negro spirituals."

Jo Ella sang in the choir (she pronounced it "chore") of a church near her home. Her remarkable voice and endless variety of material were greatly admired throughout our neighborhood. It was not unusual for people within hearing distance of our living room to stand motionless on our front sidewalk or sit silently on our porch steps during my rocking-time serenades.

I vocalized along with her, in my own way, to such favorites as "Froggy Went A-courtin'." Mother told me in later years that Jo Ella continued to sing and rock long after I had gone to sleep. However, no one in the household ever wanted to stop her or suggest that she put me to bed and do other work. Her voice was an aural treat too rare to be silenced.

There is no doubt in my mind that, in a later era, Jo Ella would have been a professional singer. For a black woman in the midst of the Depression, that was not to be. Her career opportunities were limited to housework or a similar type of job.

There was a constant emotional gap in my childhood caused by the sudden disappearance of my talented caretaker. I never knew what happened nor do I remember it being discussed.

As an adult, I asked my mother, "What happened to Jo Ella and why did she leave us so suddenly?"

"She had a sudden attack of appendicitis," Mother answered. "We took her to our doctor and paid for him to do her surgery. She was doing well and we planned for her to come back and work for us after she recuperated. Before the doctor released her from the hospital, he asked if we knew she had syphilis. Of course, we didn't. We didn't know how to handle that, but he advised us against letting her work in our home with a child to take care of."

With that one suggestion, my "second mother" and I, who loved one another deeply, were arbitrarily separated forever.

There were treatments for syphilis available at that time. So, upon hearing my mother's explanation, I mentally listed all of the things that could have been done differently. Of course, my insight came in the form of hindsight, so mental rearrangements of events were exercises in futility designed to cope with painful memories.

As my mother and I were talking over Jo Ella's disappearance and my unaddressed feelings of loss, she remembered an event that had occurred prior to my birth.

My grandmother had asked Jo Ella to go next door and borrow a cup of sugar from Aunt Julia. Jo Ella used the gate that connected our back yard with that of the Franz sisters. Soon, she returned carrying a refilled sugar container.

"I looked over at her when she came into the kitchen," Mother remembered. "She didn't say anything, but judging by her expression, she was upset. "'Jo Ella, what's wrong,' I asked.

"'I knocked on Miss Julia's door,' she said, 'and I heard Uncle Bill (the handy man) say, 'Fletcher's nigger wants to talk to you.'

"I knew that being called by that name had really upset her, so I told her that Uncle Bill emigrated from England and didn't know any better. The men he worked with when he first came over here were tough and had no education. They were the ones who taught him that word.

"'You know that Aunt Julia would never use that word, so what difference does it make?'

"'A nigger has a black heart,' she informed me. She pouted the rest of the day and there was nothing I could say to convince her that Uncle Bill's choice of words had been made out of ignorance and not designed to insult her."

This memory, held so long by my parent, seemed to contrast strongly with the decision to suddenly cut all ties between Jo Ella and a family who loved and valued her. My mother noticed immediately when she was upset and tried to come up with an explanation that would assuage her hurt feelings. Yet, unexpected news and advice from a white doctor was allowed to suddenly alter a personal relationship important to both employer and employee.

Watching the actions and attitudes of neighbors who lived on both sides of our home as they interacted with our household help revealed a sharp contrast of belief systems.

Our next door neighbors usually came for visits through back yard gates that connected our properties. The Franz sisters always greeted our current housekeeper with big smiles and stood around visiting in order to catch up on her news. They normally knew names of her family members; and when they inquired about them, their interest was sincere. It was not unusual for our cook to be handed a plate of Aunt Julia's just-baked cookies to take home and share.

Mrs. M., on the other hand, stalked through our back door with a sour expression that decorated her face as long as she was in the presence of our household helper. Looking through her, rather than at her, she exhibited what she assumed was her superiority by ordering that my mother or grandmother be summoned.

The name of our housekeeper was always well-known to our racist neighbor. She simply refused to show a non-Caucasian the respect of addressing her by name. Mrs. M. hired only white housekeepers, and often remarked that our neighborhood would be better off if each household followed her example.

The conflicting messages within the system called segregation were often relayed along flawed circuits through frayed wires as they were received by the young. I can only pass along memories of how these things affected me as they happened.

Following the laws of the day that kept the races separate, white people and black people used separate restroom facilities. Our household help used a restroom out by the servant's quarters.

There were other words used for people of color in those days. "Pickaninny" was often found in children's stories. The word referred to a black child, and traveled to the new world from West Africa. It was actually a word that came from *pequeniño* meaning "small child." As it changed, it became offensive.

Elderly people of the 1930s often used the word *darkies*. That was an older term and was in no way meant to be insulting in the minds of those who used it. There were some very popular 19th-century songs that used the term in the lyrics—"In the Evening by the Moonlight" is one that comes to mind.

Children's rhymes sometimes used pejorative terms. The rhyme Eeny, Meeny, Miney, Mo was often used as a device to choose who would be on what side in a game. My mother taught me the version she invented, and I never knew there was any other until I went to elementary school. Her version went:

> Eeny, meeny, miney, mo
> Catch a bunny by the toe.
> If he hollers let him go.
> Eeny, meeny, miney, mo

Once I arrived on a school campus, the other students informed me my version was wrong. The correct rhyme, they told me, was:

> Eeny, meeny, miney, mo
> Catch a nigger by the toe.
> If he hollers make him pay
> Fifty dollars every day.

Back at home, I asked Mother about what my friends had said. She responded that this new version I had heard was insulting and mean-spirited. It was too bad that the other children used it.

"In the future, either use the one I taught you or don't use the rhyme at all."

Another woman of color highly valued by my family was Mamie Snowden. I knew from infancy that the occasions when I was expected to look my best, be the cleanest, smell the most fragrant and wear my "best bib and tucker" were when our family planned visits to Mamie's house.

Mamie came into my father's life at his birth. It was a time of emergency for the baby, and shock and sorrow for the baby's mother, my grandmother.

Florence Vaughan married Harvey Davis Fletcher February 8, 1893, in Beaumont, Texas. They had known one another their entire lives as the children of two men who had served the Confederacy together on the front lines of Hood's Texas Brigade.

My grandmother, Florence Vaughn Fletcher

Though they emerged from totally different backgrounds, my great-grandfathers surely must have felt joy with the marriage of their offspring. My great-grandmothers, Alabama Eglantine Keith Vaughan and Julia Long Fletcher, were also best of friends. The children of each called the other "Aunt," which was a title of respect.

A son born to Harvey and Florence Fletcher in December of 1894 lived less than twenty-four hours. A girl arrived in November of 1896 and was named for a sister of each of her parents: Vallie May.

Vallie May was a beautiful child, a fact attested to by numerous old photographs and a portrait painted in the center of a jeweled brooch. Her parents and relatives adored her and were elated with the news that she would have a younger sibling during her third year.

Was it a spider bite? I cannot remember the awful story I heard in whispers a generation later. Hushed tones were designed to avoid the ears of my sensitive grandmother. Everyone knew she had never really recovered from the loss of that child with golden ringlets and big blue eyes.

Florence went into complete shock at Vallie's death on June 23, 1899. She was still wrapped tightly in her shawl of grief on July 3 when she delivered the baby boy who would one day be my father.

The space of ten days separating death and birth were not sufficient to lift the heavy sorrow nor suspend the disbelief she felt surrounding the loss of her daughter. Somehow, the infant son searching for her breast was blamed, and she turned her back on him physically and emotionally.

Through the back door, into this home filled with despair, Mamie Snowden stepped. Mamie was at that time an employee of Bill Fletcher, Harvey's father, who lived next door. As the mother of a young child, Mamie was both equipped and willing to step into an emergency job as wet-nurse.

So, William Andrew Fletcher II was rejected by his own mother and nursed into life by a black mother he would love and continue to support financially for the rest of her life.

It became apparent to both family members and medical advisors that Florence Fletcher intended to remain within the protection of her dark emotional cave, refusing entrance to her infant, for an indeterminate length of time.

Colorado was then the fashionable place to go for East Texas flat-landers in search of "the cure" for various maladies. Little was known about emotional illnesses, but it was assumed that removing a person from the scene of a tragedy and replacing that somber scenery with beautiful surroundings would restore a troubled mind to its normal state.

I am not sure if anyone else accompanied my grandmother, Mamie and "their" baby on the long train ride from Beaumont into the mountains of Colorado. The small group lived in a hotel together for the better part of a year before returning to Beaumont.

Florence appeared to be back to normal as she stepped from the train onto the railroad station platform in Beaumont. However, to those of us who lived close to her in later years, it was apparent that she would always subconsciously blame Bill for the death of the sister he never knew.

❦

Mamie's diligence, and her role as my father's guardian angel, came into play once more when my father was seven years old. Bill had grown into a happy boy with the same blond curls, big blue eyes and shy smile seen in pictures of Vallie May. Normally a healthy boy, he contacted diphtheria in the fall of his seventh year.

Since this disease was often fatal, and my grandparents had already buried two children, they were extremely worried. To add even more consternation to the situation, Florrie was expecting another child.

Two local doctors took turns coming to the Fletcher's Beaumont home to oversee young Bill's care. Many nurses of that time had no medical training of any sort; they were simply women for hire who were willing to take on unpleasant and menial chores. So, an individual who employed one of these "nurses" could only hope that they possessed some degree of focus and compassion.

This was the type of nurse who first came to the Fletcher home. One of the doctors ordered that a pipe, filled with boiling water and wrapped in blankets, be kept in Bill's bed for warmth. He had continued to run a high fever and was often delirious. Mamie had never really trusted his nurse, so she took every opportunity to come into his room and check on him. As she entered the room one morning she realized his bed sheets were thoroughly soaked in blood. Bill was unconscious, and the woman charged with his care was totally preoccupied or disinterested.

During Bill's thrashing about, she discovered, the blankets had unwound from the steaming-hot pipe lying next to Bill's leg. Skin and muscle had burned away, and the pipe was lodged against the bone.

Mamie pushed the pipe away and screamed for help. Doctors were called to deal with the horrific situation, and the so-called nurse was immediately dismissed.

Added to Harvey's other worries, he had noted with disgust that one of the two doctors was often drunk when he came to check on his son.

Florrie was kept away from the sickroom because both doctors felt she could go into labor at any time.

As the family searched for a nurse with true medical skills, Bill's condition grew worse. One evening, the doctor with the drinking problem showed up and pronounced him dead. This doctor called Harvey into Bill's bedroom and said, "I'm so sorry to have to tell you this, but your son is gone."

At that moment, Harvey reached into his pocket, extracted a pistol, cocked it, pointed it at the physician and replied, "If he dies, so do you."

The story goes that the doctor was immediately scared sober, and as my grandfather continued to stand and hold the gun aimed at his heart, he made a valiant effort to revive the seven-year-old child he had given up on moments before. Probably more concerned for his own life than that of his young patient, his last-ditch efforts proved to be successful. Bill was, once again, counted among the living.

Would my grandfather really have shot the drunken doctor? He had watched helplessly as my grandmother rejected Bill at his birth out of shock and grief over the death of her little girl the week before. I believe he knew she could not emotionally survive the death of another child coupled with the birth of a new baby. I can only venture a guess that his serious threat, combined with his finger on the trigger, convinced the doctor.

Both doctors agreed that the extent of the burns Bill had sustained while unconscious had damaged his leg to the point where he would never be able to walk if he survived. Those men of medicine had not counted on the dedication and stubborn determination of Mamie and a young woman named Polly Fairbanks.

Katherine "Polly" Gonder (later Fairbanks) received a diploma from John Sealy College of Nursing in 1898. Throughout her life, her gray eyes kept a continuous twinkle that masked a dogged determination to undertake the impossible when it came to patient care. Hired as the replacement nurse, she waited until Bill's diphtheria improved and his burns had healed to the point where his leg could be rubbed before she embarked upon a course of what today we would call massage therapy, paired with physical therapy.

Polly taught Mamie her system, so together they rubbed and exercised both Bill's legs nonstop. Though his right leg carried a terrible scar for the rest of his life, his ability to walk without a limp eventually returned.

Still recuperating, Bill was not told at first about the arrival of his baby brother, Nicholas Vaughan Fletcher. His parents knew that he would ask to hold the baby and feared he was still too weak. So, on November 28, 1906, when Bill first noticed strange cries coming from another part of the house, he called to his nurses, "It's cats! It's cats! Bring them in here."

Both of these women remained a part of Bill's life as he grew into a man. Polly Fairbanks left Beaumont and moved to San Antonio after the death of her husband. She remained close to our family; and at my birth, because new mothers were kept in bed for long periods of time, she moved in with us and took care of my mother and me.

As I grew, I enjoyed her company; she was an extremely witty individual who moved rapidly and gestured like a wind-up toy. Her energy appeared superhuman, and her supply of new jokes and riddles inexhaustible.

When Dad and my mother moved to San Antonio in the 1920s, they brought Mamie along. I have inherited old black-and-white photos showing her standing in our back yard wearing a long cotton skirt and a turban wound around her head.

She made her home with my parents, my grandmother and my uncle Nick for several years. Eventually, with advancing age, she decided that she would like to live in "a colored neighborhood."

My father located a home in one of the nicer black areas and installed Mamie, much to her delight. That's when the very important trips to visit her and restock her provisions became a family custom.

My entrance into the family added a new dimension. It afforded my parents an ever-changing entity to carry along and display. It offered Mamie an opportunity to resurrect a long list of carefully nourished rules, beliefs and superstitions related to the raising of a child.

My father chose what I was to wear—always my prettiest party dress"—the day before our planned trip; normally, any choice related to my attire was left up to Mother. He also gave Mother a long list of things to purchase prior to our crosstown trip. The list could have been titled "Surprises that are sure to delight Mamie." Daddy carried another list with the heavier and more practical items.

About an hour before we were to leave for the trip to Mamie's house, I was escorted to the bathtub and scrubbed with vigor until I turned a sparkling bright shade of pink. Then, Johnson's Baby Powder was applied and rubbed into all portions of my body below my chin.

Frilly underwear, socks and a giant hair ribbon that matched the dress Daddy had selected the previous day were laid out on the bed. I emerged from the bathroom smelling like the perfume counter at Joskee's.

After I had donned all of my going-to-see-Mamie costume, my hair was brushed until every tendril lay in the exact spot my mother had foreordained. Only after a final inspection was I allowed to go outside and get into the car.

Our family laughed on numerous occasions about the time my mother and I arrived at Mamie's with our supply of gifts, only to find we had forgotten the most important item.

The plan had been for us to visit for awhile, leave and pick up Daddy at work and then return to Mamie's house. Mamie flashed her toothless grin as she extracted and unwrapped each of the articles in the sacks.

After everything had been unwrapped and remarked about, she looked puzzled.

"Miss Aleen," she asked, "where my Bull Derm (Durham)?"

Mother answered that she had forgotten to buy it and apologized for her oversight.

"Oh, Miss Aleen, don't never come here wid-out dat good ol' Bull Derm."

Promising that we would soon return, Mother grabbed my hand and pulled me into the car. We must have been a laughable sight to onlookers as they watched a frantic white woman, dressed in her finest complete with hat, purse and gloves, holding the hand of a child who had been turned out to win "best in show." We rushed from store to store in a black neighborhood, intent upon finding a specific brand of tobacco. When we finally located a store that kept Mamie's favorite brand, Mother's delight was obvious, and she purchased every package in that happy merchant's inventory. He probably judged her addiction to Bull Durham to be excessive.

By the time we hit paydirt, it was time to pick up my father. He listened to the tale of Mother's forgetfulness, followed by her version of our speedy search, and enjoyed a laugh at her expense. We all returned to Mamie's, where Mother triumphantly displayed her stash of Bull Durham to a beaming hostess.

Mamie was extremely pleased to see both the tobacco and her "white son."

As usual, she quizzed both of my parents on various aspects having to do with the way they were raising me. They dutifully answered her questions and commented upon things that I had said, done and experienced since the last time we visited. Each minor milestone in my life, and small details into the methods of parenting being used in our home, were totally serious issues to Mamie. After all, as she and a lot of my older relatives saw it, she had raised my father. She was no longer living in the same place my parents were, so she relied upon our frequent visits to assure herself they were living up to her expectations.

The segregation stone had been cut into many facets. Black people prided themselves on the high caliber of white families to whom they were attached. Just as Mammy was horrified at some of Scarlett's lack of propriety in *Gone With the Wind*, Mamie and others, who had never endured a day as a slave, were strongly invested in the actions of members of white families with whom they shared a long-term relationship. Indeed, it was considered part of their destiny to see that future generations of that family behaved in an honorable manner designed to make their ancestors proud.

It was not at all unusual for a person of color to visit my parents with a specific request that went something like this: "Mrs. Fletcher, could you please help me locate a good family to work for? You know that I worked for Mrs. X for years. No one could have been a finer lady.

"When she died, I took a job for Mrs. Y. Now, I hates to say this, but her family is just plain poor white trash. My mother would turn over in her grave if she knew I worked for that kind of person."

The term "poor white trash" reflected upon the family's words, actions, morals and lack of integrity rather than their bank account.

My mother and grandmother always took these requests to heart and often located another "high-class fine lady" in need of an experienced and skillful helper.

Using some unique type of radar, friends in Mamie's neighborhood always knew when her white family came to call. They, too, came calling, usually a few at a time.

Women, for the most part, announced their arrival with soft taps on the front door. Mamie seemed to expect them, and they never stayed long. As she had done on many previous occasions, she again introduced everyone to her family.

The women stayed long enough to make a few pleasant remarks. Often, they would present Mamie, or one of us, with flowers from their garden. Before leaving, each visitor always walked over to me and touched me.

These touches were gentle and loving, and seemed to be part of a ritual that my parents and I did not quite understand. As I grew older, I sensed that it was a part of a long-held custom or superstition. Mamie understood what was going on and, with a series of silent smiles and nods, telegraphed to each small group when it was time to go and let others come in.

This was an expected part of our visit each time we arrived at Mamie's. Our visits were never hurried, and in one respect were rather formal. Mamie was the hostess and choreographer of the colorful parade of neighbors who danced in and out of her doorway. My parents and I simply copied their steps and followed her lead.

So, my first connections to colored folks, as they were then called, were pleasant and loving ties. It was not until I was old enough to accompany my grandmother on a bus trip to church, or a downtown movie, that I was introduced to the rules enforced by "Jim Crow Laws."

Grandmother and I usually sat very close to the front of the bus. Heavy buses used by San Antonio's public transportation system swayed and lurched a great deal during their frequent stops to pick up new passengers. Grandmother suffered from arthritis, was unsure of her balance and liked to sit down as soon as possible after boarding a bus.

I often became bored during the ride and walked down the aisle to talk to other passengers who had boarded our bus and went straight to the back. My grandmother would lecture me and say that I must not do that.

"They are not supposed to sit in the front of the bus, and you are not supposed to sit in the back. That's their part of the bus, and you need to stay in your own part. You have no business occupying a seat that's reserved for colored people."

All of my questions pertaining to the logic of people who were going to the same place being forced to sit at opposite ends of the bus were answered by "That's just the way it is," or a similar remark.

I gradually learned that colored children went to different schools from white children. They attended different churches, ate at different restaurants and sat way up in the top balcony in theaters where they purchased their tickets at a separate box office window. More questions addressed to family members were dismissed with "This is the law, and they are simply obeying rules."

I became more and more aware, as my ability to read progressed, of the myriad signs that read "Whites Only." These signs were placed above the doors of many business establishments, on restroom doors, above drinking fountains and at the doors of the larger waiting rooms at bus stations and train depots. This meant that all means of public transportation had to invest in separate waiting areas and facilities. The "Whites Only" sign for restrooms and drinking fountains led one to believe that there were other facilities for blacks. Very often, that was not the case.

To each of these cases, "That's just the way it is" was the standard answer.

The stated rationale concerning racial division of facilities was "Separate but equal." That was fifty-percent correct, as everything available to blacks was separate. However, the word *equal* was not even close to the truth.

When books and other educational equipment were scrapped by white teachers, they were passed on to the colored schools and new ones were ordered for white students. When new football uniforms were issued to white high school athletes, the worn-out uniforms were used by team members at a colored high school. So, the stated equality of education was, in fact, a system of scruffy, hand-me-downs with which black educators had to make do.

A friend of later years told me that her school in Jones Creek only went through the third grade. Her father was forced to send her to a boarding school in the Conroe area where black children were given the opportunity to progress until they earned a high school diploma.

Black people who had to travel during the 30s were often faced with no overnight lodging that would accept them. The same thing happened when they were ready for a meal—most cafes and restaurants in the South displayed a "Whites only" sign.

As might be expected among people of different colors who were not allowed to interact socially, both races held specific notions about members of the other race that were not necessarily based upon fact. My mother was convinced, for example, that all African-American children possessed amazing musical talent at birth, and were also endowed with a sense of rhythm far superior to any enjoyed by members of the white race. When we were en route to a specific destination in the car and happened to pass black children playing on the sidewalk, it was not unusual for her to pull the car over and park so that I would have the opportunity to observe their natural rhythm when they began to dance.

Days spent with Jo Ella had also convinced Mother that "Colored people have beautiful singing voices." Probably, her theories were reinforced by the movies of the 1930s, as quite often black people in a film were given a role in which they either sang or tap-danced.

Since musical films of the 30s and early 40s were often little more than a series of Vaudeville acts strung together minus any semblance of a plot, often a "picture show" would feature minstrel acts performed by whites wearing blackface makeup. Hollywood was not ready to admit that there were beautiful and talented people of color.

To view an example of this, rent a vintage film called *The Dolly Sisters* starring Betty Grable, June Haver and John Payne. In one of the film's production numbers, Haver and Grable sing "The Darktown Strutter's Ball" while a long procession of women portraying some of those "Darktown Strutters" appear in costume and slink past the camera. Each woman is obviously white with her face and body darkened by makeup.

As in its vaudeville predecessors, blacks in the movies were portrayed as happy, musical and simple-minded. With few exceptions, their roles were limited to portraying maids or other servants.

A typical song performed on stage and screen by entertainers who were either blacks or whites in blackface was "Oh! Susanna" by Stephen Collins Foster. This troubadour and writer of American folk music wrote "My Old Kentucky Home," "Swanee River," "Old Black Joe" and other beloved songs that were still being performed quite often. The original lyrics to "Oh! Susanna" were written in the style of speech Foster observed while listening to Southern Negroes speak, and were no doubt conceived of as humorous at that time.

> I came from Alabama wid
> My banjo on my knee,
> I'm gwine to Louisiana,
> My true lub for to see;
> It rain'd all night de day I left,
> De weather it was dry
> De sun so hot I froze to death,
> Susanna, don't you cry.

> Oh! Susanna, Oh!
> Don't you cry for me,
> I've come from Alabama
> Wid my banjo on my knee

> I jumped aboard de telegraph,
> And trabb'led down de ribber
> De 'lectric fluid magnified,
> And killed five hundred nigger;
> De bullgine bust, de hoss run off,
> I really thought I'd die,
> I shut my eyes to hold my breath,
> Susanna, don't you cry.

I had a dream de other night,
When ebry ting was still;
I thought I saw Susanna,
A-coming down de hill;
De buckwheat cake was in her mouf,
De tear was in her eye,
Says I, "I'm coming from de South,
Susanna, don't you cry."

I soon will be in New Orleans,
And den I'll look all 'round,
And when I find Susanna,
I will fall upon de ground.
And if I do not find her,
Dis darky'll surely die;
And when I'm dead and buried,
Susanna, don't you cry.

Most of my mother's notions concerning black people could be classified as humorous and harmless. However, on a day when Aunt Vallie, Mother and I drove into town on some errand, she made a statement that I found shocking.

We were in a small shopping area when I spied a black woman standing at a nearby bus stop.

"Look at that lady over there," I directed the grown-ups. "Isn't she pretty?"

"She surely is pretty," Mother answered, "but don't ever call a colored person a lady."

"Why?"

"Because Negro people are called women. They are incapable of being ladies."

This answer was beyond belief to me. I thought of the many instructions I had received since first learning to interact socially. I understood the type of manners and comportment necessary to become "a little lady." It was a veritable litany of actions aimed at always being considerate to others and obeying rules. So, why in the world should any female who did likewise not be called a lady?

I expressed my feelings to my mother and aunt. Aunt Vallie knew exactly where I was coming from and said so, though she did not want to interfere with my mother's instructions.

I kept on with my series of arguments that anyone who comported themselves as a lady deserved to be known as such. It was a one-sided discussion, as every opinion to which I gave voice was rebutted with the same statement: "A colored person is not capable of being a lady."

Mother's patience became exhausted, and I was reminded that a young lady does not ever argue with a parent. I left the scene of our argument convinced that her words did not match the actions I had seen her display with people of color close to our family.

There were other times Mother and I argued over this same matter. However, I could never get her to budge from the stated opinion she must have memorized as a child.

The far-reaching unfairness of Mother's views did not hit me until a time when my parents and I went to stay at my favorite destination.

I inherited my father's love for ranch life and the out-of-doors. Daddy fell in love with the coastal area of Texas as a child and planned to have a ranch there someday. In the meantime, he kept a small herd of Hereford cattle on his cousin's ranch near Port Lavaca. The Traylor Ranch was pure heaven to me, and I became excited each time I learned about the possibility of an impending visit.

There were three homes on the ranch. A single-story ranch-style stucco housed the older couple whom we called Cousin Will and Cousin Katie. Their son "Cap," his wife Mary and their two sons lived next door in a two-story white frame home. Depending on who else was visiting at the time, our family might be housed at either of these two places.

A smaller white frame home housed the Traylor's top hand, Antoine Meride. Antoine had once stayed on the ranch to act as overseer during the years when Will and Katie Traylor moved to Cuero so their four children could attend school. His grown daughter Naomi now lived with him and cooked for Cousin Katie. Naomi had several daughters, and one of them was my age.

Lillie Marie had been given a typical Texas-style double name, like so many children of that day. She and I played all day long the first day my family was at the ranch. I have pictures of us on her front porch. Another shot shows me racing a horse up to her house. That was purely because I liked being in the saddle, since her house was an easy walk from where I was staying.

In the evening, when I was called to come inside, I did the polite thing. I said, "Tomorrow, you come over, and we'll play where I'm

I learned my first lesson in prejudice the summer I played with Lillie Marie Meride on my father's cousin's ranch. Though I was welcome to spend the entire day at her house, but she wasn't permitted inside mine.

staying." That was what I had been taught to do at home—don't overstay your welcome at any one spot. Extend friends an invitation to your home.

Lillie Marie arrived at the door soon after breakfast the next morning. I don't remember whether Mary Traylor or my mother answered her knock, but as I was on my way to the door to greet her, Mother informed me in no uncertain terms that she would not be able to come inside to play with me.

"It's not proper for a colored girl to visit in the home of a white child."

I was horrified. She knew full well that I had spent the day before at the Meride's house. I felt like the breath had been knocked out of me, and wondered how my mother could expect me to hurt a friend's feelings in such an unnecessary manner.

Whether or not Mary intervened, I never knew. I was told that I could go outside and play with Lillie Marie if I wanted. So, that's what I did, and I never mentioned the reason I did not suggest playing inside, where we could have found shelter from the hot sun.

Lillie and I continued to play, out- of-doors or inside her house, each day for the remainder of our visit. However, I deeply resented the fact that a perfectly delightful friend was barred from coming inside to visit me because of the color of her skin.

⁂

There were other black women to whom I was attached during my childhood. When my mother interviewed women for household work, she never hired those who asked for "totin' privileges." This was a term still in use from a century before when slaves toted food and other items from a plantation home into the slave quarters. Mother was very generous with her employees and always saw to it that enough food was cooked for them to carry home each day. However, she understood this frequent request to mean that a household employee could "tote" home whatever she saw that she believed her employer did not need. Mother wanted to be the one to decide which items were carried through our door.

Food, shoes and clothing were the major items usually included under the totin' privilege heading. Furniture, dishes, linens and other household items were also in demand by families who had very little.

⁂

Jony Mae's employment as our housekeeper offered the perfect opportunity for Mother to enlighten me about the mysteries of pregnancy and childbirth.

Domestic servants of that era wore a one-piece black dress covered with a white apron. They also wore white organdy caps, which sat on the front of their heads and were often trimmed with black satin ribbon.

Maid's uniforms differed very slightly in design, and were in such large demand that retail clothing stores kept a large inventory. Our housekeepers always looked extremely professional in their attire.

One day, I watched as Mother adjusted Jony Mae's uniform, which seemed to have suddenly become extremely tight. My mother laughed, shook her head and told Jony Mae that they would have to come up with another style outfit.

Jony Mae was young, cute as a button, giggled a lot and did not have the slightest idea what to tell me when I asked, "Jony Mae, how come you're getting so fat?" My mother was also not eager to venture into that subject matter.

Small children always accumulate a collection of overheard bits of conversation that they file away in a mental file cabinet marked "Solve Later." It's their cold case file of kidnapped words and phrases, held captive until the mystery finally unravels. Each tiny conversational section will, at some future point, fit neatly into the outline of another puzzle-phrase accidentally dropped within the child's hearing range.

In families that openly discuss and honestly answer the questions of children, there is no need for such a file cabinet to take up valuable cranium space. However, in my home environment, it was up to me to surreptitiously collect pieces of the puzzle and, when I had gathered enough, fit them together.

I knew that Mother was extremely concerned about Jony Mae's health. That seemed strange, because Jony Mae usually sang or giggled while working in our kitchen. She surely had not complained or acted sick.

Another bit of gathered intelligence showed that there was concern that she had no husband. *Give her time, she's still young.* I overheard questions like "Where will she have it?" "Who will take care of it?" However, I found no clues that indicated what "it" might be.

One morning, Jony Mae did not show up for work. Mother answered the phone and spoke to someone in hushed tones. After finishing her conversation, she made a quick visit to my grandmother's room. I knew they were having a discussion to which I was not invited. Then, my mother called my father at work, which she seldom did.

After completing that call, she told me she had to run some errands, and I was to stay with Grandmother. That was fine with me because I was more interested in playing with my dog than I was in any adult errand.

That evening, Mother announced that Jony Mae had "gotten a baby." My immediate reaction was "Where did she get it?"

On one of Mother's errands several sacks of groceries and other supplies had been purchased. That evening, my parents took me along to the place where Jony Mae and the baby were staying. To my mother's deep concern, there was no one in the house but Jony Mae and the extremely tiny infant.

Mother had acquired an entire layette for the baby. She immediately began to change the baby's diaper and dress her in a cotton sacque. Jony Mae lay very still and watched without making any comments.

At the same time, Mother asked Jony Mae a series of questions concerning who would care for her and the baby. Jony Mae's answers were vague and sounded almost disinterested. It was obvious that Mother did not like the answers she was receiving and was becoming even more concerned.

There were no ready-made infant formulas available for purchase at that time. For the baby to thrive, the mother's milk had to be good, or she had to be able to acquire a combination of ingredients and cook up a formula. When we left Jony Mae's that night, and started the drive back home, Mother was at the point of tears.

"I just don't think that baby looks healthy," she said, "and I don't see how Jony Mae can take care of it. She doesn't look good herself. I did not want to leave her there by herself."

I wondered aloud, "Did whoever gave Jony Mae that baby surprise her?"

In the following weeks, Mother made numerous trips back to the house where Jony Mae was staying. There were no home health care agencies or social service organizations available to step in and render aid. So, Mother came face-to-face with the constant frustrations black people faced trying to get adequate medical care. San Antonio's Robert B. Greene, a charity hospital, was always overflowing with long lines of sick people waiting to be seen.

I know that my mother worked hard to find some sort of medical help for Jony Mae. Eventually, a relative showed up, and Jony Mae moved with her to another town. We heard later that her baby girl did not live.

Our household helpers were not all black. Over the years, Mother also hired housekeepers who were white or Hispanic. Minnie was a lovely young Mexican woman who used her salary to attend college at night. When she worked for us, she had a special way with animals.

My constant companion, Stormy the wire-haired terrier, died suddenly. Only days after this sad event, Aunt Lulu was being taken for a drive on a country road. A heavy rainstorm had just ended when she spied a little puppy, looking lost and thoroughly drenched, standing by the side of the road. Aunt Lulu told Marie, her chauffeur and paid companion, to stop the car and go get the poor little thing.

They drove directly to our house and presented me with a still-wet and bedraggled-looking new pet. When my father arrived home from work, he took one look at Lucky and said, "I think what we have here is a coyote! He must have wandered off from the rest of his litter."

Of course, I was totally charmed by the new arrival, so Daddy decided to take a wait-and-see attitude about the little pup who was at that time busy investigating our kitchen.

Lucky was decidedly different from other puppies our family had owned. He and Minnie formed a very close bond over the next few months. She seemed to be the only one from whom he was willing to accept any type of order. The rest of the family he simply endured and ignored.

My father was still convinced that he was a coyote, so watched him carefully for any sign that he was an unsafe pet for a small child. I soon gave him the opportunity to make a decision on that matter.

One evening, Minnie put Lucky's food in his bowl on the kitchen floor. On an impulse, I decided to hand-feed him. My plan was to pick up some food from his bowl and put it in his mouth. After all, I had done that with Stormy.

Well, I hand-fed him, alright! The minute I reached into his dish, he used his very sharp teeth and strong jaws to take a large bite out of my right hand. My parents heard me holler and "made pig tracks" into the kitchen. By then, Minnie was holding Lucky up by the back of his neck and yelling at him in Spanish. I was dripping blood and tears all over the kitchen floor.

"That's it!" announced my father. "You can't turn a coyote into a child's pet. We're getting rid of him."

Since Minnie was the only one Lucky would obey, whether she spoke English or Spanish, she asked if she could have him. That was the day when the dog's fate really matched his name. I do not believe that my father's plan of action would have landed him in the lap of a young lady who loved him.

Minnie enjoyed owning Lucky, as did the rest of her siblings. She frequently gave us glowing reports about how smart he was. According to her, he was well-behaved and a joy to have around.

Those times when Daddy drove Minnie home and was able to see her full-grown pet, he returned home wondering how long it would be before Lucky's luck ran out.

"In that Mexican neighborhood," he told us, "people know what a coyote looks like. I hope for Minnie's sake that no one decides to take a shot at him."

There may have been another reason Minnie wanted Lucky around. Josephine, her diminutive mother, worked for us several days a week as a laundress. She had been widowed when her sheriff husband was shot and killed while performing his duty. After her husband's death, Josephine moved her large family from the Rio Grande Valley to San Antonio in search of work.

It was not unusual for outlaws, as well as law-abiding people, to cross the Texas-Mexico border by swimming the Rio Grande. San Antonio was the favorite destination of these illegal immigrants because it was large enough to offer a person the opportunity to disappear. The Mexican-American population made it easy for "wetbacks" to blend in. Minnie and her mother were both acutely aware of the outlaw element that often showed up near their home. So, a watchdog, or watch-coyote, was a plus.

Lucky performed that service for the family for several years after Minnie graduated from night school, left our home and took a job as a teacher. Josephine always told us about everyone's progress. One day, she came with bad news. Lucky had died after a neighbor fed him poison. Minnie's heart, she said, was broken.

Illegal aliens arrived by the truckload, in full sight of the authorities, once cotton-picking season rolled around. Human cargo, ranging in age from toddlers to great-grandparents, were packed into open-air trucks like cattle to cross the Mexican border in quest of work.

These poor people had no cover from the wind or blazing Texas sun as they stood up for the long, sweltering rides along highways heading north. Housing, food, sanitation and general treatment on the various ranches and farms, where they worked from dawn to dusk, depended upon the hearts and humanity of the owners. No laws protected these workers in the 1930s and '40s. Exploitation and abuse were common, and society in general simply looked away.

El Campo was one of the first Texas towns where residents got together and jointly said, "We will no longer stand by and watch such inhumane treatment of our fellow human beings." Other Texas towns soon followed their example. All of the changes put in place to help migrant workers were strictly voluntary in the late 1940s. It would take decades before laws were passed in an effort to insure humane treatment for individuals within this labor force.

Workers were paid in cash at the end of the week. I remember seeing parents lead their children into local stores after being paid. Big brown eyes gleamed and petite fingers pointed at their selections. In a short time, most of the money earned by a week of backbreaking labor had been spent on candy, soda pop and other treats that brought smiles to the faces of the young. Children, of course, never saw the inside of a school because they worked beside their elders in the fields.

Some of the better jobs available to men of color in the 1930s and '40s were with the railroads. Passenger trains were still elegant, and travelers were met by "Red Caps"—the luggage handlers—as they arrived at the bustling railroad stations.

Black men had been connected to railroads since slaves laid the original rails in Maryland in the 1830s. A century later, Pullman porters were the elite jobs available to them. At first, their only compensation came from the tips received for the many tasks they performed. A decision by the Supreme Court eventually changed this by ruling that porters were, in fact, Pullman employees and as such had to be paid a salary.

However, though black men held such skilled jobs as firemen and brakemen on the railroads, all colored men were designated "non-promotable." So, society in general, and certainly railroad hierarchy, shared my mother's opinion that people of color were not capable of advancing beyond a certain rank. Strict rules were in force to make sure they never received opportunities for promotion as white railroad employees did.

Many Pullman porters were laid off during the Great Depression; but after the beginning of World War II, a huge number of jobs re-opened for troop movement and "sleeper service."

The training porters received was extremely exacting, even finicky. They were on call twenty-four hours per day for the duration of their trip. Once they received baggage from the Red Caps, they were available to assist their passengers by bringing drinks or snacks, sending telegrams when the train reached a station, making appointments in the diner or the barber shop and helping sort through luggage.

Uniforms worn by Red Caps and Pullman porters were extremely colorful and military in design. Their bearing and manner of movement as they executed their duties was also reminiscent of soldiers on parade.

Porters expertly tended to the needs of the passengers until they reached their destinations. They announced that the dining car was ready to serve by strolling through each car and sounding a soft gong. In the evenings, they saw to it that seats were converted into private berths where passengers were lulled to sleep by the click-clacking wheels of the train. As travelers slept, their shoes were polished to a mirror shine.

Most of our family's train travel was done for the purpose of visiting relatives in Beaumont. We usually took a train that left in the evening for the simple enjoyment and novelty of sleeping while in route.

In the morning, while travelers enjoyed breakfast in the dining car, their berth was converted back into a comfortable seat. The white-gloved porters were so professional that each and every conversion was accomplished in the manner of an experienced magician—now you see it, now you don't.

Restrooms and the plush upholstered seats were kept spotless. Passengers were coddled and spoiled by these professional caregivers until the final "Knock-em-off," or brushing down, a traveler received upon detraining.

There was another variety of prejudice, which I first encountered while visiting a fourth-grade classmate's family. Anti-Semitism had never been a bias held by any family members or close friends, as far as I knew. As my new friend June and I played a game of jacks on a red-striped linoleum floor, I overheard a conversation between several adults who sat at the kitchen table drinking coffee. The gist of their gathering seemed to involve casting slurs at Jewish people in general and trying to outdo one anther by telling crude "Jew-jokes."

That evening at supper, I repeated their conversation to my parents. Daddy quickly pointed out that such remarks were ignorant, offensive and not at all based on fact. He then named several families who were friends of ours and asked if I thought any of them fit the descriptions I had heard that afternoon. I answered, "Of course not."

"Well, then, in the future, steer clear of June's house if that's the way they feel."

Dad went on to explain that there were some organizations that would not allow Jewish people to join their membership.

"These groups brought a lot of old prejudices along when they came to America. I guess they are just afraid of anything they don't understand. It's called fear of the unknown."

The visit to June's was the only time anti-Semitism intruded into my life until I was in my sophomore year at the University of Houston. Nineteen-fifty was the first year the university had dormitories on campus. Actually, the construction was not finished when the fall semester began, but we moved in anyway; and the builders were forced to crawl over and around us just as we had to carefully maneuver past a conglomeration of cables and extension cords stretching from a temporary power source.

Some controversy had caused a work stoppage during the preceding summer, so only one of the four dorms was close to becoming habitable when September rolled around. This situation left the university with a weighty problem. It would be several weeks, maybe months, before flooring and electrical work could be completed. The students whose housing checks had been accepted had every right to move in prior to the beginning of the fall semester.

Could these young folks handle walking on tarpaper floors without tripping over the myriad extension cords needed for power tools? How about moving around and reading by flashlight beams in the evenings? September in Houston is hot and humid; and these were, we were told, the first dorms designed for central air-conditioning in the nation. With no electricity, that luxury would have to be forfeited.

The university had an even bigger problem—some of us who stood on the sidewalk with our luggage and listened to a frantic construction foreman yell instructions to his crew were female and others were male. There were no coed dorms anywhere in the United States, but University of Houston administrators were faced with the necessity of creating one instantly. They did their best to keep that situation under wraps until a second dormitory was finished months later.

They kept it so quiet, in fact, that no one bothered to explain to us about hallway doors, used as partitions at night but kept ajar during the day for the benefit of flooring and electrical subcontractors. Few of us realized that some power-that-be materialized each evening to close and lock these doors.

Any stairway within the building could be used as a route to my fourth-floor room during daytime hours. Returning from a date one evening during the first week of classes, I took the stairs I normally climbed. As I walked down the hall in the direction of my room, I realized several facts at once. The sound of water rushing through pipes indicated showers were being taken in a lot of bathrooms. Quite a few students were singing in the shower—and each of the singers was a baritone!

Previously, I assumed the fourth floor was occupied by girls only. I ran towards my end of the hall and was stopped by a locked door separating me from the room I sought. Hurriedly retracing my steps downstairs and outside of the building, I eventually found someone who explained that each floor was partitioned in this manner because of the administration's desire to have campus athletes live onsite. That was when I learned that more than eighty-five percent of my dorm mates were male

This was a strange thought for a student who had spent her freshman year at Texas State College for Women (now Texas Women's University) in Denton. We women, housed in a few rooms on the north corner of each floor, were actually residing in the men's dorm.

Word of this situation soon spread through the entire student body, so local students teased us constantly. The fact was, despite being humorous, our shared living remained innocent. The only boys who wandered into the girl's section and found their way to my room were seeking someone to sew buttons on ROTC uniforms.

My roommate and I did enjoy the small groups of tipsy males who stood beneath our window each night and serenaded us. Their favorite, and oft-repeated, song was the popular "Good Night, Irene."

The U of H was a privately funded college during the years I attended. Campus sorority and fraternity groups were local and rather low-key. I had not planned on joining a sorority, but as the first women to dwell on campus, we were both a novelty and a desired addition to these organizations.

I had been elected president of the Women's Dormitory Council, a new political title on campus and one that, at first, represented only a small contingent of north-corner-dwelling females. A few months later, we were moved into our new dorm and joined by a throng of new residents.

Sororities wanted the holder of that office among their ranks, so I was royally rushed. Some groups even assigned stalker-type girls to keep reminding me of why their particular Greek letters stood for "pick of the litter."

I had an aversion to "Rah-Rah Team" cutesy-coed groups who gathered in the campus cafeteria and pulled every type of shenanigan to call attention to their clan. While attending various soirees, I eventually met a small group of gracious, mannerly and rather reserved young women who called their organization Pi Delta. Their members proved to be excellent conversationalists, able to discuss subjects other than football and those who played it.

As I accepted invitations to rush parties, so did my roommate, Blanche Levy. I thought it strange that we never bumped into one another at some of the events but decided that there were so many girls out there that rush parties were split into several groups and held on separate occasions.

Blanche knew what I failed to grasp—because she was Jewish she would only be asked to join the one sorority on campus specifically for Jewish girls. I was absolutely incredulous when she explained this after we each had joined "the group of our choice." Blanche was a delightful individual with vibrant red hair and a personality to match. Certainly, any organization would have been lucky to claim her.

Anti-Semitism quietly raised its ugly head a number of times during the next few months. Blanche and I were in the habit of meeting for lunch in the campus cafeteria most days. On numerous occasions, I was stopped as I entered the dining hall by members of my new sorority.

"Come over and sit at our table."

I always politely thanked them for the invitation and told them I was planning to eat with my roommate.

"Why doesn't she sit with the Jewish girls? Then you can come join us."

Though these words were actually spoken as a directive, I pretended to understand them as a question.

"Because we like to have lunch together" was my truthful but less than tactful response. I obviously did not fit into the category of "good pledge material."

I certainly was not trying to avoid these pleasant young women. On days when Blanche and I had conflicting schedules, I often ate with them.

This situation caused Blanche and me to realize that, as far as sororities went, we were square pegs attempting to fit into round holes. Addicted to independent thinking and acting from our hearts, we were both poor candidates to perpetuate and support an artificial system of separation based upon ancient ethnic beliefs.

Though Pi Delta's membership included lovely young women whom I enjoyed knowing, I lost track of my sorority sisters after college graduation. Blanche and I, however, formed a sister-like bond and remained the closest of friends until breast cancer caused her untimely death.

⁓✢⁓

Though my parents abhorred anti-Semitic sentiments, Mother just didn't "get it" when it came to skin color. Our society gradually became more enlightened and tolerant, yet many of her generation refused to acknowledge that their long-held racial beliefs had been flawed.

My mother demonstrated the lingering fallacy of her values when one of my daughters planned to try apartment living prior to enrolling in

Sam Houston University. Autumn chose to remain in Pasadena and work for a year between high school and college. Her favorite coworker at her bank-teller job was a black girl named Sheila.

Both girls thought the numerical amounts on their first full-time paychecks looked bountiful. Elated with this sudden prosperity, they decided to share an apartment and try living away from home.

What could offer a more realistic lesson into the art of managing money? Autumn had the full approval of her parents and three siblings. Her grandparents thought this would be a good learning experience also —that is, until my mother learned that Sheila was black.

Mother insisted that my father leave his La Ward office immediately and drive her to our Pasadena home. When they arrived, she stalked through the kitchen door into our family room and plopped into a chair without her normal greetings to grandchildren. We quickly ascertained that she had driven for several hours to demonstrate that she was not speaking to us.

Her cold lack of response to our greetings, refusal to make eye contact and the stubborn set of her jaw made it very obvious that she was angry about something. My father was his old sweet self, so we could only wonder what burr was under her saddle.

Realizing that she had gone to a lot of trouble to sit in our midst and silently pout, I understood that sulking without an audience does not make much sense. I also knew that she expected me to ask questions like "Are you upset about something?" This would give her the opportunity to vociferously express her views and vent her spleen. I refused to play that game, so we left her alone to ride her high horse. In the meantime, we enjoyed visiting with my father while Mother continued to glare at us though eyes narrowed to slits.

After a while, each of our family members caught on to the fact that she was not-speaking to Autumn the loudest, which in turn made clear the reason for her behavior. My children had been taught that everyone is the same on the inside, however, so I was not interested in having them hear her thoughts on racial issues.

Actually, Mother's petulant actions while caught up in her own melodrama were so ludicrous that the rest of us were required to suppress laughter while observing them. She rendered a magnificent soliloquy of silence.

Her performance that afternoon reminded me of Emma, and a foolish decision Mother made when I was still a child. Each of us has heard the old saying, "Cut off your nose to spite your face." I never hear, or read, those words without thinking of my mother and Emma.

Emma was what other black people used to refer to as a "high yellow." Her skin was very light, and if she had chosen to do so, she probably could have passed for white. She was, as far as I can remember, the last full-time housekeeper our family employed.

Emma and Mother worked well together, and if my mother had been asked, I think that she would have described Emma as the perfect household helper. She seemed to know exactly what needed to be done without any discussion of the matter.

There were a lot of discussions between my mother and Emma, but the subject matter usually had nothing to do with household chores. I could overhear their conversations, and there was a distinct difference in the relationship between those two women and the ties my mother had had with other employees through the years. Anyone who did not know the rules of segregation would have sworn that the two women exchanging views were close friends.

There came a morning when Emma did not show up for work. It was assumed she had missed her usual bus and would arrive on a later one. A telephone was a luxury item not found in the homes of those employed as domestic help. Since Mother could not call Emma, she worried about her all day long.

Emma did not come to work the next day, either. To not show up for work, or send a message by someone else, was not her way of doing things. Finally, Mother received a phone call.

I could tell that it was Emma, and that Mother was very relieved to hear her voice. Overhearing only one side of the conversation, I was able to glean that Emma's daughter had been arrested and taken to jail. Emma's absence had been caused by having to go to the police station and make arrangements to bail her out. Evidently, public intoxication had been the cause of the arrest.

I could hear the difference in Mother's attitude change from one of relief over Emma's safety to anger over the fact that she had not called sooner. My mother had absolutely no knowledge of dealing with jailhouse procedures. Emma had probably been forced to wait her turn in lengthy lines, which she dared not leave or she would lose her spot. She may have had to visit friends and neighbors to collect bail money. Surely, a black woman having to deal with white police was in a precarious position.

Mother began speaking in superior tones, repeating that it was Emma's duty to inform her employer immediately if something happened that would keep her away from work. I believe, now that she was no longer frightened that something terrible had happened to Emma, her fear was being released as anger.

Emma had spent close to forty-eight hours at the jail. She was probably exhausted, frustrated and desperately in need of understanding and sympathy. What she did not need at that moment was a sanctimonious lecture from a white woman who was protected from unpleasant worldly issues by a devoted husband.

I could hear the raised voice, though not the words, coming through the phone. Whatever Emma said angered Mother more, and she banged down the receiver. After hanging up, Mother informed no one in particular that Emma must be fired for "talking back."

Bits of conversation overheard in the community flooded my mind. *I told that woman she had better not sass me again. I just won't put up with an uppity Negro!* Such words were not unusual at that time. I had just never associated them with my mother. If she used the words *uppity* or *sass*, she was referring to me arguing a point with her!

Emma was an intelligent woman and not a child who needed to be told how to act or talk. I hoped that Mother's sudden decision to fire her would be replaced with a more understanding and logical attitude overnight. However, when Emma arrived the next morning, spotless in a neatly pressed uniform, Mother had an expression of icy resolve on her face and a check written for severance pay in her hand. There were a few formal words spoken, which I did not hear.

Emma was there only minutes before she accepted the check and left crying.

"I sure does love you-all."

Thus, my mother, in following a mindless system long in place, symbolically cut off her nose to spite her face. By a poorly thought-out decision, as with the one involving Jo Ella, she erased from our household a person who certainly did love us, just as we loved her.

Mother now found herself without help during a war era when blacks were able to get numerous jobs that had never been open to them before. Wages had risen, and she could not compete with salaries being paid by various new war-related industries.

I always hoped that Emma applied for and received a much better job. Mother interviewed a number of women after Emma left but never found one she wanted to hire. Probably, she regretted her hasty decision many times over the next year.

Meantime, the world around us, as well as our personal situation, was changing rapidly.

Alabama Eglantine Keith Vaughan (my great-grandmother) with her three daughters: L to R May ("Duckie"), Addie and Florence (my grandmother). May and Addie were the reclusive Vaughan sisters who spoke baby-talk to one another and close relatives. They didn't speak at all to anyone else.

Archibald Nicholas (A. N.) Vaughn, owner of the first newspaper in Beaumont TX, *The Beaumont Banner*, shown wearing his Confederate uniform.

y paternal great-grandmother abama Eglantine Keith (Mrs. A. N.) aughn. She lost both parents on e journey to Texas.

Capt. K. D. Keith, Alabama's brother and a member of Speight's Battalion and hero of the battle of the "Cotton Clads" near Sabine Pass.

My great-uncle Emmett Fletcher, Harvey's brother, who used his brother's widow's financial ignorance to defraud my father of his inheritance.

My maternal grandfather Dr. Thomas Benjamin Haynes. His payment for medical services often came in the form of kittens, puppies or a cake.

Lavinia Parker Haynes, my maternal grandmother, in one of the few photos she didn't find and black out her face.

My uncle Nick and my father, caught in business attire by a San Antonio street photographer

My parents circa 1922, the year they married.

My uncle Nick and Ima (Bean) Fletcher during World War II

Harvey Davis Fletcher, my grandfather, who pointed a pistol at the inebriated doctor treating his seriously ill son and said, "If he dies, so do you."

Hugh Phillipus Jr. and I face a 1930s paparazzo on our first day of school. Hugh and I often played violin together onstage

I performed at San Antonio's Municipal Auditorium when I would much rather have been doing other things.

My grandmother Florence and I, also captured by a San Antonio street photographer.

Freshman Duchess for 1950 at the Texas State College for Women's annual Redbud Festival. TSCW is now Texas Women's University

CHAPTER FIVE

WORDS THAT HAUNT US

Answering our doorbell became an almost nonstop activity during the Depression years. The parade of men of all ages who asked for food and drink, a handful of change or if we had any jobs available was a constant reminder that my father was lucky to have a job and we were blessed to be able to enjoy a comfortable life.

No man who said he was hungry was ever turned away from our door. He was asked to go to our back porch, where he was able to sit in the shade and consume a sandwich or a plate of leftovers from our icebox. A cup of coffee or a glass of iced tea was offered, also.

Remembering the never-ending procession of men who found our home, I am amazed at the ability of my mother and grandmother to always have food to offer. For instance, homemade biscuits, cornbread, corn dodgers or corn pone were served with each of our meals. Any leftover breads were paired with other ingredients to make sandwiches. Sliced bread, available in grocery stores after 1930, was used mainly for breakfast toast or French toast.

One evening, friends Paul and Lucille Muret were visiting our family when Mother made a remark about the unusual number of men who had come to our door that day. Paul was a newspaper reporter who possessed an encyclopedia-like brain filled with little-known facts. After Mother finished speaking, he arose from his chair and said, "Let me go check something."

He walked out to our front curb and looked down. He turned and gestured for the rest of us to join him. Pointing to an innocuous-looking mark made by a chalk-like substance, he said, "This is the reason for the crowd at your front door."

He went on to explain that hobos always tried to help one another. Large numbers of men rode the rails in search of a job, temporary or permanent. Some banded with others who were down on their luck and lived in camps near the railroad tracks. Often, entire families existed in those camps. The women and children usually remained at the campsite while the men walked into town in search of anything to ease their situation. Few of these people had known what it was like to live as a tramp or beggar prior to the Depression.

Homeless men developed a series of code marks with which they left messages for others in their hapless circumstance. A chalky rock capable of marking a cement curb could easily be found and carried. The mark placed on our curb simply meant "These people will help you."

Paul looked for, and quickly found, another type of mark in front of a neighbor's house. We followed him over and could immediately see the difference.

"This mark," he told us, "means 'don't waste your time at this place.'"

Front doors were usually left ajar to allow ventilation during the warmer months. However, screen doors designed to keep insects outside could be kept locked with a simple latch. Newspaper articles warned housewives not to open their doors to the beggars who made the rounds daily. Most of these men were truly desperate, and would have been among the work force if they could have found an available job. However, a criminal element had developed within their ranks. Sympathetic people who opened their door to offer food had been assaulted and robbed.

There was a time when someone in our household was careless and forgot to latch the screen. I walked into our living room and was startled to find a dazed-looking older man staggering around in circles.

I ran to get Mother then watched as she gently but firmly took his arm and guided him back out onto our front porch. We were fortunate that this poor fellow was simply overwhelmed by confusion and meant no harm.

Two men for whom our door was always opened were the Fuller Brush Man (a well-known title at the time) and a spectacular salesman who represented the Workshop for the Blind. Our family used products sold by both of these individuals.

Pat, from the workshop, was a handsome blond man with curly hair and a sunny disposition. He carried an armload of sample brooms, mops and other household utensils that blind people at the workshop had expertly crafted. These products were known to be superior to those available elsewhere, and Pat was proud to be able to offer them to his customers.

In the morning, a car from the workshop brought him to our general area of town and stopped to let him out. He was told when and where to expect to be picked up that afternoon. From that point on, he was on his own, with only a white, red-tipped cane to rely upon.

Pat had memorized the location of every house in his territory and immediately identified the person who answered the door by the sound of his or her voice. My father looked forward to his visits because they both enjoyed discussing world news. Pat was on top of each current event and provided Dad with an astute conversational partner. We always offered Pat something to drink and ordered the items he told us about whether they were an absolute necessity or not.

Each of us loved him and thought he was a wise and outstanding individual. As a very young child, I told Mother, "His color (aura) is the prettiest I have ever seen." Of course, she did not understand what I meant and chose to think I was referring to his abundant blond hair.

Each remark Pat made was cheerful and positive in nature. His visits left us with a special glow, as if he had reached inside each of us and lifted our spirits. If I were to speculate about angels sent to earth on a mission to inspire others, Pat would surely come to mind.

Feeling about Pat as we did, we were overjoyed on the day he told us of his engagement to a young woman, also blind, whom he had met at the workshop.

Of course, we could not afford to purchase items from every salesman who came to our door. My mother and grandmother were perfect examples of kindness and graciousness when they dealt with the constant parade of men. Their remarks allowed the individual salesman to feel good about himself, even if he did not make a sale. They always thanked those who sought to sell pencils, light bulbs or similar items for demonstrating their wares and gave a logical reason why we did not need any at that moment.

I often heard, "Thank you for showing me your pencils, but I just bought a box at the store yesterday." To my young mind, it was the "thank you...but" combination that worked.

One day, our doorbell rang when I was the only one inside—Mother, Grandmother and the housekeeper were all occupied in the back yard. Feeling confident as the miniature lady of the house, I walked to the door and asked, "May I help you?"

The salesman standing on our porch grinned and proceeded to give me his pitch about a new musical studio about to open in our area. As he closed his memorized litany, he asked, "Now, you would like to take piano lessons wouldn't you, little lady?"

I knew what this question called for. I responded politely, "Thank you for asking, but I would rather take violin."

Those few words would haunt me for years to come. I had never even given the violin a thought; I simply chose my answer in order to turn him down politely. He rolled his eyes skyward, whispered, "Praise God," and then all but turned cartwheels down our front walk. He looked so happy as he departed that I decided I must have done my job well.

That same evening, as our family relaxed together in the living room, two strange men suddenly appeared on our front porch. My father went to the door, where one of the men began a lengthy narration. This account turned out to be a heart-wrenching tale of Daddy's little daughter who had always yearned to play the violin.

As my father listened, they communicated the fact that the two of them had undertaken the journey to Kayton Avenue hoping to make her dreams come true. They represented a new music studio in our area that would have a special class teaching violin to talented small children.

I was as shocked as my parents listening to these two dramatically, but accurately, reproduce the words I had spoken to the salesman earlier in the day. Like the chorus of a favorite song, they almost sang my words over and over again. Of course, they added their own innovative twists, which soon had my parents in a state of astonishment that they could have so blatantly overlooked this secret desire of mine for four whole years. What could I say? "Your kid's a liar?"

The screen door was unlocked, the men stepped inside and events transpired so rapidly that I don't remember having a chance to speak at all before a quarter-sized violin was placed into my arms and I was patted on the head and congratulated.

Twice-a-week group sessions and an hour of practice each day were a fact of my life from that day forward.

Our tall, stooped and reed-thin teacher, Mr. Richard Weckel, was a soft-spoken man. This kind gentleman had been given the totally impossible job of taking a room filled with noisy four- and five-year-olds and coaxing them into making sounds that could be tolerated by the human eardrum. The initial session was packed with wiggling, squirming students from wall to wall. Mothers sat in a line of folding chairs at the back of the studio and smiled proudly. Probably to Mr. Weckel's great joy and relief, there were fewer students at each new session.

Small children and violins are not necessarily compatible. Most of the young ones gathered at this music conservatory had only two things in common—their parents had somehow been able to scrape together enough Depression dollars for their lessons, and they had a strong aversion to sitting still and pushing a bow across violin strings.

Hugh Philipus Jr. and I were probably the only two students who managed to sit still and attempt to follow Mr. Weckel's instructions.

Knowing how to mind adults was not the only thing Hugh and I had in common; we were both only children. Being in this category was formidable for a girl, but it must have been harder for a boy.

Our mothers quickly found each other during the first day of lessons. Hugh's mother was a pretty redhead, and I believe that Hugh may have had red hair, too. Peggy Philipus poured so much hair oil on top of his head prior to combing each hair into place that the actual color was disguised.

There was an old description often used to describe someone who dressed to perfection. Hugh always appeared to be "right out of the band box." His clothes were freshly laundered and starched enough to stand alone. Worse, Peggy tended to dress him in white outfits. That meant he had to refrain from indulging in any activity that might have involved a spot of dirt. He also had to abstain from forms of entertainment that resulted in creases or wrinkles.

I would have loved to coach him in the art of climbing trees and other tricks that I had learned in order to get out of a parent's viewing range. Peggy sometimes brought him over to our house so the two of us could play while she visited my mother. However, she never let him out of her sight, so we were limited to playing indoor games under her protective and ever-vigilant gaze.

Hugh was one of the nicest children I ever met, and I hoped that he one day learned to make use of escape routes so important to constantly monitored only-children. In the meantime, we both turned our attention to learning to play the violin.

Despite this constantly-in-motion group of young musicians, the Institute of Educational Music presented "The Junior Musicians of America" in concert at the San Pedro Little Theatre November 29, 1937, at eight p.m.

The carefully-filed-away program says I played "Sleepyhead" by H.G. Brox, "Golden Poppies" by Anton Nelson, "The Little Sandman" by Brahms and "Mary Jane Waltz" by Fred Heltman. I was five and fit the title of that first selection.

Soon after this concert, Mr. Weckel called my mother at home and asked if he might be able to come over and visit us that evening. My parents were curious at this request but were too polite to ask for a reason.

When he arrived, he told them that he would no longer be teaching at the conservatory. He proceeded to inform them that, out of his group of students, only Hugh Philipus and I would ever be able to play the violin.

"Vallie has real talent," he told my parents. "You should place her in private lessons. I have someone I would like to recommend to you. If she will accept your daughter, you can expect her to become a professional musician."

I felt true sadness to be telling this nice teacher goodbye. As first violin for the well-known Woodroffe String Quartette, he would surely not miss the group of unruly children making those ear-splitting squeaks. I had grown to love Mr. Weckel who, having found himself unable to make a living at his chosen profession, was leaving it to sell insurance.

My parents acted upon his suggestion, and I was taken to be auditioned by the famous, stern and forbidding Mrs. Golda Morgan Niggli. She lived in a marvelous old home in San Antonio's King William District. The atmosphere of the place, as I walked through the front door into a classically furnished room with a high ceiling, was extremely serious.

The energy in the home relayed the message that individuals who lived there conducted their lives rigidly and without humor. As I let my intuition speak, it announced there was an essential ingredient missing in this house devoted to musical development. There was emptiness—a vacuum—begging to be filled with the feeling of pleasure.

It is difficult for me to look back at the many years I spent practicing, and performing at events I loathed. What a shame that I did not have the courage to say loud and clear, "I do not want to be a classical musician. I want to write and play my own music—and it's a different kind."

A student who planned to devote his or her life to performing professionally could not have asked for a better instructor. I loved music and constantly wrote songs, both music and lyrics—country songs, ballads, folk songs and show tunes, but not classical. Mrs. Niggli told Mother, as my lessons progressed, that my compositions were excellent and someday I could pursue songwriting. However, she wanted me to stick to the works of classical composers for a number of years. So, Mother sat by my side during lengthy home practice sessions and stopped me when I began playing my own songs.

When students arrived for their twice-a-week lessons, they were expected to come early and sit quietly in the parlor until Mrs. Niggli emerged from the music room. As the previous student departed, she would gesture for the next one to come in quickly. There was no smile of greeting or small talk whatsoever. Both student and teacher got right down to business.

Once I became a part of Mrs. Niggli's stable of young musicians, my childhood freedom was sharply curtailed. It was as if I had applied for work, landed the job and suddenly been handed responsibilities normally assumed by individuals far beyond my years.

The first hurdle I had to overcome was the approximately twice-a-year judging by a panel representing the National Federation of Music Clubs. The more serious music teachers continually entered their best students in this nerve-wracking procedure.

Nothing we were asked to do would have been a problem at all if the teachers themselves had not been so totally invested in having their students show up as "top of the heap." I cannot remember all of the categories and sub-categories on which we were judged, but some are still lodged in compartments of memory. Our entrance upon the stage, general posture, style of bowing, fingering, stage presence, timing, touch, and many musical inflections on which a judge could base an opinion were taken into consideration.

Each time I entered this professional torture chamber I was a nervous wreck. I always received Superior and Superior Plus ratings, which pleased my teacher and my mother no end. Most of the judges added written remarks about my outstanding stage poise. I probably appeared to be so poised because my insides were frozen stiff.

If a student was capable of playing at a level beyond his or her years, Mrs. Niggli firmly pushed that individual. Most of my assigned pieces were selected to develop and show specific skills, so the compositions were intricate instead of melodious.

Tears ran down my cheeks and onto my instrument when I was allowed to play a beautiful composition. These were periods when I literally existed outside of my body and simply let my spirit soar while exquisite sounds flowed through my violin.

After entering public school, I was often asked to perform during assembly or at other special programs. Rather than take a chance at having an unskilled pianist as my accompanist, Mrs. Niggli drove across town to my school to accompany me. Thus, a simple elementary school program was entered into as a professional commitment.

From early elementary school through junior high school, I do not remember a single program that I was not a part of. I had undertaken the job of making my teacher and mother happy but did not have the heart of a performer. My constant desire was to simply sit in the audience and watch others perform.

I will admit that my parents saw to it that I was given ample opportunity to function as a spectator, seated in San Antonio's Municipal Auditorium. We had season tickets for each opera and classical concert that arrived in our city, so I was exposed to world-famous talent of the 1930s and early '40s. Through some connection made by Mrs. Niggli, I was ushered backstage after each performance to meet the star entertainers. I believe she realized that I had absolutely no ambition to become the classical star she thought I was capable of becoming. Her plan seemed to be that I would be suddenly infused with desire for fame by sharing a small segment of time with these singers and musicians.

The performer and the song that touched me the deepest was not classical in nature. It was singer James Melton's rendition of "The Hills of Home." Even today, I can think about his voice singing those lyrics and tear up in an instant. The song was actually written about the hill country near San Antonio, so the message reaches heart-level in the guise of memory.

My favorite opera was *Carmen*, with Rise Stevens's fiery portrayal of the title role. I must admit, I was more fascinated by the handsome horses on stage than by most of the human performers.

As our driver and escort, my poor father was trapped into attending all of these events. I'll never forget his reaction to Grace Moore's death scene in *La Boheme*.

Moore was extremely rotund to have been cast in the part of a heroine supposedly dying of lung cancer. Daddy grew more and more impatient as "Mimi" continually collapsed onto her bed and appeared to be dead, only to pop back up like a Jack-in-the-Box and sing for ten more minutes.

Totally exasperated, he finally said in a stage whisper, "I wish that fat woman would hurry up and die so we can all go home!"

The audience seated within earshot broke into delighted laughter, as if he had given voice to their thoughts.

To give me practice in playing with an ensemble, Mrs. Niggli asked Mother to deliver me to her studio on occasions other than my twice-a-week lessons. I was inserted into an existing group of adult musicians, which I found rather daunting. Everyone was considerate; in fact, I was treated as an adult. Once more, I was surrounded by a group of serious professionals when I would rather have been home climbing trees.

Mrs. Niggli often featured her younger students in recital at her 221 King William Street studio. A yellowed old program found in my mother's desk shows that my solos were "Slavic Dance" by Ondricek, "Hungarian Rhapsody" by Kovacs, "Puppet Show" by Trott, "Minuet Op. 78" by Schubert, "First Aire Varie" by Charles Dancla as well as Adams's "The Bells of St. Mary's" with an ensemble.

I suppose every musical studio of that day had a student "loaner." I was continually being loaned out to play in programs presented by other music studios with names like Tekla Staffel School of Piano or Meta Hertwig, Steinfeldt College of Music or Miss Emma Jackson, Progressive Series Pupils. The feeling among piano teachers seemed to be that each piano recital needed a token violinist.

There came a time when I had grown to the point I was ready for a full-size violin. Mrs. Niggli located a specific violin in the possession of an individual who bought and sold a few outstanding stringed instruments. At her behest, my parents took me to his studio, where the violin in question was placed into my arms.

There is a deep connection between a musician and the instrument he or she chooses. I felt no joy, wonder or possessiveness as I played several pieces. The owner of the violin sensed my lack of connection with that particular violin.

He left the room and soon returned with another instrument. "Perhaps you should try this one," he said as he carefully handed it to me.

After playing a few notes, I fell madly in love with the feeling of that violin in my arms and with the vibrant tones it produced.

I assume the others in that room recognized my altered state of awareness, because I had gone somewhere else and continued to play one selection after another. Playing was effortless, and my feelings ecstatic.

The man and my father left the room together as "my" violin and I bonded in a musical mating of souls. I have no idea what that instrument must have cost or how long it took my father to pay for it.

A time came when I was expected to play my own solos at the Municipal Auditorium. Old pictures show me garbed in a pink taffeta evening gown, and frankly, I remember the dress more than I remember the performances. I always managed to do what was expected of me but took no joy in the procedure.

Actually, this was not the first time I had performed a solo in that auditorium. Prior to, and along with, total immersion into violin-related activities, I took dancing at San Antonio's Bonner Dance Studio. The Bonners enrolled students as fat little toddlers and started them out turning somersaults on a mat. This was not nearly the serious situation that becoming proficient on the violin called for. Mr. and Mrs. Bonner taught dance together, and they were an interesting and rather flamboyant pair.

I first appeared with a large group of fellow dance students who were stretched clear across the auditorium's massive stage. As one of the two youngest dancers, I was placed at the extreme right end of the line, since we were lined up by size and the tall kids were in the middle.

I had to loudly sing, "I am a spectator." I was answered by the short guy at the other end of the line, "I am a spectator!" Then everyone sang out, "We are the spectators...the fans!"

Back to me; "I love a good ball game." Other short guy; "I love a good ball game." Everyone; "We now take our place in the stands." We were all doing step, shuffle ball-change, hop, step, cross-kick and other assorted tap steps as we sang our parts.

Once we finished our song, we switched to a stylized dance version of playing baseball. I think everyone on stage had a fine time. My chorus line experience must have really impressed me, because I still remember both the song and the steps of our 1935 ball game routine!

In later shows, I was one of the solo dancers. I actually don't remember much besides being fitted (having to stand still) for costumes. As an intentional echo of '30s-era films, our dance costumes, complete with hats, had every tacky floral adornment one could imagine attached.

Dancing was fun, and since we were free to express ourselves with constant movement, I did not mind these performances at all.

I totally forgot about these early childhood events after my parents and I moved into our ranch home in the late '40s. This home, finished in 1861, had a large room upstairs for walk-in attic storage.

One day, I was trying to locate a particular case of art supplies for a college class. I walked to the back of this dimly lit attic and was suddenly confronted by a child in full costume. After conquering my initial heart-stopping fright, I realized it was a lifesize cut-out of me on a stand. Once upon a time, it had served as an advertisement for San Antonio's Kidnight Follies. I had no memory of having seen it before, but my parents had hung onto it as a symbol of my momentary stardom.

Along with the child-sized stand, Mother had taped tickets reading "The Bonner Studios of Dancing present 'The Kidnight Follies,' a musical review at the Municipal Auditorium, Thursday May 19, 1938 —8:15 P.M."

If the freedom and spontaneity of dance classes had transferred over into the world of a child violinist, I would not have resented it so much.

Guests in our home sometimes asked, "Does Vallie still take violin?" They were simply trying to make conversation and could have just as easily asked, "Do you think it's going to rain?" That was all it took to get Mother up from her chair and on a search for me.

When she found me she would say, "Get your violin. They want to hear you play." Of course, that was the last thing on the mind of the person who had asked that innocent question. I understood that, but soon learned it did no good to argue with my mother. Our guests were condemned to a short concert.

I always thought, "Hopefully, the next time you come over you'll know to keep your mouth shut when it comes to musical matters."

Mother never learned how to say "No" when it came to organizations calling with requests for me to play. Without consulting me, she appointed herself my booking agent, and I often found myself on stage performing at events for groups I'd never heard of. I always hoped that Daddy would put his foot down and say, "Enough is enough!" He finally did when Mrs. Niggli, probably with my mother's collusion, made plans to send me on tour.

This was a national tour, but I never learned the extent of the travels or who else was involved due to Dad's intervention. He finally spoke up and said, "An elementary school student needs to be at home with her parents."

I was extremely grateful.

⚜

My neighborhood friend, Georgia Lee H., was a marvelous pianist. She and I often played popular pieces of the day together and enjoyed ourselves in the process. This was done in our own homes, and we often hammed it up by singing the songs.

We could both play anything in the field of pop music by ear, so others in the neighborhood gathered and made requests. On these evenings, I could switch between performing on the violin and playing the fiddle.

When World War II began in December 1941, a Downtown USO was opened in San Antonio. Georgia Lee was in her teens, so she was thrilled when we were asked to join the group of entertainers who would play for the men in military service.

My friend Merry Tom's brother-in-law thought it was a good joke to teach Merry Tom and me risque verses to popular songs. Merry Tom and I were too naive to catch on. I later taught these verses to Georgia Lee, who was no wiser.

As we took song requests from the servicemen, we usually simply played while they sang. But there were other times that we sang songs, such as "Pistol Packin' Mama," belting out all of the naughty verses we had carefully committed to memory.

Neither Georgia Lee nor I had the slightest clue as to the meaning of our lyrical double entendres. No doubt we both looked as innocent as we were. When the servicemen, along with my father, erupted into laughter, we assumed they were simply enjoying our performance.

⚜

When our family took vacations, I was intensely disgruntled if I found out that Mother and someone at our destination had pre-arranged some type of concert or recital. One summer we were about to leave for my favorite spot, the Traylor Ranch owned by Dad's cousins. I was fed up with being joined at the hip with my violin case, so I managed to sneak the case out of our car's trunk and hide it under the living-room sofa. I believed my furtive actions had solved my problem, but Mother must have suspected my intentions.

With Dad behind the wheel and me in the back seat, my mother paused prior to getting into the passenger seat. She either had a sudden psychic flash or my expression gave me away. Turning around, she walked to the back of the car and opened the trunk.

"Where is your violin?"

"I'm not going to take it."

"Well, we'll all just go inside and wait until you decide to find it and put it back into the trunk."

We did go inside, where I hoped I might get some help from my father. After all, he had to drive, and it was a long trip to this ranch located between Port Lavaca and Palacios.

Mother unknowingly seated herself on the sofa directly over my violin. She picked up a magazine and pretended to read, as if she didn't care if we waited all day.

I was too eager to get to the ranch; so my patience gave out, and I reluctantly retrieved my violin so we could leave. I knew there was no truth at all to Mother's tales of everyone waiting to hear me play. That was a case of wishful thinking on her part, combined with guidance from Mrs. Niggli, who wanted to make sure I got in plenty of practice throughout the summer.

I don't mean to imply that every moment of every performance on the violin was an unhappy occasion for me. Like the impromptu request programs at the USO, there were times I was involved with some enjoyable events.

Our Girl Scout troop sometimes had opportunities to put on shows. I loved writing shows, and would undertake whatever role I was asked to play during these informal occasions.

Probably the most challenging role came about when I was asked to portray a musical wind-up toy. The setting was supposed to be the interior of a toy shop at night. Each of the toys, in turn, would come alive and do their own thing.

The idea was for me to go around and around in a circle while playing a piece on the violin. Like an actual wind-up toy, I would eventually begin to turn and play more slowly until I came to a complete stop. At this time, the scout portraying the shop's owner would cross the stage to wind me up. Then the process would begin again.

We did not have any type of revolving stand, so I had to invent a way of turning in a continuously smooth-flowing circle by the way I moved my feet. Wearing the same pink evening gown I'd worn while performing classical solos, I looked the part of a traditional ceramic toy.

To coordinate undetected foot movement while playing a pretty melody was definitely a challenge. I had to slow both my turning and playing simultaneously and eventually come to a rather jerky stop in mid-note.

The real show of talent, however, came when I managed not to burst into giggles as I was being wound-up. Knowing exactly what she was doing from my reactions during rehearsals, my "owner" always inserted the key into the most ticklish spot on my ribcage then proceeded to wind it.

These original performances, in which the spotlight was shared by many, were a lot of fun and often hilarious. No one was uptight, unless it was a Scout leader who took herself too seriously.

Our friends the Dukes belonged to a church that needed someone to provide music during the service. The Reorganized Church of Jesus Christ of Latter-Day Saints had broken off from the main branch of the Mormon Church many years before over disagreements with the leadership of Brigham Young. Their congregation in San Antonio was small and comprised sincere and interesting individuals.

I attended church with the Dukes for several years and played the violin in the sanctuary during Sunday services. The people at this little church constantly expressed their appreciation, and time spent in their midst was always a joy.

When my father quit his job in San Antonio and purchased the Agricultural Implement Company in El Campo, Mother and I each received the news differently.

My first thought was "Halleluiah! No more Mrs. Niggli, violin lessons or performances!"

Mother expressed consternation in ways that revealed her feelings were the opposite of mine. She immediately began making inquiries into who was the best violin teacher in the El Campo area. The Heavens smiled upon me. There were *no* violin teachers there!

Having been an only child surrounded by adults at home resulted in teachers and family friends often remarking about me being mature beyond my chronological age. My total immersion into the field of professional music, from my fourth through fourteenth years, gifted me with experiences, whether desirable or not, that only increased my self-confidence and maturity level.

At the time of our move, I had just entered my teens. I felt adamantly opposed to skipping past peer-group experiences as a teenager in the manner I had been forced to miss many childhood activities. If I had truly had any ambition at all towards a career as a professional violinist, no teacher could have surpassed the opportunities afforded me by Mrs. Niggli. I was sorry to have disappointed her with my personal desires, which did not match the plans she had for me. Though her demeanor was stern and all business, I'm sure that she did have affection for me and her other students.

I warned my mother and father that they were not to tell anyone at all in our new hometown that I could play the violin.

"I won't play any more performances," I announced. "I'll still play at home and anywhere else that I personally find enjoyable. But don't make any plans for me to perform."

Daddy moved to El Campo in 1945. Mother and I stayed in San Antonio for me to finish out the school year and for her to sell our home. I made several trips to visit Daddy, and by talking to new friends I could tell that he had not mentioned the word *violin* in connection with me.

Unfortunately, our cousin Mary Traylor knew the head of a woman's musical association in El Campo. She passed on news of my musical accomplishments about the time of our move.

Mother was overjoyed to learn this, I'm sure. I hastened to reaffirm, "I am not going to do any sort of performing. So, please remember that." I planned to be sitting in the audience during shows at school or elsewhere.

We moved in June of 1946, and had barely unloaded our furniture into the two-story duplex Dad rented before Mrs. Stewart, president of the El Campo Music Association, called Mother. They booked me to perform for one of their association meetings the following autumn. I was not informed of this, so was able to enjoy a life filled with freedom during the summer.

119

When time for my appearance before the association rolled around, Mother finally told me about it along with the news that she had arranged for me to be taken out of school the day of the music club meeting. Her words hit me like a recurring nightmare and sent me into a spell of extremely negative déjà vu.

I argued long and loud against performing, but as usual, Mother prevailed. However, this time I made my own plans for what would occur when I showed up with my violin to play for the women's meeting.

My mother was essentially a timid person who was not comfortable in social situations unless it was among family or close friends. My previous performances had given her some sort of a social structure to hide behind. Just as the violin is the voice of a symphony orchestra, I somehow functioned as her voice in public. I had, however, reached a point where I was no longer willing to serve as her "prop."

I assumed that parental pride was what drove my mother to constantly accept new appearances for me. Since she was totally unwilling to listen to my pleas for no more violin gigs, it was obvious that I would have to deliver that message in a musical, rather than a conversational, manner.

My creativity turned in the direction of designing a performance that would drive home the point that I did not intend to be a violin virtuoso ever again. I also intended this program to engender a sudden and permanent end to Mother's career as my ever-eager booking agent.

If a violinist is capable of drawing a bow across strings and producing enchanting melodies, an experienced violinist is also skilled at creating sounds so discordant that they assault the human eardrum.

I offered no resistance on the day she drove me to play for the members of the El Campo Musical Association.

During our years of playing duets at home, Georgia Lee and I had sometimes experimented with creating awful-sounding music. We had often rendered ourselves, as well as any neighborhood listeners who gathered to join in our foolishness, weak with laughter. Armed with skills that could create some alarmingly inharmonious tones, we often produced a horrendous hootenanny just to see our friends collapse into gales of laughter.

With total focus and determination, I entered the meeting of the El Campo Musical Association under false pretenses. The women were cordial and expressed intense desire to hear me play. Each of them was simply an innocent bystander trapped in the fallout generated by a family tug-of-war.

I followed my plan to the letter, so the poor women were bombarded by sounds learned during my staged horrors with Georgia Lee. My bowing style was borrowed from the wind-up toy that needed a re-wind. Everything about my performance was jerky, flawed, aurally invasive and amateurish.

From a memorized repertoire of familiar classics, I chose to play "Twinkle, Twinkle, Little Star."

The expressions on the faces of the assembled clubwomen registered shock, disbelief and dismay. I did not dare look in my mother's direction. After I ended my performance, I noted that her skin color had turned beet-red, probably from humiliation and rage.

We had previously been invited to join the club members for lunch and had planned to stay. Mother had a sudden change of heart and decided that I needed to be in school, so it was necessary for us to leave.

Since I had been the ultimate obedient child all of my life, Mother was undoubtedly in a real state of shock. She probably had a burning desire to strangle me, yet she was amazingly quiet as she drove me to school. I felt that my actions had clearly spoken for me, so I also remained silent.

However, now that I finally had her attention, I wasn't quite finished. After I got out of the car and closed the door, I leaned inside the car window and told her, "If you ever book another event for me to play, that was a preview of the performance I will give."

I expected repercussions in the form of punishment at home. Daddy refused to be drawn into our conflict, since he felt that my feelings had been made perfectly clear prior to our move.

Without his support, Mother tried many ways of pressuring me into extended practice sessions, to no avail. Because I had learned how to drive, she threatened no more use of the car.

That was fine with me. By then, I had made good friends at school who would see that I got anywhere I needed or wanted to go.

The no-win dimension in this battle of wills was my mother's tendency to take a mile when given an inch. Each time I played the violin for sheer pleasure, she materialized with demands that I turn a joyful occasion into a professional practice routine.

Surrendering to others who chose to groom me as a professional musician was a horse I wished had never been saddled. The ride threatened to become never-ending, and I believed there was a need to stop and dismount. Sadly, I felt that there was only one way to end this constant battle of wills. I placed my violin into its case and refused to ever touch it again.

I had taught myself to play Aunt Vallie's Steinway piano, so I was able to continue enjoying music by playing that instrument. My ability at the keyboard was limited, so requests to perform were never a problem.

If this chapter contains a moral, it would have to be: "Use extreme caution in responding to the person at your front door." That's the Kayton Avenue version of "Be careful what you wish for. You may get it."

CHAPTER SIX

ILLNESS AND INTUITION

As I hovered above the hospital roof, I was able to look right through it into the emergency room. Guardian angels had suddenly appeared, scooped me up and allowed me to share their vantage point.

I felt rather intrigued as I watched the actions of a small crew of medical personnel frantically working around the small body on the table below. I was rather put off when I realized a doctor was shouting at others around the table.

He's not using good manners, I thought.

Since communication in that love-filled reality is not verbal, the angels received my thought. They made me aware that he was a fine doctor, who shouted directions because he was very concerned.

Many times, in the years that followed, I heard my mother tell friends, "We almost lost her when she was two." I have no memory of the actual illness. Only bits and pieces of overheard conversations stayed with me. I can still hear terms like "totally dehydrated" and "critically ill," spoken in my mother's voice.

I was unconscious upon entering the hospital and didn't awaken until a physician inserted a large needle into my abdomen. The pain caused me to open my eyes, and then close them again quickly due to the blinding light that illuminated me for the doctor's benefit. I realized that I was surrounded by people wearing white coats and masks.

Immediately, angels appeared and took me up with them. I was completely comfortable in their company as they explained, without spoken words, that I was to stay with them for a while.

"When it is time, we will take you back and you will be fine."

I was wrapped in a cocoon of such blissful feelings that I did not question my situation at all. What would a two-year-old have asked? Besides, I was allowed to soar with my Caretakers. This was an activity I loved and tried to emulate on earth for years to come.

Prior to this, no one had spoken to me about angels. Neither of my parents attended church, and whatever spiritual beliefs they held, they kept to themselves. I don't believe the spirits I refer to as angels had wings, but they were most assuredly angelic.

Continuing to watch the scenes play out below, I finally saw the small body placed on a gurney and rolled out of the emergency area through a door leading into a hallway. The gurney was pushed around several corners and then into a room where my parents sat next to an empty bed. It was then that my angelic caretakers escorted me into that room, where I suddenly felt my spirit re-entering the body of the child as she was taken from the gurney and placed into the bed.

From my mother's written records, I know that this occurred on May 19, 1934. This memory is so vivid that these things could have transpired yesterday. Yet, I never spoke about it to anyone. Near-death experiences were not talked about then, nor were they the subject of scientific studies as they have been for the past three decades.

There are certain similarities, or shared after-effects, identified by persons who have done in-depth studies of individuals who have experienced NDEs. I honestly don't know how many of these characteristics I would have developed without the NDE, since I was so young.

If you have listened to an old-fashioned radio while turning a circular dial, you may have reached a frequency where you began hearing broadcasts from two separate stations at the same time. A similar situation followed my hospitalization. From that day forward, I was tuned in to both a physical and a spiritual realm.

None of this kept me from being a normal child filled with questions and plotting mischief. However, there was always a contemplative inner world about which I did not speak. Inner voices sometimes spoke, and I listened.

The cause of my early hospitalization was said to have been a severe allergic reaction. The doctors were never sure what caused it, though my mother blamed a single square from a Hershey Bar I had eaten. Eager to find something to blame, the doctors said, "Okay, make sure that she never eats chocolate again." I believe that they were way off base, but I abstained from chocolate during my entire childhood.

Whatever the cause, I must have gone into anaphylactic shock. As an adult, I've had a few emergency room visits with this reaction as a result of an unknown allergy. I'm probably lucky that the 30s-era doctors were able to bring me out of it. Still, they *did* have some unusual help.

In any case, my psychic ability, which is a gift all infants receive at birth, was increased tenfold after that experience. I believe this intuition, sixth sense or whatever term one prefers to use is the voice of spiritual guidance. In many cultures, this gift is honored and supported.

Unfortunately, in our Western world, most people do not understand this ability. Parents try their best to either fight or ignore the actions of children who are listening to this inner voice.

This voice is the best source of information, guidance or warning we will ever receive. Each time I chose to ignore the advice I was receiving, something occurred that made me deeply regret that decision.

Certainly, there have been charlatans who have discredited the field of psychic ability with their actions. Perhaps it is because of flamboyant dress or mannerisms, or choosing to run a con game, that these people often receive more notice than a quack doctor, unbalanced psychologist, crooked cop or pedophile teacher might engender.

I never heard the word *aura*, referring to the colors in a person's electromagnetic field, until I was an adult. As a small child, I saw the colors around everybody, and often referred to my mother's friends as "the pink lady" or "the blue-and-gold lady." Mother believed that I was referring to the color of the clothes they wore. She taught me all of the color names when I was tiny, so she became upset when I called a person by what she perceived as the incorrect color.

"Why do you call her the pink lady when she is wearing a green dress?"

I would respond, "I mean her color." This answer only confused her more, so I eventually stopped speaking of colors or trying to explain.

I also observed the etheric radiance around trees, plants and all living things, and assumed everyone else knew what I meant when I talked about "the glow." They didn't.

In the field of precognition, I received most of my information through dreams. I knew who was coming to see us, or perhaps who we would go visit. I saw groups of people talking and heard every word of their conversations. Within the next few days, these people would gather, and my pre-dreamed conversations would transpire.

I must have looked like a spectator at a tennis match, always turning my head to ascertain the trajectory of the ball. In this case, it was a matter of turning to the person I knew would be the next to respond.

None of these pre-dreamed events were particularly dramatic, or life-changing, as we often see on television.

After I closed my eyes at night I saw a series of scenes before sleep arrived. The scenes changed quickly and sometimes were prophetic of events in my life. Once I went to sleep, I soared through the air in my dreams, just as I had done along with my heavenly escorts.

I was so convinced that I could soar while I was awake that, when I was old enough to climb trees, I launched a career of ascending to the top of garage roofs in order to jump off. I assumed that while I was in mid-air my soaring mechanism would kick in and off I would go. Garage roofs were my launching pad of choice because I was less likely to get caught during my furtive climbs than I would have been on the roof of someone's house.

After scouting the neighborhood for a garage with a nearby tree, I shinnied up and hopped over to the roof. Those angels must have still been looking out for me because I jumped off some pretty high rooftops and never sustained even a minor injury.

Another recurring dream featured my ability to play music. Quite often, I saw, felt and heard myself playing beautiful selections on a large and magnificent pipe organ. My dream-time repertoire was quite extensive, and the playing itself was effortless. So, I became convinced that if I could only locate an available organ, I could put my hands on the multiple keyboards and immediately create spectacular music.

Needless to say, pipe organs were not as plentiful as garage roofs. Once in a great while, I was able to bribe a young friend into taking me to his or her church. After I had been led into the sanctuary, I would make a beeline for the organ. Anticipating the sound of majestic music when my hands and the keyboard connected, I found that my talent as an organist was another portion of my dream life that did not translate into physical reality.

I was as disappointed over the fact that my musical attempts did not fill the atmosphere with glorious sound as I had been over my failure to soar while awake. Still, a glimmer of hope remained alive that one day I would find that special pipe organ or garage roof, and a miracle would occur.

In a third, and far less flamboyant, repetitive dream I was in a car that turned off a paved highway onto a caliche country road. This winding road was slightly hilly and lined with trees. As the car crossed a bridge over a flowing creek, I became aware that just around the bend ahead I would arrive at a piece of land that was my special place.

I was always filled with excitement as we rounded that curve; however, that was where the dream inevitably ended. I would awaken filled with frustration because I had not been allowed to see that magical spot.

I felt that this country road actually existed but had received no clue as to its whereabouts. So, each time one of my parents turned our car off the blacktop onto a caliche trail, I felt a sense of excitement. Would it lead to "my place?"

I felt this sense of anticipation on many newly traveled roads in East Texas as well as the southwest Texas Hill Country. After I became an adult and turned my own car onto unpaved country roads, I would suddenly become tense and alert for scenes I might recognize from this repetitive lifelong dream.

It was not until I reached my fifties that another driver turned down that long-sought road. I was visiting a part of Texas where I had never been and with which I was completely unfamiliar. My mindset at the time was one of total disinterest. I had ceased hoping to find my special place and was neither mentally nor emotionally involved with this side trip.

Preoccupied with my own thoughts, I suddenly realized that the car was crossing a bridge over a flowing creek and just ahead there was a sharp bend in the road. This was so much a part of that oft-dreamed sequence that I began to wonder if I had fallen asleep during the drive.

Suddenly,, the car made a left turn, leaving the road and heading through a gate and onto a piece of land that I immediately knew was meant for me. My thoughts zoomed from, *This drive is a waste of my time* to *Oh, my God! This is the place!*

At the time this occurred, I was enjoying an extremely happy life in Austin. I had no thought of leaving that wonderful city or the numerous friends I was fortunate to have in that area. Nevertheless, an unexpected decision to leave that well-loved city and move to an equally appreciated rural area was made the instant our vehicle drove through the gate. I knew I would build a home on this land to which I felt a lifelong psychic connection. It was a momentous turning point I never regretted.

As an older child, I stopped jumping off rooftops hoping to soar, and no longer expected to excel at playing pipe organs. But I was elated to realize this one dream was actually a prophecy that required a lifetime of observation and patience prior to fulfillment.

⌘

Psychic ability was my constant childhood companion, whispering information all of the time. Some of my remarks startled the individuals to whom they were made. Often, they surprised me as well.

It was a simple case of hearing my mouth speak words that my thoughts had not formed. The inevitable response from others would be "How on earth did you know that?" Since I had no logical explanation, I eventually learned to hold my tongue.

When quite young, I puzzled over the strange experience of watching someone begin to disappear before my eyes. If I was alone with that person, I would wonder if something unforeseen was happening to my eyesight. However, when I was in a group and only one individual seemed to be leaving the realm of physicality, I came to grips with the fact something unusual was actually occurring—an extraordinary event to which I was witness.

When this occurs, the outline of a person becomes blurred and his or her body dissolves into dancing molecules that grow dimmer as one watches. In a social situation, it is difficult not to stare in fascination at the transformation taking place in the space the person is leaving.

I kept waiting for adults in the group to comment on what was taking place. Why didn't they ask, "Mary! Where on earth are you going?" Eventually, I realized that I seemed to be the *only* one who was observing Mary in the process of disassembling.

It's like viewing a painting by an artist from the school of Pointillism except, in this case, the juxtaposed dots of pure color are not static. These tiny fragments of energy constantly move about, sometimes fade away and later return.

Perhaps that person's thoughts or dreams have taken him far away from the group, and the body is attempting to follow. I have never witnessed a person's total disappearance, but have observed clear images diminish into soft shadows. Energy particles fade and become extremely indistinct, and then they gradually return to full brilliance until that person is once more physically a part of the group.

Only once did I feel free to ask a person if she realized she sometimes partially disappears from the physical plane. I waited for a time we were alone to broach the question.

This particular friend is a psychiatric nurse, writer and poet, so I assumed her background experiences would cause her to have an open mind. I was correct. She was both intrigued and amused by the question.

My guess is that her spontaneous partial exits from physical reality are a result of a total preoccupation with her current project coupled with an astounding ability to tune out her surrounding environment. Both are enviable talents.

As a child, I found that individuals who listened to their intuition tend to recognize one another. One summer, a Girl Scout volunteer arranged for my troop to spend several weeks at a lovely ranch in the hill country. This place, we were told, had a great swimming hole. Rope swings suspended from giant oak trees would take us out over the middle of the Guadalupe River, where we could jump in.

Each troop member was impatient to board the chartered bus as we stood surrounded by our camping paraphernalia. Prior to allowing us to board, a pre-trip meeting called by the leaders took place so they could inform us about rules that must be followed.

As the other girls and I continued to fidget, only half-listening to a litany of familiar regulations, they told us something very odd.

"There is a crazy woman who lives there. She is the wife of the owner and isn't a danger to anyone, so just try to avoid her."

Now, that was a strange thing to announce. During the bus trip we all speculated about what "a crazy woman" would look like. None of us, it seemed, had ever seen one.

Upon arrival, we saw a couple and their teenage daughter standing in front of a picturesque stone ranch home. As we stepped down from the bus, each of the three greeted us. The man was nice, his wife was lovely and the teenager was "an older woman" to us.

We kept waiting for the crazy woman to show up. Then we remembered that she was supposed to be the wife of the owner. How in the world could this sweet, delicate woman be given such a title?

As days went by, filled with numerous activities, I felt drawn to our hostess. She was a fascinating conversationalist, extremely interested in, and knowledgeable about, indigenous plants and animals. Once, she called me to come out on a side porch and look at her "babies." Pulling a chair over for me to stand on, she told me to look into a basket swinging from the roof. Inside was a bird's nest filled with just-hatched baby birds.

A major rainstorm howled through the countryside that night, complete with high winds, dramatic lightning bolts and rolling claps of thunder. The next morning, the sarcastic teenage daughter was in the kitchen loudly complaining that her mother had been up all night checking on the welfare of the baby birds. The tone of her voice conveyed the message "She's totally insane."

Near the end of the first week, when everyone had a free period, our hostess approached me and asked that I accompany her to a special place. I was rather leery thanks to the stories we had heard, though we had certainly witnessed no strange actions on her part. Still, I must admit that I was uneasy about being the only one to go with her.

We were headed, she told me, to a natural waterfall where fairies played. She added, "I think that you will be able to see the fairies, but I doubt if any of the others can."

We hiked for quite a distance and finally reached an absolutely breathtaking vista. The waterfall, flowing from beneath a group of large stones, was spraying a fine mist into the air.

I felt edgy, and anxious to get back to the group, so just took a quick glance around and told her that I saw no fairies. I was too polite to add that I did not believe such a thing existed. In fact, I had long been an adult before I ever heard of nature spirits. Traditional and conservative people whom I respect, usually organic gardeners, have told of seeing these tiny beings. I'm sorry in retrospect that I was not more open and mature in my actions, and less tied in to peer-group acceptance, during that hike to the waterfall.

In order to cooperate and show appreciation for her invitation, I should have sat on the ground quietly and not have been in such a rush to return to the group. I have no idea if I would have seen anything out of the ordinary, because I'm more clairsentient (I feel things, know things) and clairaudient (an ability to hear paranormal voices and sounds audibly) than clairvoyant (an ability to visually experience). In later years, I found plenty of opportunities to experience events with each of these abilities.

By the end of our visit, I realized that people called this sensitive individual crazy because of her willingness to act upon her intuition. Her friends, and surely her bitter-tongued daughter, did not operate as she did; thus, they judged her to be mentally unbalanced. She truly deserved someone with whom she could share that special intuitive knowledge she possessed.

⁂

𝔐y father was considered psychic by his friends because of the extremely accurate predictions he made concerning politics, governmental upheavals and unexpected events that occurred throughout the world. I believe his predictions were, rather, based upon his common sense paired with formidable knowledge and constant reading in the fields of history and government. His negative predictions regarding the formation of the United Nations organization and the fallacy of the United States reconnecting with old world views that they came to this land to get away from have played out just the way he said they would.

At work, there were several occasions when my father's intuition caused him to twirl around quickly in his desk chair just in time to bear witness to a tragic event.

Dad's office was located on the fifth floor of the Frost National Bank building. His desk was positioned in a manner that his back was to the outside wall as he worked. After the stock market crash of 1929, economic conditions in the United States contributed to numerous individual financial disasters. Over a period of time, concerned people visited bankers on the first floor of my father's building and received devastating news pertaining to their loss of funds. A few of these people took the elevator to the top floor, walked out to the roof and, still in a state of shock, ended their life by jumping off.

Dad, who at the time of this occurrence had been involved in paperwork, later described a sudden feeling that made him whirl around to face the window—just in time to see a man falling past the fifth floor. These occasions haunted him, and were difficult to dismiss from his thoughts.

⁂

𝕴 received numerous inner urgings to do, or not to do, various things as a child. One dire warning that sticks in my memory concerned a birthday party.

Like all children, I loved attending birthday parties and partaking of games, sweets and the favors we were given to take home. Billy and

131

Wayne Schneider were children of a family who lived across the street on Kayton Avenue. These brothers shared the same birthday, so their parents traditionally threw a big blowout to celebrate.

Now, I liked both of these boys and played with them often, but when the Sunday afternoon of their party came around, everything that had to do with my inner guidance shouted, "No! Do not go!"

Too young to know what "a sense of foreboding" meant, that's exactly what I had. I told Mother, "I can't go to that party."

She informed me, "You are being ridiculous. We've already purchased gifts, and you are not going to be allowed to hurt the feelings of the Schneider family by not attending."

My arguments did not end there. Mother and I kept at it for probably close to two hours. She quizzed me over and over about why I was being so difficult. I could only repeat, "I just should not go."

When it was time to change into my party dress, I began to cry. Now, crying was something I seldom did, but I was totally frustrated at being unable to make my mother understand that something bad would occur if I attended that gathering.

Mother was no more susceptible to my tears than she had been with my fruitless attempts to make her see the situation from my viewpoint. Once party clothes were donned, she took my arm and escorted me across the street.

The first hour of this soiree was spent in playing the usual party games in the family's back yard. Every activity was organized and directed by a number of adults. As the games came to an end, I saw several women carrying large trays emerge from the home's back door. Each tray held a variety of refreshments that the women placed on a decorated patio table.

Across the lawn, Wayne and one of his male guests were in the midst of a loud argument. It soon became obvious that, whatever the bone of contention, the two were not playing. Their angry voices became louder. Suddenly, Wayne picked up a large rock and slung it with all of his might.

I have no idea where he was aiming, but the rock slammed into my mouth, splitting my lips and breaking one of my upper front teeth. I could taste the blood and feel pieces of the tooth landing in the bottom of my mouth.

Wayne's mother walked over and opened my mouth. Once she saw the damage that had been done, she went into hysterics. Grabbing my arm, she pulled me across the street, yelling at the top of her lungs. My mother opened our front door to see Mrs. Schneider crying wildly and the front of my dress covered in blood.

When Mother looked at the ugly, diagonally broken tooth, I thought she would faint. She must have replayed in her mind the hours she had spent listening to me say, "Please don't make me go."

This party calamity affected my life for years to come. It also affected the finances of my family with nonstop dental bills. There was no cosmetic dentistry as we know it today, and dentists did not have access to the type of crowns, temporary or permanent, that allow people to look normal even if there is a broken tooth involved. Our dentist covered the tooth with bright yellow cement and then wrapped a large silver band around it. I was to wear this hideous addition to my mouth, he told my parents, until I stopped growing. That would be about age sixteen, he estimated. I was nine or ten at the time, and sixteen sounded like old age.

My smiles and laughter were suddenly turned into an unattractive sight that engendered a lot of attention. Both adults and children constantly asked, "What happened to your tooth?" Adults normally shook their heads with expressions of pity. Children were quick to make rude and insulting remarks. I had only to look into a mirror to agree with them.

I reached my full adult height of five feet and two inches at age eleven, so when I entered my teen years, we found a dentist who was willing to recap the tooth with a porcelain crown. I was thrilled and relieved to be rid of the ghastly yellow cement and tin band. However, it took me a while to break the habit of covering my mouth each time I laughed.

The years of embarrassment and discomfort for me, as well as the constant drain on my parent's finances, could have easily been avoided if my mother had accepted my intuition.

Though I was comfortable with my psychic ability during childhood, something happened to make me hate having it after I entered junior high school.

I have no way of describing Mrs. F. other than to say she was totally sadistic and thrived upon seeing her physical education students humiliated and physically injured. I believe she hated being female. Her hair was cut like a man's, she wore men's shoes, and her movements were very masculine in nature. She scorned the use of makeup and was adamant that her students must forgo makeup also.

Most of us wore Tangee Natural lipstick, often applied in route to school so our mothers couldn't see. Before entering the school gym, each of us tried to wipe away all traces of pink left on our lips.

Once a week, Mrs. F. instructed the girls in her class to sit on the floor of the gym for "inspection." Her assistant followed, holding a paper separated into many categories, while Mrs. F. examined our heads, teeth, ears, skin and fingernails. She then turned our heads from side to side to make sure our faces showed no vestige of makeup.

As Mrs. F. bent over each girl, if she encountered anything she did not like, she would yell, "Cross...cavity! Cross...pimples! Cross... dandruff! Cross...B.O.!" or "Cross...lipstick!" Her assistant was expected to mark a cross down in the proper column, in order to lower the girl's grade.

Of course, most of these things were really in the school nurse's realm, but Mrs. F. could not resist an opportunity to ridicule her students and cause them embarrassment. We were all terrified of her and never disputed her word. Several times, she saw a just-completed filling in my mouth and called it a cavity. I accepted the lowered grade rather than argue.

We were at an age when skin eruptions were likely to occur. A few of the girls had severe cases of acne, which they suffered enough from without having this unkind woman heap public derision upon them.

Often, a group of outside instructors came in and taught Red Cross First Aid classes. In those days, we learned artificial respiration and how to handle various types of broken bones and wounds until a doctor could arrive at the scene of an injury. Class members were always elated to have Red Cross instructors in our midst because we felt that somehow they protected us from Mrs. F.

Mrs. F.'s actions, as she coached us in games, were sometimes dangerous. I did not read minds, but I could intuit her intent. She would set up situations where a student could not help but sustain a physical injury. Mrs. F. always protected herself by being onsite, so events would be perceived as bad choices made by students. She absolutely loved seeing these girls hurt.

Mrs. F. always chose a perpetrator and a victim. Her choices of girls to be injured were usually the most shy and physically weak. I once warned a friend named Annie to be careful when I realized that our coach had selected her as the next victim.

As I talked to Annie, our teacher was explaining to an extremely large student, who was also an excellent ball player, just how to sling her bat after hitting the ball. Then, she told Annie to play catcher.

The muscular girl hit the ball with all of her might then slung the bat backward as she had been instructed. All of Annie's front teeth, top and bottom, were knocked out. Mrs. F.'s eyes glowed with elation, and I felt physically ill.

Sweet and shy little Annie came from a family who could not afford the services of a dentist. I only hope that they received some sort of financial help since the "accident" occurred at school.

Being one of Mrs. F.'s students for two years changed my life in several ways. As a younger child, I had been extremely active in each sport I had an opportunity to play. With no hesitation, I threw myself into every game with eagerness and tremendous energy.

Playing various sports under Mrs. F.'s direction, I began to dislike participation in team sports intensely. I also found that I could not watch any sort of organized sporting event without becoming anxious and apprehensive. In later years, I refused to attend most high school and college football games because I found myself holding my breath awaiting an injury to one of the players.

After being a reluctant witness to a series of physical disasters caused by the nefarious actions of this depraved woman, I decided I could no longer bear having pre-knowledge of events that I had no ability to change. I put up some sort of an interior wall that blocked all of the messages from that ever-present inner voice. This was like choosing to ignore an old and valued friend. When that friend tried to speak to me, I turned away and refused to listen to the words.

Many years later, after a second near-death experience, this wall was knocked down, allowing my ability to come back, many times multiplied. This time, I was mature enough to accept it, and work through the layers of disappointments and disillusionments I sometimes experienced, until I reached a level that some would describe as insight.

CHAPTER SEVEN

MEDICAL NOTIONS
AND NOSTRUMS

Certainly, children of the 1930s caught a lot of things besides intuition. The many pharmaceuticals of today were then only dreams in research scientists' heads.

With the exception of smallpox, there were no vaccines for contagious diseases. Hot water bottles and ice bags were the most frequently used painkillers of the day.

Most of my friends and I were healthy, but one friend was extremely delicate. Helen Elizabeth, the great-niece of the Franz sisters, had asthma and was forced to live her life as an invalid. She was seldom able to enjoy the companionship of someone her own age, so I would often be asked by her parents to come visit her. While driving me across town my parents would remind me that any games we played must be the quiet, non-physical type.

Helen Elizabeth's skin had a blue-grey pallor, and stories were told about how she turned totally blue and stopped breathing during her asthma attacks. I always tried to follow the instructions I was given before being taken upstairs to her room. Basically, that was letting her win any game we played so she wouldn't get upset.

My mother was the daughter of a horse-and-buggy doctor who practiced in the late 19th and early 20th centuries. To a great extent, she continued to use the same mixtures as curatives that her father used a generation before.

Allergies to things one inhales were not recognized in the thirties. My frequent "bad colds" were actually caused by the fact my father was my favorite companion and a constant smoker. In later years, I was diagnosed with an allergy to cigarette smoke.

To relieve my stopped-up nose and chest congestion, Mother smeared Vicks Vapo-rub on my chest and back and dabbed some on my nostrils. Frequently, she also dosed me with her magic brew—a hot toddy. Mother was an absolute teetotaler but always kept a bottle of bourbon on hand "for medicinal purposes."

This remedy was made by pouring bourbon into a cup then adding boiling water, sugar and lemon juice. She mixed a strong concoction, and the memory of its taste and smell kept me from accepting any form of alcoholic drink until I was in my mid-thirties.

To stop the hacking cough that so often accompanies a cold, Mother also devised her own cough medicines, which actually tasted better than those on the market. Honey mixed with lemon juice or lemon juice stirred into brown sugar were the two she preferred.

I always hoped that the Vicks and her cough syrups would fix me up, because I knew what would come next if they didn't. A favored medical treatment when all else failed was a mustard plaster, and it was no fun to endure.

Recipes available for an old-fashioned mustard plaster differ in the amounts of each ingredient to be used, but the major ingredient in all of them is dried mustard seed. To this, flour and warm water, or warm oil, are added to make a paste. The mixture was spread on an old piece of flannel and applied to my chest. It burned like heck! After my chest had been cooked by this counterirritant, I was told to turn over, and a new plaster was applied to my back.

Some old recipes indicate the mustard plaster can be left on all day. That would be pure torture. I would guess fifteen or twenty minutes would be all a child could stand. Children with sensitive skin might begin to blister before that.

My habit of climbing trees often put me in close proximity to yellow jackets or wasps who resented my intrusion. Mother used damp baking soda applied directly to the skin around the stings. When we swam in coastal waters, she used the same remedy for jellyfish stings.

Smallpox was still a feared disease in the 1930s, and parents were urged to see that their children were given the vaccine to keep it from spreading. I may have been the most vaccinated child in the San Antonio area.

My doctor tried twice each year, but the vaccinations would not take. When I entered school, medical papers had to be shown to prove that I had been vaccinated to no avail. Often, students were lined up so school nurses could check vaccination scars. Finally, my fifth vaccination, given September 27, 1939, resulted in an extremely tiny reaction that I was allowed to count as a scar.

No proof could be given, but we assumed that I must have inherited immunity. During the early years of the 20th century, when my grandfather was treating patients with smallpox in Beaumont, my mother and her younger sister, Ella Victoria, both caught the disease. They were lucky, in that they had light cases and neither was left with extensive scarring. Mother survived with one small pox scar near her hairline.

I never knew if immunity to such a disease could be effectively inherited, but up until my adult years, when smallpox vaccinations were discontinued, no more scars would form after that one tiny reaction.

⌘

My fellow elementary school students and I passed around the usual communicable diseases that children were then expected to contract. There were no childhood inoculations for mumps, measles or chicken pox, and while a vaccine against whooping cough had been discovered it wasn't in widespread use until the 1940s.

Mumps swelled my cheeks and neck on January 29, 1942, but was not so bad to endure. However, I had contracted a very severe case of "red measles" (rubeola or "ten-day measles") on February 7, 1940.

I've heard of strange cravings all of my life but never experienced any except during the course of this illness. The entire time I was sick I begged, pleaded and became totally disagreeable to my elders because they would not bring me a plate of Mexican food and a bowl of potato salad.

Now, in a state of wellness I loved both of these dishes but would not have chosen to eat them at the same time. However, like a drug addict denied her fix, these foods were all I could think of night or day.

The doctor worried about the extremely high fever I continued to run. I don't know if my temperature triggered those powerful cravings or not, but I continued to squirm and kick and holler like an obnoxious junky being forced to quit Mexican food cold turkey.

I've wondered since then if there might have been some ingredient in these dishes that my body actually needed. In any event, all I was allowed were the usual pallid bowls of Jell-o, chicken broth and milk toast.

Today, I cannot enjoy a plate of Mexican food, or a serving of potato salad, without remembering how badly I wanted those things while broken out from head to toe with red spots.

Children's tonsils and adenoids were removed far more regularly in those days than they are today. I parted with mine August 1, 1936, in an effort to stop the frequent cases of tonsillitis I had endured. The bowls of ice cream I was given to eat for days afterward were an extremely rare treat.

❧

Many of my friends had to endure large doses of castor oil, taken for "spring cleaning." Thank goodness, I was never given any. However, when the mood struck, Mother was apt to back me up against a wall and administer a spoon of milk of magnesia followed by a spoon of Nujol. Swallowing this duo of nasty flavors kept me gagging and sputtering for the next thirty minutes. I still get a bad taste in my mouth today each time I walk into an antique store or flea market and see a display of the cobalt blue glass bottles that once held liquid milk of magnesia.

Most of my acquaintances were also given cod liver oil for the same reason children are given vitamins today. The fish taste was pretty bad, but it went down easily.

Mother's charts comprising what other mothers were told to do with their young ones indicate that I was introduced to Mead's Cod Liver Oil, teaspoon twice a day, at the age of three months. Doctors preferred fat babies, probably because plumpness was considered a sign of thriving health in a time with a high rate of infant mortality. And during one conversation Mother had with pediatrician Dr. Sidney Koliski he told her, "I thank God for every constipated baby!" Many infants were lost at that time due to an inability to cure infant diarrhea.

Physician-prescribed sun baths were considered a health benefit, and resulted in mothers following a strictly timed routine. I took my first sun bath in a bed pushed up against a window on June 12, 1932, my parent's tenth anniversary. By the next month, I began to receive short sun baths outside. Time in the sun was to be increased by one minute each day until a fifteen-minute time limit was reached.

I'm sure that every young mother did not take the advice of her child's physician as seriously as mine did. Because of her copious notes and almost obsessive record-keeping, I know the exact dates on which I was introduced to numerous foods.

On June 7, 1932, I was allowed my first taste of orange juice (2 teaspoons twice daily). An ounce of this fresh-squeezed juice was diluted with an ounce of sugar-water. A month later, on July 8, I could eat two teaspoons of Mead's Cereal twice daily. At six and a half months, October 7, 1932, vegetables and applesauce were introduced.

Scraped beef, lamb patty and chicken breast were added to my diet at sixteen months—August 10, 1933. Baked or broiled fish entered the picture a few months later on October 17.

Holstein milk was discontinued, and I was switched to Grade A raw milk April 10, 1934. Mother was instructed to boil the raw milk for two minutes.

I saw so many references to "Maltine" spread throughout Mother's records that I decided to see exactly what that was. Maltine "is recommended as a palatable, stable and uniform extract of malt of high diastatic power, differing from other malt extracts in containing in addition to the virtues of malted barley the nutritive principals of wheat and oats." It is used as a "digestant, nutrient and adjunct infant food..."

While reading the manner this children's drink was made from the same barley malt and fresh hops combined in alcoholic beverages, I remembered that my Maltine drinking friends and I often experienced cases of hiccups!

In retrospect, I admire both the careful prescribing of foods and diligent record-keeping that resulted from the collaboration of a young pediatrician and a first-time mother.

❧

The various scrapes, scratches, cuts and skinned knees familiar to active children were doctored with mercurochrome or iodine. Most of us did not object when bright red mercurochrome was applied, but we were ready to take off and hide when we saw the dreaded brown iodine bottle appear.

Iodine, when applied to a raw wound, compounded the felony by burning like wildfire. School nurses favored painting young students with gentian violet. This wasn't as bad as iodine, but the deep purple color stained our clothes and skin and lasted through several baths.

Children who lived in rural areas sometimes had more than iodine to worry about. A friend in Hico used to spend summers with his grandparents in tiny Carleton, a farm community. He remembers his grandmother pouring kerosene, or coal oil, on all of the scrapes and cuts he and his brothers sustained. Others in this area speak of being given a spoonful of turpentine with sugar in it when they complained of a sore throat.

It was not unusual for ranchers and farmers to use the same liniments to treat family members that they used on their animals. More familiar as they were with feed stores and veterinarians than physicians, when money was short, keeping the stock healthy took priority.

❧

I remember talking across the driveway to Mrs. M. in the early summer of 1941. My mother told her that I had a bad cold, and she admonished me to "Take good care of yourself because a lot of people's colds have been going into a really severe form of pneumonia."

I assured our neighbor that I was getting better and would not get pneumonia. Before I knew it, I was semi-conscious in our bathtub as family members poured ice over me and my pediatrician stood in our hall calling one overcrowded hospital after the other. As he tried to locate a private room, an ambulance waited in our driveway. The date was June 12, 1941, my parent's nineteenth anniversary.

In those days, pneumonia patients were placed under an oxygen tent, which covered most of a child's body. The tent was kept oxygenated by a large tank filled with ice. Gauges on the tank had to be watched constantly and ice added frequently. Antibiotics had not yet arrived upon the pharmaceutical scene, nor were there intravenous drips to keep one hydrated.

When a hospital room was finally located, my parents hired a special nurse, and one of my parents, usually Mother, was also in the room at all times.

I'll never forget the first nurse who came to stay. This young woman stood beside my bed and talked nonstop. Her constant chatter irritated me, and I began feeling sicker. Too weak to say anything, I would have loved to ask her to be quiet. Breathing was becoming more and more difficult.

Mother looked through the tent and saw that perspiration was pouring down my face. Our chatty nurse had been so preoccupied with telling us about her boyfriend taking her to Garner Park that she ignored the needles on the gauges and had allowed the tank to totally run out of ice. That nurse was promptly dismissed, and though future special nurses were more attentive to their duty, Mother began checking the gauges herself.

I was unable to speak the first week I was in the hospital, so we relied upon the sign language Mother had taught me when I was tiny. Though too weak to hold my hands in the air, I was able to rest them on my chest and respond to questions about my feelings and needs. She acted as interpreter and relayed my answers to the medical personnel.

During my second week in the hospital, I began to respond to treatment and gradually get better. We later learned that two different groups had formed extemporaneously and prayed for my recovery.

Aunt Annie Franz, our next door neighbor, worked for Fox Photo in downtown San Antonio. She stood up in her office one day and said to the people at the other desks, "I can't stand it—I'm so worried about my little neighbor. Will you pray for her with me?" They all did, then and there.

My nine-year-old cousin, Jimmy Land, asked the same thing of some of his playmates. The thought of him leading other children in prayer still touches me deeply. I believe that these prayer groups, combined with a new "miracle drug" called sulfathiazole allowed me to get well when others with this same form of pneumonia did not make it. This was an era when more than 100,000 people a year died from that disease in the United States.

Certainly, that case of pneumonia changed some big plans my family had made for the rest of the summer of 1941.

My parents and I had been invited to spend the entire summer on a cruise of the Bahamas with Dad's cousin Jack and his wife Mary. Jack and Mary Fletcher had sailed to many wonderful places throughout the world on their yacht, *The Escape*. They believed we would enjoy visiting the Bahama Islands. Dad planned to be with us during his two-week vacation while Mother and I would remain on board the rest of the summer.

This truly would have been an unusual trip. The former English King Edward VIII was at that time the Royal Governor of the Bahamas. He and his wife, Wallis Simpson, for whom he abdicated his throne, had been sent as far away from England as possible. Edward's marriage to a twice-divorced American socialite had created a scandal and was considered an embarrassment to the British royalty.

Their home in Paris was deemed unsafe because World War II had already started in Europe. So, from 1940-45, the Duke and Duchess of Windsor, a famous couple in European high society, were sent to be bored to death in the Bahamas.

I remember listening to the radio with my family on December 11, 1936, when Edward VIII made his famous abdication speech. "I have found it impossible to carry the heavy burden of responsibility and to discharge my duties as king as I would wish to do without the help and support of the woman I love" were words that became famous throughout the world.

Mary and Jack were introduced to the Windsors while *The Escape* was docked in Nassau. The two couples, along with others who sailed in on luxurious yachts, continued to socialize the rest of that summer. I'm sure a nine-year-old would not have been included in these elite gatherings. Mother would have felt out-of-place because she did not drink, and the atmosphere was one in which most of the partygoers remained well lubricated. However, she and I could have taken some memorable pictures with the family Kodak.

To make me feel better about the illness and recuperation that caused me to miss that trip, Mary and Jack mailed me a check for one thousand dollars. The size of that gift was mind-boggling to a nine-yea-old who received a fifteen-cent weekly allowance. Of course, my father put it safely into a college savings account.

꧁꧂

None of my friends suffered from any of the forms of emotional or personality disorders we hear so much about today. My friend Mickey, however, did have an older sister, Alma, who would go into hysterics when a thunderstorm blew through our area of town. After trying a series of remedies, their mother found that reading to her from the Bible would calm her down. So, at the first sign of lightning, Mickey grabbed the family Bible and ran to find her mother so she would not have to endure thunderclaps accompanied by Alma's screams.

In one instance, taking precautions against a prevalent malady backfired at a time when I was an active Girl Scout. Some friends and I were planning to go to camp, where swimming in the river would be one of our daily activities. This meant we were required to take typhoid shots that came in a series of three.

Our friend Stella Duke told Mother about her girls, Rosemary and Patsy, screaming, crying and carrying on like wild children when they took their first shot. Mother informed her that I took mine in a very adult manner. So, Stella asked if she could borrow me to act as a role model.

Mother and Stella conspired to take the three of us together to get our second shots. My part in the conspiracy was to show the others how to act.

My first shot had not hurt at all, so I was comfortable with my assigned role. When the doctor administered my second shot, it was a humdinger, and I thought my left arm might fall off. Of course, I did not dare let on that it hurt. Rosemary and Patsy watched me display a big fake smile and decided to take their shots without resorting to any more drama.

Our group left the doctor's office, got into an elevator, and I immediately passed out cold. Carried back into the doctor's office, I awakened to a very strong smell and realized a nurse was holding a vial of "smelling salts" under my nose as the doctor explained that I had undergone a reaction to the typhoid vaccine. So, my career as role model was extremely short-lived.

The next ten days were spent in bed as I endured a case of shot-induced typhoid fever. It was not unusual, we were told, for people to react to the vaccine by getting a mild form of the illness. Rosemary and Patsy, on the other hand, had absolutely no problems after their shots. When we went for our third and final shot, they were eager beavers and I was the one who was extremely leery.

⚜

Pediatricians and family doctors still made house calls during the '30s and '40s. People made appointments to go to their doctor's office for check-ups; but if a person became ill, the doctor would arrive at his patient's home carrying a black leather medical bag.

Mother always insisted my first word was "Dada" and the next one was "Car." Number three was "Buick." Like most youngsters of that time, I enjoyed being taken for a ride. So, one day Mother accepted an invitation to go driving in the M. family's just-purchased car.

There were no safety features such as seatbelts on cars then. This particular mid-thirties model had a front windshield that rolled open and out with a crank. I've never seen another like it, and can only speculate that it was designed to provide passengers with a cool breeze.

My mother occupied the passenger seat, and since special seats for infants and small children did not exist, I stood on the floor between her and this front window. While we were driving along one of the roads, we passed a place that highway workmen had recently resurfaced. I did not feel it at the time, but a piece of the asphalt-based tarvia they'd used blew into my right eye.

The next day, my eye was painful, swollen, tearing and red. It was a weekend, but our ophthalmologist met us at his office in the Nix Hospital. He had my mother hold one finger up in the air and told her not to move it. Then he told me to stare directly at her finger and not to move my eye even one iota.

Both of us managed to do what he asked as he broke into heavy perspiration and concentrated on cutting the foreign body out of my eyeball. He used no local anesthetic, so I assume there was none available. I still see the small black dot this surgery left in my right eye.

Plymouth and Ford roadster convertible coupes, as well as a few other models, featured rumble seats where today's cars have trunks. All models of automobile had wide running boards on which people often stood and clung to the side of a car as it was being driven. So, injuries from passengers riding outside of a car were frequent.

As a neighborhood, we were aware and concerned if any of our neighbors became ill. Pots of soup were often cooked and delivered to the home of anyone who was under the weather. However, no one caused more concern than Mrs. Wallace, who lived on the other side of the Franz home, when she was diagnosed with breast cancer.

Members of the Wallace family were devoted to their Christian Science theology so would not accept the services of a doctor. Christian Science Practitioners came often, but terrible moans and screams could be heard through Mrs. Wallace's open bedroom window as her cancer progressed. Neighbors were horrified as they listened to this woman, who was obviously in tremendous pain yet receiving no medical care to alleviate any of it. They also understood that the situation was based on religious beliefs that were purely the business of family members.

Most of the other Kayton Avenue families tried to help by preparing meals for the family and having frequent conversation with their two grown daughters to ask what else might be needed. Catholic, Protestant and Jewish prayers were offered daily on our block for our neighbor who was bound with endless ribbons of pain.

Christian Science Practitioners continued to show up daily, but the heartbreaking screams never stopped. So, this was a summer we all suffered emotionally and with great sympathy until Mrs. Wallace made her transition.

Another illness that became a shared neighborhood dilemma was introduced by a woman named Fannie Root. My parents first met Mr. and Mrs. Root when they moved to Kayton Avenue and began taking their meals next door at the Franz sisters' home. The Roots, an older couple who lived at 704 Kayton, on the New Braunfels Avenue end of the street, were also boarders.

George Root was quite successful in the insurance business. The couple left Alabama, where they had married in their mid-twenties, and moved to Texas where his business continued to thrive. Fannie often mentioned to the other boarders that she had agreed to marry George only after he promised she would never have to cook or do housework. Since George was totally smitten, he hastened to agree to her terms.

Fannie liked to show off her expensive designer outfits, worn with custom-made shoes. Nothing was too good for George's little doll. The couple had no children, so she willingly reigned as queen of the castle.

George Root passed away in the mid-1930s, and his elderly wife was left with a more than adequate inheritance for that period. As time progressed, though, as Fannie continued her habit of taking walks down to our end of the block, neighbors noticed that both her appearance and actions had changed drastically. Fannie Root's fashion-plate appearance had been discarded, and she roamed the block looking totally unkempt. Her short, salon-coiffed hairstyle had turned into long, dirty and matted strands of hair hanging past her shoulders. When she stopped to talk to neighbors, they were forced to turn away from her disagreeable odor.

Our family ate supper at six o'clock each evening. Normally, no one came to the door while we were eating because just about every family on the block was also enjoying their evening meal.

Fannie began ringing the doorbell each evening just after our family sat down at the dining table. As was her normal custom, Mother asked the cook to set an extra plate so that Mrs. Root could share our meal.

Our guest always arrived wearing an ankle-length gray wool coat covering whatever else was worn beneath it. This coat looked like it had been purchased for a winter's trip to a northern climate, and was certainly out of place in warm San Antonio. Yet, she refused to remove it.

A repugnant odor immediately blotted out the delicious smells coming from the dishes on the table as Fannie entered the dining room.

146

Suddenly, she was the only one at the table who displayed a hearty appetite.

It was obvious that Fannie knew exactly when and where she could get a good meal. She began showing up "just in time" for the noon meal, also. Finally, my father put his foot down and said, "I'm tired of coming home from work to enjoy my family and having to sit with that stinky woman. From now on, we are going to close and lock the front door before we sit down to eat."

A closed door did not deter Fannie Root. She rang the bell incessantly and angrily called out to us. When she got no answer, she would eventually head next door to the house of Julia and Anna Franz, hoping to find *them* in the midst of a meal.

Neither our family nor the Franz sisters had neglected Fannie since George's death. Mother, Grandmother and the Franz sisters had spent many hours taking food and other items to her home. After she lapsed into a lack of cleanliness, they offered to help her take a bath. She always informed them she had just taken one. Offensive body odor and dirty clothing disputed her statements.

Finally, my grandmother, Aunt Julia, Aunt Annie and Mother ganged up on her. Working in tandem, they were eventually able to get her undressed and into the bathtub as she protested at the top of her lungs. Their first major job was to get her hair de-tangled and attempt to get a comb through it. Fannie, like a small child, was not cooperative. She shook her head from side to side, so it was inevitable that her mane had to be cut before it could be washed. The tub was drained of dirty water and refilled with fresh several times before her captors pronounced her clean.

As a little child, I was taken along to Fannie's house for some of these bathtime trips. I sat in the living room and cringed at the sound of loud splashes from her angry kicks, accompanied by continuous howls of objection to this "unnecessary" procedure.

Certainly, these neighbor women were doing their best to contend with a woman who had mental problems. At that time, there was not a public mental health facility to contact. There were no home health care agencies that could send someone to visit and make recommendations. She would either receive help from those concerned friends or continue to wander the streets dirty, disheveled and searching for a meal.

For many months, those four women saw to it that Fannie Root was given frequent baths and her dirty clothes and linens were laundered.

They took turns taking her food and restocking her household needs so she did not show up at their tables with such extreme regularity.

"What has happened to your household help? Did you stop paying them? Do you have enough money left to take care of yourself?" Fannie Root was either unwilling or unable to answer such questions posed by concerned friends. She quickly displayed symptoms of paranoia, voiced as suspicions of their motives, when one of them attempted to glean information in order to ascertain exactly what she needed.

I have no idea what her mental diagnosis would be today. She surely knew who she was, who we were, and was sly enough to plot exactly where to be at what time in order to get a seat at a table filled with good food.

Her neighborhood caregivers were devoting many hours to Mrs. Root's plight, but it was obvious that she needed a legal guardian. By doing some detective work, my dad learned that Fannie had a nephew in another state. He was able to locate him and inform him of his aunt's condition. Eventually, the man came to San Antonio and took over the job of selling his aunt's home and seeing that she went to a place where she could receive constant care.

It seemed that George, the devoted husband who had allowed Fannie to play the roll of a dependent, spoiled child as he took care of her every need and desire, had managed to cripple her by not allowing her to develop her own abilities and resources. George Root's death suddenly jerked Fannie out of an effortless existence when she was in her seventies. Though she was still physically healthy, she could not cope with an environment in which she was required to take on any responsibility.

These were days when multiple generations within a family normally remained close geographically. As relatives aged, other family members stepped in and provided whatever care was necessary.

I often remember Fannie Root's pitiful visits to our house at a time when any strange actions on the part of an aging individual were referred to by the catch-all term "senility." I cannot imagine what would have happened to her if it had not been for the efforts of my family and the Franz sisters. Though the Public Health Service had a Division of Mental Hygiene at that time, the National Institute of Mental Health was not formed until 1949. People unlucky enough to exhibit symptoms of mental illness in the 1930s were simply stored in buildings referred to as lunatic or insane asylums.

Like the field of mental health, preventative medicine and preventative dentistry, except within an individual doctor's practice, were not yet upon the horizon. Though I complained about the way our dentist fixed my broken tooth, it was the unattractive materials used to which I objected. He was actually ahead of his time in seeking to save a healthy tooth.

Many people who visited a dental office returned home without the offending tooth or teeth. Whether from lack of funds or fear of pain, people often endured dental problems far too long before seeing a dentist. It may have been for this reason that most dentists of the day were quick to suggest replacing problem teeth with dentures.

I knew a number of middle-aged people who suddenly acquired a George Washington-style jutting lower jaw from the day they were fitted with dentures. Nan-nan, my maternal grandmother, normally refused to be photographed after ill-fitting dentures changed her looks in this respect. If she was included in a group picture, she would later seek out the offending photos and black out her face.

There were times I felt that I was spending far too much time at the dentist's office. The problem was that materials used to fill a cavity would fall out, so dental patients would have to return again and again to have the same tooth refilled.

My grandmother's doctor visits were made seeking relief from pain caused by arthritis. Other than that, my family members were seldom ill, with the exception of Mother's tendency to come down with a case of "Christmas flu." I believe this illness, which seemed to arrive with Santa Claus, was brought on by fatigue from making numerous platters of holiday cookies, divinity and pralines along with her ever-present dread of entertaining.

Mother was an excellent and gracious hostess, yet she was also a perfectionist who doubted her own abilities. She often crawled into bed just before a large group of relatives arrived at our home for Christmas dinner. My father, grandmother and I always managed quite well without her.

Many of the popular beliefs pertaining to health concerns seem naive, if not ludicrous, today. My great-aunt Vallie and I both suffered from what we called "foot aches." A severe ache began in the balls of our feet then

149

progressed into the calves, thighs and buttocks. The pain was so intense, it was virtually a migraine of our lower limbs.

Neither of us had a clue as to why these powerful aches affected us from time to time. No one else in the family was bothered with a similar ailment. Assaults of these debilitating aches often awakened me from a sound sleep in my younger years. My parents responded to my moans and groans by rubbing my feet with Absorbine Junior.

There were no pain medications made for children at the time, so it was not until years later that I was allowed half an adult aspirin. Family friends spoke of my aunt's aches in a manner to indicate they felt it was a shame for such a nice lady to have to put up with foot and leg pain.

In my case, friends dismissed these aches as "growing pains." Children who complained of aches and pains in their limbs were automatically saddled with that diagnosis. I'm not sure when or why society developed the theory that a child's growth should be painful.

In any event, as in the case of my aunt, these aches have continued to plague my adult life at times. Using reverse thirties-era logic, as a grandmother, I am evidently undergoing intervals of "shrinking pains."

After my grandmother's death, I used her pretty ivory-colored bedroom suite both in our San Antonio home and later in our El Campo duplex. During the spring of my senior year in El Campo High School, the wooden headboard of that bed helped me sound an alarm that all was not well.

Following a Saturday spent shopping in Houston, my parents and I returned to El Campo tired enough to settle for an early supper and bedtime. Sometime during the night, I awakened and realized I was extremely ill.

Trying to call out to Mother, I found I couldn't make a sound. Neither did I have the strength to move my body. Fortunately I had gone to sleep with my right arm above my head resting on a pillow.

Knowing that I needed medical help, I thought of knocking on the bed's wooden headboard, believing the sound might travel down the hall and reach my parent's bedroom. Thanks to the position of my arm, all I had to move was my wrist.

I was able to make some feeble knocking sounds and hoped that they would eventually awaken my mother. Finally, I heard her call, "Val?" Unable to answer, I kept knocking.

When I had first awakened, I was simply very ill and weak. In a short time, severe lower abdominal pains were added to the equation. I had suffered several bouts of abdominal pain in previous months. The family consensus was "stomach-ache," a catch-all diagnosis of the day. None of these attacks had lasted more than a few hours, so they were dismissed as nothing serious.

Mother showed up at my bedroom door and turned on the light. I must have looked horrible because she turned on her heel and headed for the phone to call the doctor. In a very short time, a sleepy Dr. Johnson was by my side.

After examining me and listening to whispered answers to his questions, he suspected either appendicitis or mesenteric adenitis (an inflammation of the lymph nodes in the abdomen that causes them to form "kernels"). He drew blood from my arm, then returned to his office to do a blood count. We soon received a phone call saying an ambulance was on its way.

In many small towns, a hearse was used for both transporting bodies to the cemetery and patients to the hospital. A schoolmate of mine worked at the local funeral home as a mortician's assistant. Suddenly, this young man was by my bedside lifting me. I was conscious enough to realize that he carried me down the flight of stairs, out the door and placed me into the back of a hearse. Feeling as I did, I was not sure of our destination.

Surgery was scheduled early the next morning. Mesenteric adenitis *was* the culprit, but my appendix was also removed "just in case."

Hospitals kept their patients much longer back then. Registered nurses were not trapped behind desks doing paperwork. They were the ones who expertly cared for patients in their rooms. Nurses not only gave each patient a good "bed bath" each day, they gave expert rub-downs. A patient could be assured that his or her nurse would bring lotion to the bedside and massage the limbs and body parts not affected by illness, injury or surgery.

When we first arrived at the hospital, the only empty bed available was in the charity ward. The friend who had chauffeured me in the hearse, however, only knew he had left me in *some* sort of ward. Not remembering clearly, because of having his sleep interrupted, he announced at school that I was in the Wharton County Hospital's maternity ward.

I was transferred to a private room after my surgery and stayed in the hospital for what I remember as a week to ten days. My weight dropped well below my normal ninety-seven pounds, so by the time I was allowed to go back to school, I did not look very "maternal."

CHAPTER EIGHT

THE FASHIONS OF THE DAY

A trip to the foundations department of a '30s-era department store would take a family of today into unknown territory. Displayed on assorted wide-eyed mannequins one would see extraordinary undergarments made of thick, unfamiliar materials.

This department, like the others within the store, would be filled with smiling sales clerks inquiring if they could help you. All a customer need say was "I would like a ..." and the clerk would be off gathering each item that fit the customer's description within her area of responsibility.

When the desired items were gathered, the clerk led her customer into a large private fitting room equipped with comfortable chairs and places for the customer's own clothes to hang. The clerk immediately began helping her customer undress—unzipping zippers, unsnapping snaps and untying sashes.

Shopping was my mother's hobby, so being taken along on her pilgrimages through San Antonio's best department stores meant I learned the routine at an extremely young age.

The foundation departments of that day equipped Mother with her girdles and my grandmothers with their corsets. These women were slim and petite, yet each slavishly followed the fashion rules of her youth.

In the early 1950s x-ray pictures of my grandmother Haynes were used as a teaching tool by doctors at Houston's Hermann Hospital. She was then in her eighties and, as the widow of a physician, received special attention while undergoing treatment for cancer. The older doctors explained to their young residents that when they came across an x-ray with a totally deformed ribcage like the one in the pictures, it was caused by a woman's having worn a tightly laced corset when she was young.

The heavy elastic garments that saleswomen helped their customers struggle into looked terribly hot and uncomfortable. The corsets were inset with steel or whalebone stays, which meant the wearer had better have extremely good posture or take a chance on getting pierced when she bent over. Corsets were also equipped with laces, which had to be pulled tight and tied. For a Scarlett O'Hara-type result, a second person was needed to pull on the laces.

Materials with the ability to stretch were not yet upon the scene, so women who donned the formidable girdles of that day had to master the ability to wiggle, squirm and pull at the same time. Only after this torso-twisting maneuver had been completed and the woman inhaled and held her breath could a girdle be zipped.

Fitters came in to make sure that undergarments were exactly the size and type the individual customer needed. An assortment of flare-legged panties that reached to mid-thigh, petti-pants and camisoles, full slips that hung from the shoulders and brassieres were carried in for the customer's inspection once the girdle or corset had been decided upon.

These foundation garments had long garters to which ladies hooked their silk stockings. White cotton stockings were required for nurses and by my grandmother Fletcher, who wore them underneath her regular silk ones in cold weather. Nylon pantyhose did not exist, even in dreams.

During the winter months, many individuals, especially those of my grandmother's generation, wore a cotton or woolen one-piece garment called a union suit. These were equipped with a "trap door" to facilitate bathroom visits. The silk garments I called "panties" were referred to as "step-ins" by my grandmothers.

To obtain her stockings, a woman had to leave Foundations and instruct the elevator operator to take her to the Hosiery floor. Elevators were run by store employees who had memorized each and every item for sale in individual departments. As the elevator moved in slow jerks between floors, the operator sang out the number of the next one along with the various departments located there.

Gathering clothes for a woman's wardrobe was a slow and detailed procedure. A trip downtown meant that women were already adorned with hat, purse and gloves plus all of the unseen accoutrements worn beneath their dresses. These items had to be removed in order to try on clothes and then re-donned prior to leaving the fitting room and progressing to another floor or store.

Women's fashions were affected by the stock market crash of 1929. Flapper-style boyish-looking outfits dropped totally from sight, and '30s-era magazines featured styles with a much more feminine look. Hemlines dropped dramatically, and there was a return to the natural waistline. Necklines received more attention with the use of wide scalloped or ruffled collars. Long puffy sleeves, fabric flowers and bows were used as accents on evening wear.

Dresses rather than suits or separates were the style of the day. Most were made with a neck zipper (also referred to as a slide-fastener) in back and a side zipper under the left arm. Many had large, decorative buttons and sometimes a sash that tied in the back. Dress materials were pure cotton, silk or wool with the exception of a few new rayon creations called "artificial silk."

In a decade remembered for financial ruin, readers may be surprised to know that fur garments of all kinds were worn day or night. Not only were fur capes, stoles and coats in style, but many garments sported fur trimming. I was often allowed to play dress-up in one of my grandmother's shoulder furs. However, I steered clear of her full-length black fur. I'm sure that many small animals met their maker so that coat could be created. As a small child, I assumed someone must have skinned a bear to get that much fur.

My father once returned from the Traylor Ranch with an unusual gift for me—a small rug made from wildcat skins. Mother told me in later years, "We saw you looking at the rug with tears running down your cheeks and asked what was wrong. You answered, 'I'll bet that poor old wildcat sure is missing its skin.'"

So, having admired black bears at the San Antonio zoo, I felt great sympathy for the animal that, in my imagination, had been deprived of his fur so my grandmother could have her winter coat.

Slacks and shorts for women did not become popular until the mid-1940s, although jodhpur-type riding pants or proper attire for specific sport needs could sometimes be found in specialty stores during the '30s.

It was not until the World War II years that American fashion designs became truly unique rather than copies of European haute couture. Cut off from the fashion centers of Paris and London, US designers concentrated on sportswear, and New York eventually became the sportswear capital of the world,

Little girl's dresses in the '30s featured fewer zippers, more buttons and almost always a sash tied with a big bow in back. In warm months, children often wore a one-piece cotton garment called a "sunsuit."

I felt prettiest and most feminine when my mother brought out a pinafore for me to wear over a dress. White organdy, with stiffly starched flounces at the shoulders, they remained my favorite attire until I grew too old to wear them.

Like our elders, girls wore several different pieces of underwear. Both sexes wore undershirts, and little girls added a full slip. Most of the dresses purchased for me were made from print fabric. Once I became old enough to select my own clothes, though, solid color fabrics were my choice.

For some reason, a bright-yellow wool dress appealed to me shortly after I had taken over as dress-selector. Living in a warm climate, I had never before worn wool next to my body. This was one of the worst choices I could have made.

I wore my new dress to school one morning and felt very well attired. By noon, I was beginning to itch. At the end of the school day, I ran most of the way home and was coming out of my dress by the time I walked inside the front door.

I thought that the itching would stop once the woolen dress and I parted company. Unfortunately, a combination of the dress material, and possibly the bright-yellow dye, triggered an intense allergic reaction over my entire body, even in places that had not come in contact with the fabric.

There were no antihistamines to take then, so Mother rubbed my body with all sorts of lotions, creams and some kitchen liquids she hoped would stop the itching. None of them worked, and I began frantically clawing my skin from the bottoms of my feet to the crown of my head.

After several hours of misery, I looked up and was astonished to see Mother advancing with her remedy of last resort—a bottle of Phillips Milk of Magnesia. As she poured that vile liquid over me and proceeded to rub it into my skin, I erupted into hysterical laughter and asked if she thought that was going to "eliminate" the itch.

It turned out that itch relief required the services of our doctor, who administered an injection strong enough to totally knock me out.

After that, I cringed and quickly turned away from the sight of bright yellow in any form. I could never tolerate even a small amount of that color in either my closet or home surroundings. I also learned to appreciate the beauty of woolen materials from the safe distance of a magazine layout.

In many Depression-era families, only the oldest girl and oldest boy received new clothes. Their clothes and shoes were passed down to younger sisters and brothers. Once their contents had been used, cotton flour and feed sacks, manufactured in various colors and prints, were washed and used by many a rural family to make dresses for women and little girls and shirts for the males in the family.

My mother mailed my outgrown party dresses to East Texas for her niece's children. My outgrown everyday outfits were carefully wrapped in waxed paper, put into paper sacks and placed atop garbage can lids to be claimed by the families with children who roamed San Antonio's alleyways searching for food and other hand-outs.

I always hoped that Vivian Jean's mother would be the first to find the clothing my mother left. I formed a mental picture of my secret friend wearing the items in the paper sacks, and the imaginary bond between us became tighter.

⋙

Business men wore a double breasted suit with a vest and generous-cut long trousers. These suits were normally made in charcoal, steel- or speckled gray, slate, navy or midnight blue. Because London was the official center of men's fashion, suit designs carried names that referred to British royalty. My father used to laugh at the sales pitches used by suit salesmen as they waxed eloquent concerning Prince of Wales checks and Windsor or Kent double-breasted designs. As an avid historian, and typical middle class American customer, he considered those male royals to be rather dull-witted.

Blazers, named for the blazing colors of jackets originally worn by late 19th-century English university students, also became popular in America during the 1930s. A totally American suit, the Palm Beach, was designed during this decade and became available in light weight materials like seersucker, silk shantung or linen.

In order to help department store clerks unfamiliar with London style trends, *Apparel Arts*, a men's magazine designed for the fashion trade, was founded in 1931. This soon became the salesperson's bible when seeking to advise American consumers.

Strangely enough, European gangsters created a huge influence on the men's fashion industry in the '30s. In striving to appear like businessmen, gangsters took every detail of the suits they wore to the extreme. Broader stripes, bolder plaids, more colorful ties, wider shoulders and trouser bottoms and narrower waists were their signature. They also liked their felt hats in a variety of colors never before worn by traditional businessmen.

New York designers, who only imitated European designs in those days, were then obliged to turn out similar versions of the style for other men. Instead of calling it Mobster Mode, they waxed creative by naming it the "Broadway look." By the early 1940s, this look had segued into the highly flamboyant zoot (or zuit) suit, which became both a popular song and desired image for adventurous young men. An overly long and loose coat, baggie trousers with a narrow ankle, quadruple-wide hat brims and hanging pocket chains of a greatly exaggerated length announced that this was a costume with a message. Materials used were often in wildly bright colors.

Men who would never think of donning that style of clothing still enjoyed singing, "I wanta zuit suit with a reet pleat...." As children, we did our own version of jitterbug to the music of that song and took pride in emulating the distinctive walk adopted by wearers of this clothing innovation.

This humorous style led to a "hep cat" style of moving and dancing and generally poked fun at traditional male attire and customs. Hollywood films spread the image nationwide, and zoot suits became even more colorful and wilder. Young men of minority races embraced the style a lot more readily than typical Caucasian teens—parental edict was probably the most important reason that white teens were kept out of zoot suits.

It was considered important to keep leather shoes and boots looking new, whether they were or not. Shoe polish and shoe brushes were staples in every home, and stands where a man could obtain a professional shoeshine were conveniently located in many areas of town. Barber shops and hotel lobbies were seldom without a shoeshine stand; large cities had numerous stands scattered out-of-doors so men walking between destinations could pause and obtain a quick shine.

My father and his golfing buddies always wore the traditional and colorful Scottish glen plaid golf knickers, as well as the standard Tam o' Shanter cap, when they left home for the golf course. Shorts and the casual attire of today would not have been tolerated on a 1930s golf course.

In each part of town there was a store specializing in shoe repair—shoes were not discarded when they began to show signs of wear. Footwear was well-made from leather, and was worn for a lengthy period. As shoes began to age and new soles, insoles or heels were needed, the custom was to make a visit to a cobbler for repairs.

Tennis shoes were used for playing tennis, beachcombing or boating. Athletic footwear, with its many subdivisions, was not yet an acknowledged category. So, everyone knew better than to wear tennis shoes away from home unless headed for the shore or the tennis court. The tennis shoes of that time were made of canvas and used for their nonslip rubber soles. None contained any specified type of extra support that designated a particular form of use. Running shoes were whatever an individual wore while sprinting to catch a bus.

Our family purchased footgear at a store across from the Alamo called The Guarantee Shoe Store. A large x-ray machine, on which people could stand and see the bones of their feet inside a shoe, drew customers who believed this device guaranteed them a superior fit. Customers always asked for their special shoe salesperson, and there was seldom any waiting before that individual materialized.

My feet were shod with the help and advice of a delightful woman called Mrs. Brooks from the day my first pair of high-top, lace-up white leather shoes was purchased. Mothers of that day would have been mystified at the sight of a Velcro-closure, so a great amount of time was spent in lacing and unlacing children's shoes. Mrs. Brooks always measured carefully and made sure those shoes were neither too tight nor loose and that toes were not too close to the end of the shoe.

Parents bought high-top shoes that covered the ankles of their young children in the belief that this would make their ankles stronger. Only in the summertime were most children allowed to wear "barefoot sandals."

There having been no warnings to the public concerning the possible dangers of frequent x-rays, like most children who came into The Guarantee Shoe Store, I spent a good bit of time standing on the x-ray platform admiring the bones in my feet.

Women's shoes had a rounded toe and thick heels. Spectator pumps —two-tone shoes, usually in white with navy—became very popular in the early '30s. Slip-on, lace-up and buckled shoes were also worn.

I must credit whatever taste I have in combining colors to my mother's shopping routine. When we shopped for my clothes, we purchased the dresses first and then proceeded on to other departments to find matching socks and hair ribbons. Mother dressed her one child as if she were wrapping a gift. As a finishing touch, she always placed a great big bow on top.

The prettiest and dressiest clothes I owned were gifts from relatives. These thoughtful individuals, who frequented elegant specialty shops in the United States and Europe, often sent me little girl's clothing fit for royalty. My problem was, each time I asked to wear one of the gorgeous outfits, Mother responded, "Oh, no! We must save it for a special occasion." So, throughout my childhood, almost every one of these gifts hung in my closet, unworn, until it was outgrown. Since Mother had raised no other children, she never seemed to grasp the fact that the next growth spurt was always just around the corner.

People of my generation always receive a culture shock when walking in an urban area or observing casually dressed folks who gather in airports or near other forms of public transportation. In the '30s, people entered these areas only after they were dressed in proper business or travel attire.

Only the roughest segment of society hung out in smoke-filled Depression-era bars. Couples wore formal gowns and tuxes or good quality business suits to enjoy drinks and dinner in nightclubs, luxury hotels or country clubs. Anyone dressed otherwise would have been denied entrance.

With this more formal manner of dress, when away from home couples behaved in an equally formal way. A man always offered his arm to the lady, and she kept her arm linked through his as they maneuvered down crowded boulevards or across hotel lobbies. The rhythm of their dual focus and dignity of their "couple-ness" always held a special fascination for me. Today, as I watch the preoccupied darting about of individuals following their cell phones down crowded supermarket aisles or airport concourses, I become nostalgic and yearn to observe the flow of those stately silhouettes once more.

Millinery stores and departments flourished during the Depression and for two decades after. Both men and women wore hats when away from home. Classic films shown on television today are accurate in their depiction of hats with veils, semi-veils, colorful feathers and other types of adornment.

I did a lot of walking around department stores while my mother was seated at one of the many dressing tables within a millinery department. Sales clerks brought hat after hat, each of which she surveyed from the front and both sides while making use of a large hand mirror. Her hat wardrobe included a plethora of berets and pillboxes as well as brimmed hats. Towards the end of the decade, turbans came into style.

Mother looked so beautiful in hats that Aunt Vallie painted her portrait in a Flapper-era pink cloche. Her delight in shopping for, as well as buying and wearing, headgear, however, was not passed on to me. Though little girls were dressed as miniature versions of their mothers back then, when I grew up, I found that I truly disliked both shopping for clothes and wearing hats. I would often be the only young woman at social events who was bareheaded.

My future mother-in-law, who loved and looked wonderful in large-brimmed hats, often tried to diplomatically point out my lack of fashion decorum. I'm sure she thought that I did not dress appropriately, but while wearing a hat, I felt more like a circus clown than a fashion plate.

While I was still quite young, Joske's installed an escalator. Probably, management felt this innovation would be a more efficient way of moving shoppers from floor to floor. It actually served as a wonderful babysitter for shoppers accompanied by impatient offspring. Children in San Antonio considered these "moving stairs" in the same category as an amusement park ride, so they were content to step onto the escalator and ride up and down, over and over again. A woman could shop to her heart's content and, when finished, stand next to the escalator until it delivered her child.

Easter time was a special shopping occasion when family members renewed their spring and summer wardrobes. Spring coats, a dubious need for those living in San Antonio, had to be obtained as well as the traditional new dress, shoes, hat, purse and gloves.

I'll never forget one year when my friend Merry Tom Blue and I both went with our mothers to search for Easter finery. We did not make a joint trip nor did we discuss what we had in mind prior to our shopping sprees. More than likely, we went to different stores. When we got together after our shopping trips to compare our new attire, though, we were stunned. Our outfits were identical. Merry Tom and I had selected duplicate navy blue dresses with white pique collars and matching spring coats. White straw hats trimmed with navy grosgrain bands, white purses, navy socks and white patent leather dress shoes completed our matching apparel. No doubt, this was an excellent example of close friends having similar likes and dislikes.

✤

During a typical day at home, women wore "house dresses" made of cotton. Since doing laundry was such a time-consuming job, they usually also wore an apron covering the entire front of their dresses when they performed housework. Shoes with a thick semi-high heel, worn with anklets, were the normal footgear.

When a woman remained in bed to have breakfast, read or recover from an illness, she wore a bed-jacket over her nightgown. Most women of leisure had a wardrobe that included a number of frilly bed-jackets. These bits of fluff were made in children's sizes, also, so I received a few of them as gifts. Certainly, the handwork was delicate and lovely, but I had other ideas about what to do with leisure time.

Aunt Vallie and Mother often wore lovely imported silk Japanese kimonos at home. Trying to be patriotic, they discontinued this practice after the United States was attacked by Japan in World War II. I missed admiring them as they seemed to float gracefully around our home in these colorful outfits.

Prior to selecting attire for the day, the women of our house saw to their grooming by making use of personal favorite toiletries. If hair needed washing, Kirk's Castile Soap or Pear's Glycerin Soap was used. Since most homes did not have a shower, we shampooed our hair while sitting in a chair next to the tub and hanging over the side.

Mother and Grandmother were brunettes, so their rinse was made by mixing vinegar and water. Since I was blonde, squeezing fresh lemon juice into warm water created a rinse for my hair.

My father and Uncle Nick chose Packer's Pine Tar Soap for a good shampoo to protect against scalp and skin problems. They prepared to shave by lathering up with their genuine badger-bristle shaving brushes and various types of shaving cream. They then worked for close shaves with safety razors equipped with double-edged stainless steel blades. The finishing step was to slap on a small amount of Lilac Vegetal After Shave to brace the skin and close the pores.

In 1919, a man named Charles Doppelt designed a kit to hold his grooming essentials and protect them from the rigors of traveling. My father and uncle kept their toiletries stored in their leather Dopp kits inside our bathroom closet. They were both minimalists and needed very little space for personal belongings.

A popular gift for women of the '30s was dusting powder. Mother and Grandmother each received several large containers with giant powder puffs for Christmas and other occasions. So, numerous round dusting powder boxes were stacked in that same bathroom closet next to a hot water bottle, used if one caught flu, and an ice bag, kept on hand for headaches, sprains or muscle strain.

Many bottles of perfume lined the tops of our dressing tables. Probably the world's best-known perfume at that time came in a cobalt blue bottle and was called Evening in Paris. Introduced by a company called Bourjois in 1929, it could be purchased at dime stores for twenty-five cents. For Depression-era women with a larger purse, the identical scent was sold in department stores in expensive Baccarat bottles with crystal stoppers.

Honeysuckle-scented White Shoulders and I both made our debuts in 1932. My Sin, Bond Street and Coty's Emeraude, L'Oregan and L' Aimant ("mysterious and soft") were all perfumes of the '20s that remained popular favorites.

Monteil of Paris brought out oriental-scented Royal Secret to tempt women and tantalize men in 1935. The most interesting full page perfume advertisement pictured a young woman collapsing with passion as she was in the embrace of a handsome young man. The message read "Promise her anything, but give her Arpege."

This ad also featured a grand piano and a violin. Evidently, it played sweet music into the ears of American men, who flocked to perfume counters and parted with their hard-earned Depression dollars to purchase bottles of Arpege. No doubt, they hoped for the same passionate reaction from their beloved, once she dabbed her wrists with this sultry scent.

However, the story behind Arpege is that of French designer Jeanne Lanvin, who created the scent inspired by love for her daughter. The gilded figures on the Art Deco Arpege bottle depict Jeanne and her daughter going to a ball and symbolize motherly love.

French perfume designer Lucien LeLong sought to revive elegance in the bleak thirties with his Indiscret. It caught on quickly, as did hand

and body moisturizers Jergen's Lotion and Hinds Honey and Almond Cream.

Camay, "the soap of beautiful women," or Woodbury Soap, "for the skin you love to touch," washed our faces. Our clawfoot tub's soapdish held Lifebuoy, the world's first deodorant soap. Lifebuoy commercial spots on radio featured a foghorn voice bellowing "Beeeee-Ooooohhh!" Another voice then explained that this stood for body odor...which no one would have if they removed dirt and germs with Lifebuoy. Not to do so would surely be a tragedy.

Underarm deodorants had not yet made the scene, so this ad campaign introduced the American public to the idea that their body odor might be offensive. Adults were probably shocked by this possibility. Children everywhere tried to outdo one another by imitating the "Beeeee-Ooooohhh" foghorn sound. A white, greasy form of Mum Deodorant became available to the public in the early '40s. I thought it smelled worse than "Beeeee-Ooooohhh."

Mother or Grandmother would place a tiny dab of one of their perfumes on my arm if I made a special request. However, the only scent they believed appropriate for a child was Johnson's Baby Powder. Any type of loose powder sent me into a series of sneezes, so to avoid being inundated with Johnson's, I had to grow old and swift enough to grab a towel and run away from Mother when I emerged from the tub.

Mother used Lady Esther loose face powder, a powder-type rouge and lipstick, which she referred to as "lip rouge." She normally finished dressing by donning a set of matching beads and clip-on earrings.

My grandmother's skin care involved always wearing a sunbonnet if she went into the back yard to tend her flower beds. This protective garb had been the habit of women in her generation, and her skin was absolutely flawless, probably because it had always been shielded from the sun.

⌘

A Polish immigrant to the United States, Max Faktor, is considered the father of modern makeup. Prior to coming to this country, he served as a cosmetic expert for the Russian royal family and their Imperial Russian Grand Opera.

In this country, Factor (the spelling was changed by a clerk on Ellis Island) began creating "flexible greasepaint" makeup to be used by movie actors. When "pancake makeup" became available to the public, women flocked to stores, believing they could look like movie stars. This thick makeup, applied with a wet sponge, may have looked elegant under strong film-type lighting, but it lost its allure when viewed in daylight.

Women who applied the first pancake released to the public tended to use a heavy hand and choose inappropriate colors. Mother never tried it, but a number of her friends suddenly acquired faces in shades of orange on top of their white necks. These women soon learned, to their dismay, that, after a short time, whatever color they originally applied eventually turned orange.

CHAPTER NINE

FOOD AND EXERCISE

A book called *The Helping Hand for Every Day's Want, A Complete Collection of Recipes for the Kitchen, Bath, Toilet, Laundry, Household, Sick Room, Garden and Farm with Etiquette* always stayed within my grandmother's reach. This book was written in 1908 by C.H. Coldwater of Lake Charles, LA, and was received via the mail for $1.50.

Along with social rules like "It is forbidden for a gentleman to shake hands with an unmarried lady," the book contained recipes for making complexion soaps, and lengthy instructions for washing fluids and starches for your "clothes boiler."

At our home, washing was done out-of-doors by our laundress, or "washwoman," Josephine. Using the water hose, she filled two wash tubs that sat on a stand over an open fire. When the water was sufficiently hot, she placed the dirty clothes, separated by color, into one of these large galvanized steel tubs. She first washed the clothes using a washboard and a bar of lye soap. Next, she would transfer the clean clothes into the other tub and rinse them, changing the water often.

Due to the routine in our household, water in the tubs had to be dumped out often and the procedure started over. Our bed linens and towels were changed every day, so there was always a large wash. Since cotton blends and wash-and-wear materials were not even a dream yet, everything had to be starched and ironed.

Bluing, used to whiten clothes, was added to the last rinse, and later, starch was added to the water in a clean washtub. When clothes were totally permeated, they were taken out of the tub, wrung dry and placed into a large laundry basket. Josephine would then carry the baskets filled with wet clothes and linens and hang them on clotheslines to dry.

This process worked well with the cottons used at that time. However, delicate lingerie, clothing and embroidered guest towels would not have survived long, so they were washed with bars of Ivory soap in indoor sinks.

Many women supported themselves by doing washing and ironing for others in their own homes. After our family left San Antonio and moved to the small town of El Campo in 1946, we used the services of one of these home-based laundries that employed several women. Clothes were all hand-done and beautifully ironed.

World War II offered employment and decent wages to a number of women who had always worked as household servants. So, wringer-type washing machines, used in the northern states for years before they found acceptance in the South, began to appeal to housewives who suddenly found themselves without a washwoman. Brand names like Bendix and Maytag joined the jargon used by radio announcers.

These were not the throw-the-clothes-and-soap-in-and-forget-it automatic washers of today. Someone had to heat water to pour in, attach rubber hoses when it was time to drain and feed one piece of clothing at a time through the wringer while keeping one's fingers clear of the mechanism. It was also necessary to chase the machines across porches or basement floors—balance and stability were not virtues the designer had kept in mind.

When a few of these button-breakers and zipper-squashers found their way into the southern states, they were placed on back porches. The same attitude prevailed that had once been prominent when bathroom facilities were designed to go inside homes. It was just not proper to do certain things indoors. My father once offered to buy a washing machine for Mother, and she was totally insulted. After pouting for a week, she reminded him that Southern women do not do their own washing.

Several years later, after a move to their ranch home, she was very happy to have a modern machine installed. There was no one available to work as domestic help, and it was a *very* long drive to the nearest laundry.

I mentioned in another chapter that I only knew two people who were overweight during my childhood. Everything people did during the '30s exercised their body parts. Kitchen utensils that blend, peel, chop, grate, stir, puree or open had not yet been invented. That meant all these chores were done by women by hand. One could not purchase any mixes or items that were pre-prepared, with one exception that probably inspired today's pudding mixes. My*T*Fine Pudding and Pie Mix, introduced in 1918, was added to milk and cooked on the stovetop. It was one of those rich, creamy comfort foods mothers like to serve small children.

Dough for biscuits, pie crusts and cookies were made from scratch then rolled out with rolling pins. Biscuit cutters were an essential in every Southern home, as well as an assortment of cookie cutters in imaginative shapes. Meals were created from fresh foods that had to be trimmed, peeled, beaten or stirred by hand. My grandmother wielded a kitchen hammer with vigor, and was our expert at tenderizing meat on the large wooden cutting board. Muscles were kept firm by lifting and carrying heavy cast iron pots and skillets.

If a family planned to eat meat loaf, meat patties, Italian meatballs or sausage, a cast iron meat grinder about nine inches long was clamped onto the kitchen counter. The proper cuts of meat for the process were fed into the top, and a good deal of strength was needed to turn the handle and produce ground meat.

When fried chicken was on the menu, a whole fryer was cut up by the cook or housewife. My mother often laughed about the first time she tried to cut up a chicken.

"I offered a prize to anyone at the table who could identify the piece they were eating!"

For special summer occasions, many families owned a hand-cranked ice cream maker. Women first cooked delicious custards, then poured them into a steel container, which was placed inside a heavy wooden "bucket" filled with chopped ice. At that point, the cranking began non-stop. The crank had to be kept constantly in motion or the custard would never freeze into ice cream. No one could have asked for a more strenuous arm exercise. The person doing the work normally "cried uncle" and hoped someone would show up to relieve him.

Because my mother had a problem with swallowing certain things, she assumed that I did, too. She strained my food (no baby foods were available in stores then) for a very long time.

Mae West's "peel me a grape" has always been a joke signifying the speaker's indolence and desire to be waited on. Not with Mother! I loved seedless green grapes, which I was allowed to eat only after she peeled each one. Nor did it ever occur to her that I had not inherited her aversion to swallowing anything related to pills or peels. If I needed an aspirin, she crushed it for me to take with water. The taste was terrible, and I could have easily gulped it down.

Then I had a taste of a "real" bowl of vegetable soup, and I refused to eat strained food again. That day, Mother was in the midst of straining my vegetable soup as I sat at the dining room table in my high chair. The phone rang, so she stopped and went into the hallway to answer it. The soup smelled wonderful, and I was hungry, so I decided to take the feeding process into my own hands.

Probably, guilt feelings of doing something not on the agenda is what allows me to so easily recollect sitting in that high chair and reaching out for Mother's bowl of soup—the two bowls were sitting side-by-side as they cooled. Both were within my reach, but hers looked much better than my bowl of formless mush.

I managed to transfer the bowl onto my tray with a minimum of spillage and dug into it with my Mickey Mouse soup spoon. By the time Mother finished her conversation and stepped back into the dining room, I had mastered chewing and swallowing whole vegetable bites magna cum laude.

❧

If our meal menu could be reproduced, readers would assume that our family must have all been morbidly obese. Rich gravies, cream sauces, puddings and pies were everyday fare. Yet our family, and relatives who consumed similar meals, remained slim due to a combination of genetics and the physical activity inherent in our lifestyle.

The only electric appliance in the kitchens of that day was a two-door toaster. This appliance was not automatic, so when one side of the bread was deemed sufficiently brown, the door had to be flipped open and the slice of bread turned over. This style of toaster had no timer or any sort of automatic device to pre-select a degree of darkness. It was up to the person involved in making toast to watch it like a hawk. If the operator turned away for an instant the toast could burn black.

Boiling water from a teakettle was poured through an aluminum or enamelware drip coffeepot, which was then placed on a gas stove burner to keep the coffee hot. Milk was not yet homogenized, so the bottle could be shaken to distribute the thick yellow cream at the top or the cream could be poured off and placed in a cream pitcher. We shook our bottles and purchased the rich cream separately.

If someone was asked, "Would you like cream in your coffee?" that's exactly what they got. No milk-in-a-cream-pitcher or some sort of nondairy substitute. Heavy cream was used constantly over cereals and fresh berries and to complement desserts. It was used in making gravies, soups, sauces served over fresh vegetables and sweet and tart sauces for puddings.

Milk left out to sour and thicken, called clabber, was a favorite of the females in our household. This tastes similar to buttermilk but is thicker and must be eaten with a spoon. Mother served this dish with sugar and cream, and I usually asked for a second helping. Neither Daddy nor Uncle Nick would touch it. I think the name got to them.

When cakes or anything else that required whipping or beating were made, either a wire whisk or handheld rotary egg beater was used. So, it took a long time of turning the beater before egg whites intended for meringue became stiff enough to add sugar. This was just one of the ways homemakers of that day got exercise during the process of meal preparation.

All forms of chopping, mincing, slicing, grating and blending were also done by hand—no pre-cut ingredients could be purchased in a bag or processed by some appliance. A cook was limited to food grown fresh locally, since freezers and frozen foods were not even figments of our imagination.

San Antonio, which began as a tiny settlement formed around Catholic missions, had and has a large Catholic population. In the '30s and '40s, Catholics were still expected to eat fish on Friday, so we could rely upon fresh fish being rushed into town from the Texas coast towards the end of the work week.

Like our Catholic neighbors, we looked forward to Friday meals planned around fresh seafood. Both fish and meat for the rest of the week were purchased from a neighborhood meat market or butcher shop. We ate a lot of T-bone steaks, roast beef, fried chicken, ham, pork chops, meat loaf, beef stew, bacon, veal cutlets and, of course, our Friday fish. I was served calves' liver broiled in butter "for your blood."

Actually, I loved it...as long as the ketchup bottle was close by. Daddy had our sausage made from venison and pork somewhere in East Texas.

Mother was a natural vegetarian who required far more fruits, vegetables and desserts than meat. My father, who kept a herd of cattle at his cousin's ranch, teased that she was "not a patriotic Texan."

A highly honored staple in our diet was grits. Hominy grits was not just an edible commodity, it was our second language. We knew that this form of Southern sustenance had traveled west with our ancestors and often been the one provision that kept whole families alive in route. A bowl of grits, topped with plenty of melted butter and salt, was a breakfast worth getting up for. Ham steak served with grits and red-eye gravy could be enjoyed any time of day.

In my late teens, I split with a suitor from New York who could not refrain from making disparaging and condescending remarks about the grits I consumed in the University of Houston's Oberholtzer Hall cafeteria each morning. Joe evidently thought his remarks were humorous. Actually, it was the name he disliked, since he refused to taste even a teaspoon of that dish which so thoroughly reflected my heritage.

When I graduated from strained baby foods to the real stuff, my taste buds emulated those of my father, and I wanted good steak. I turned my nose up at vegetables until Mother embarked upon a challenging training program with the utmost patience.

She observed that I loved the juices, or pot liquor, created as vegetables cook. I would happily eat a bowl of green bean juice, black-eyed pea juice, carrot juice or whatever. So, she started a game with me. I was given a bowl of pea juice, for example, that contained one black-eyed pea. To get the juice, I had to eat the pea. She followed suit with all of the other vegetables, and there was no cheating. She kept score. If I ate one slice of carrot, the next time carrots were served, I had to eat two slices. Playing this game, I eventually learned to love vegetables.

Mother's carefully followed training routine was an unqualified success with two notable exceptions. The East Texas standard duo, turnips and greens, were on our menu about once a week. That was one dish I could not endure.

One of Mother's specialties was cream of tomato soup, which everyone at the table but me cheered. She, of course, started with fresh tomatoes, and the dish took a long time to prepare. One day, I visited the home of a friend and was asked to stay for lunch. Anna Nell's aunt served tomato soup. Knowing that I was expected to use good manners, I steeled myself to eat it. To my surprise, I enjoyed it.

When I told Mother that Mrs. Wolters had served some good tomato soup, she immediately called and requested the recipe. Mrs. Wolters laughed and told her to open a can of Campbell's Tomato Soup and add a can of water. My mother was absolutely floored that I preferred canned soup to her treasured family recipe.

Obtaining fresh vegetables in the 1930s was easy—they came to us in a wooden cart pulled by a horse. The growing season for farmers around San Antonio and the Rio Grande Valley is mercifully long.

Before my birth, my parents became customers of a hard-working truck farmer who began his slow journey into San Antonio early each morning before daybreak. This farmer guided a large gray horse that pulled a cart heaped with just-harvested produce onto Kayton Avenue several days a week. Housewives listened for the clip-clop sound of hooves, and were usually out at the curbs by the time he brought his wagon to a stop. He never began his homeward trip until the back of his cart was empty.

When I was a few years old, I remember the proud farmer showing up driving a secondhand truck and wearing new overalls. We were all glad that becoming motorized would make his trips back and forth easier and his work days shorter. However, I missed getting to pet his faithful old horse.

That fascination with his gentle horse caused me to run outside with my grandmother as she prepared to select vegetables. She and the farmer might have been reading from a script. Their dialogue seldom differed from day to day. "What do you have today?" always started their conversation. The farmer would then recite a memorized litany of legumes; he knew from experience which items of produce she would, and would not, purchase.

❧

Our family continued the eating habits of our East Texas ancestors, since neither my grandmother nor my mother ever chose to experiment with new tastes. They stuck to menus used in the homes of their childhoods. So, we ate a lot of greens, carrots, sweet potatoes or yams, green beans, black-eyed peas, asparagus, cabbage, turnips, celery, lettuce, spinach and beets. Sometimes we consumed mashed Irish potatoes on days we had fried chicken, and French fries along with Friday fish. But, like our progenitors, we really preferred rice and gravy.

Two vegetables Grandmother never selected, though the farmer always called out their names, were cauliflower and broccoli. I wondered what they tasted like but did not get to enjoy them until years later when I left for college.

When Mother requested a soup bone from our butcher, she received a bone with a great deal of good meat, usually brisket, attached. Dog bones, with a lot of meat still clinging to the bone, were given away to regular customers. The same thing happened with ham bones used to flavor pots of dried beans. They always contained a great deal of ham to enjoy with the beans.

My one attempt at selfish eating, sometimes called "greed," taught me an immediate and long-remembered lesson.

After graduating from my mother's vegetable training program, I found that my all time favorite was spinach. As I had seen Popeye do in movie cartoons, I once consumed an enormous amount of spinach for a little girl. Unlike Popeye, I did not acquire large muscles. In fact, I was unable to even keep it down.

Almost a hundred percent of my days were lived with several pairs of adult eyes trained in my direction. My every action was monitored, and I knew full well that I had better "be a little lady."

One evening, I wandered past a table in the kitchen where steaming serving dishes sat awaiting their transfer into the dining room. I presumed that Minnie, our cook, had wandered off to tell my mother that she was ready to serve supper. There was no adult in sight.

Seizing the opportunity, as well as a fork, I stood next to the kitchen table and ate the entire contents of a large serving dish filled with spinach. Everyone's portion was promptly shoveled into my happy mouth. By the time my parents walked into the kitchen and my deed was discovered, my stomach was in full-scale revolt. I ran into the bathroom with Mother in hot pursuit. Not only had my ladylike manners been cast aside, but my stolen spinach was also tossed.

This act was selfish in more ways than one. Fresh spinach was always filled with the sandy loam soil in which it grew best. That meant the preparer had to stand for a long time filling, draining and refilling the sink in order to wash away all of the sand particles before the spinach leaves were placed into the cookpot. Minnie also had fried and crumbled bacon and boiled and chopped eggs to be added to the top of the serving dish at the last moment.

So, I was taken immediately back into the kitchen once it was ascertained that no lasting harm was sustained during my Popeye-like binge. I gave my apologies to Minnie as she suppressed a smile. I told her I was sorry for not honoring all of her hard work and promised that I would never again give a repeat performance.

⚜

We ate wonderful, made-from-scratch biscuits every day unless the meal called for cornbread, corn pone or corn dodgers. I much preferred the cornbreads to biscuits, and still bake them often today.

An old and valued Southern custom had a place at our table, though my mother had refined it as much as possible. Sopping our buttermilk biscuits in meat drippings made into thin butter gravy, and at times thicker gravies, allowed one to truly continue enjoying the flavor of the meat. Whenever these delectable gravies were served, a nappy (a small, shallow china dish) was placed next to our bread plate so that we had our own supply of gravy and would not make a mess.

I sometimes visited homes of friends where everyone sopped out of one central gravy dish. That habit resembled a competitive game with an untidy ending guaranteed. Because I always heard my mother's rules of etiquette whispered into my ear at such times, I never became a player.

Another custom, dating back to the 19th century, was still used in some rural areas of Texas and other states. It was started, supposedly, by working-class tea drinkers in the northern regions of England. Their accepted routine was to pour a little of the hot liquid from the teacup into the saucer, blow on it to cool it and then swallow it with a noisy slurp before repeating the procedure.

This custom was brought to the United States by English immigrants and adopted by coffee drinkers. In the manner of their tea-drinking ancestors, they transferred small amounts of coffee into their saucer and proceeded to blow on it until it was sufficiently "saucered and blowed." Then, they slurped it straight from the saucer.

On trips away from home, I had plenty of opportunities to watch groups of elderly men sitting around a domino table or potbellied stove in a rural store, partaking of this coffee-slurping ritual. Years of practice must have increased their skill, because I don't remember ever seeing a drop of coffee spilled.

⚜

At home, all meals were eaten at the dinner table. No one filled a plate and took it off somewhere. Whether or not a formal blessing was spoken, we were thankful for our food. After each meal, family members went into the kitchen, one at a time, to express their appreciation to the cook.

The only time I ever sat at a table where sparse servings were dished out by the hostess, we were visiting my father's wealthy cousin in Beaumont. Our cousin's wife was tight with food, and second helpings were not allowed. If one opened the door of the refrigerator in search of a drink, they would find it almost totally empty. Shelves and cabinets, originally built to hold food, were well-stocked—with every brand of liquor and cocktail mix imaginable.

It was hard for me to understand the difference in priorities exhibited by my father and this cousin to whom he had been so close all of his life. A few more years of maturity brought about the realization that the distribution of food was controlled by their respective wives, and therein lay the difference.

This cousin and his wife owned beautiful homes in several locations and a seaworthy yacht. They enjoyed the company of friends and loved to party. Though they were generous in most respects, food was handled in a miserly fashion.

The only time liquor was served in our home was during the holiday season, when Mother whipped up some of her unbelievably rich eggnog. This was one of those dishes where the eggs were beaten with a hand-held egg-beater until they were stiff. Her eggnog mixtures could not be poured. They were served with a ladle and best consumed with the help of a spoon.

When Mother filled a sterling silver punch bowl with her concoction, she was very generous with the amount of Kentucky bourbon she added "for flavoring." My teetotaler parent evidently believed that there was some sort of dispensation granted during the holiday season that exempted bourbon from the liquor category if it was served in eggnog.

I've been unable to locate my mother's original eggnog recipe to share with those who think eggnog is planted in plastic cartons and sprouts during the holiday season. However, my friend James C. C. Williams of San Augustine has graciously shared his formula, which must be very similar. James is a former United States diplomat and connoisseur of fine food and drink.

EGGNOG

12 eggs, separated
1 cup sugar
1 cup bourbon
1 cup cognac
teaspoon salt
3 pints whipping cream

Beat egg yolks with sugar until thick. Slowly add bourbon and cognac. Chill several hours. Whip egg whites with salt until stiff. Whip cream. Add whipped cream and egg whites to the egg yolk mixture. Chill one hour. Sprinkle with nutmeg just prior to serving.

James adds that for thinner eggnog you can pour one cup of milk into the batch. If you do that, you won't enjoy an eggnog like the ones we consumed in the '30s. If you do decide to make it in the manner of Mother and James, on the other hand, pre-select a few designated drivers for your guests.

⁂

Homemade preserves and jellies were always served with biscuits in my home. My favorites from a large field of these sweet delicacies were mayhaw jelly and fig preserves. Mayhaws are berries that grow on a small tree in East Texas, so we had to rely on visits from relatives to obtain them.

Fig trees grew in our back yard to the delight of resident wasps and yellow jackets. It was obvious that these pests loved our figs as much as we did and were willing to fight over ownership. Someone picking figs while trying to avoid getting stung resembled a person playing a game of dodge ball.

Though our family employed a housekeeper-cook, both my mother and grandmother were very much involved in certain kitchen duties. The art of home canning was still used, to one degree or another, in most homes. I don't remember anything being canned in our kitchen but fig preserves and mayhaw jelly.

It must have been a cold, rainy day in East Texas when my Grandmother Fletcher was taught the art of "putting up" preserves. Her lesson began after whoever taught her had pulled down all of the windows. for the rest of her life, pulling down the windows remained the first step of the canning process. In hot weather San Antonio, when the figs in our back yard had ripened and been picked by family members dodging turf-protecting yellow jackets, our kitchen was turned into a sauna.

My mother often told the story of how many times she tried to convince Grandmother that figs could be cooked and preserved with the windows open. Her arguments were pointless, so she and our cook worked beside Grandmother, totally drenched in perspiration, until the last jar of fig preserves was capped. Only when this procedure was finished could a breath of air be allowed in through open windows.

I must say that my mother used the same good manners and respect for elders she taught. Knowing in advance what she was in for, she nevertheless abided by her mother-in-law's strange rules and took part in the preserving process year after year. Certainly, our family appreciated the outcome when served over melted butter on hot biscuits.

I was fascinated by cooking and kitchens and always wanted to be given a chore so I could feel helpful. My elders were afraid that I would hurt myself, as some kitchen tools were rather dangerous. Mother always took a protective stance with hands ready to grab any tool I might touch.

Turning an egg beater or the handle of the meat grinder were considered some of the safer kitchen chores, so when I was old enough they were happy to share those jobs with me.

Mother's menus always included fresh fruit salads topped with her own mayonnaise, which was creamy in color and tasted absolutely delicious. This was one of the dishes I was allowed to hand-whisk as oil and fresh eggs were blended. The first time I tasted mayonnaise from a jar on sliced white bread was when I entered elementary school and ate in the school cafeteria.

Citrus fruit was purchased by the case from a local Baptist preacher we called Brother Boucher. To supplement his meager salary, he made trips into the Rio Grande Valley and returned with huge crates of luscious grapefruit, oranges, lemons and tangerines. Hand-squeezed orange juice was enjoyed daily for breakfast. Lemon and mint from our garden were always served with iced tea. Grapefruit was enjoyed at breakfast, and tangerines made a great between-meal snack.

Aunt Julia Franz taught my mother, who passed on the knowledge to our cooks, the art of making Cajun gumbo. A Louisiana native, Aunt Julia would only use gumbo filet that family members sent from St. Martinville. She made believers of Mother and Grandmother, so this imported ingredient was always kept on hand. Though gumbo can be made by using many kinds of meat, it was the seafood gumbo that I loved best.

It was the custom for housewives on our block to share special dishes with neighbors from time to time. We often enjoyed one of Mrs. Goldstein's good kosher soups or a German dish from the Schneider or DeWaal households.

Favorite restaurants for ethnic foods were Schilo's downtown, where we consumed thick split pea soup, and La Fonda on Broadway, which turned out superior Mexican food. Minnie's Mexican food was also delectable, and we appreciated her culinary skills.

During the years she was in our employ, my parents tried hard to get her to teach me to speak Spanish. Minnie had worked hard and long to learn English and was proud of her ability, so she was not eager to teach me anything but Mexican folk dances and songs with Spanish lyrics. Entering the kitchen through the swinging door from the dining room and attempting to cross the floor could be dangerous when Minnie and I were in the midst of one of our whirling, foot-stomping Mexican-dance routines. We eagerly provided our own musical accompaniment, to the delight of the rest of my family.

Probably one reason my elders were not especially eager for me to be in the kitchen was a shared memory of the time I decided to be of help when no one was around. My intention had been to aid the cooks of our household, but instead, I created a long lasting mystery. Awakening from a nap to find my mother and grandmother still napping and Minnie in the back yard helping her mother hang clothes, I undertook the role of Good Samaritan.

I had watched as Minnie peeled a plethora of fresh fruits and vegetables. Knowing that I was not supposed to touch knives, I decided that I could be of service by "peeling" the cans in the pantry.

Before I was discovered, I had dedicated myself to this chosen task with great determination. Several shelves were filled with neatly aligned silver cans, their paper labels on the kitchen floor at my feet. My mother laughed each time she re-told the story about all of the "surprise" dishes our family ate during the months following my good deed.

Our family loved eating the pecans grown in our back yard as well as walnuts we purchased. The only way to enjoy these delicacies was to use a nutcracker to crack the shell then carefully extract the nut-meats with a pick designed for that purpose. This was a lengthy procedure, and one best tackled with the entire family gathered at the table to help. The job could not be hurried if one hoped to skillfully extract an entire pecan half. Small pieces of the pecan were used also, but the halves were valued for decorating the tops of cakes and cookies. At Christmas, Mother made a special treat using pecan halves, dates and cream cheese rolled in sugar.

Using a can opener meant that one had to stab a hole in the top of a can and then, with a steady up and down movement, saw around the top of the can until it came off. This tool caused a lot of wounds, not only with the knife-like portion but by creating serrated edges on can lids that easily cut hands.

Each time I walked into the kitchen and prepared to fix something to eat, my mother invoked her habit of standing next to me with hands outstretched to prevent what she obviously thought would be a catastrophe. Because of this, I did not get an opportunity to begin my cooking career until after our family moved to El Campo.

While living there, I received an invitation to spend several weeks at a Port Alto beach cabin owned by the Stockton family of Louise. Pat Stockton and I were friends, and I totally enjoyed spending time with her entire family. Her father, like mine, loved to tease us and often declared we were, "Ol' Val and Ol' Pat...the same mean." (Two of a kind)

In addition to Pat's younger siblings, her two maiden aunts were going along on this vacation. They had their own cabin but would take their meals with us because they had never learned how to cook.

The first night we arrived at Port Alto, the Stocktons received a telephone call that turned out to be a death message. They decided it was necessary to leave the next day and drive to West Texas. That meant we would all have to go back home and abort our planned vacation, since Mrs. Stockton was the only one who could cook.

"I'll do the cooking," I volunteered on an impulse.

"Oh! You can?" asked a relieved hostess.

"Sure." I didn't lie and indicate I had ever done it before—I was just positive that I would be able to do it. Besides, I loved the beach and the waters of the bay and had no desire to leave them behind.

So, the Stocktons left us money to buy groceries and rules to follow in looking after Karen and John Haywood, Pat's sister and brother. Pat's aunts were sweet and interesting chaperones for two fourteen-year-old girls.

As I had always imagined, I loved cooking. The salt air and bay breezes kept our entire crew continually hungry, so I received a great deal of practice in meal preparation. The aunts were most generous with compliments about what I served, so I never told them they were my guinea pigs.

The weeks at Port Alto flew by, and before we knew it, Pat's parents were back and it was time to return to town. I never mentioned my kitchen exploits to my parents. However, a few weeks later, Mother and Dad ran into one of Pat's aunts in downtown El Campo.

"Oh, I just can't begin to tell you how much we enjoyed Val's cooking," she gushed. Her words rendered both parents speechless.

⁂

"Elbow grease" was the engine used to keep the house swept, mopped, dust-mopped, vacuumed and cleaned in those days. The many varieties of cleaning products now on the market were not available to make the job easier. Vacuum cleaners were extremely heavy and difficult to move from place to place.

Removing accumulated dust from room-sized rugs and carpets, used atop hardwood floors, had previously been done outside. The rugs were hung over a sturdy clothesline and, using a tool that resembled a tennis racket, thoroughly beaten. The person doing the beating had to dodge clouds of dust emitted during the process.

Upright Hoover vacuums, made by a former saddle manufacturer, dominated the market. Murray Spangler, who suffered from asthma, designed a machine for collecting dust. Hoover acquired the rights to Spangler's invention and proceeded to refine his new "electric suction sweeper."

Hoover introduced the slogan, "It beats as it sweeps as it cleans."

In England, Hoover's machines carried a royal warrant and were used on the prestigious ocean liners of the 1930s. In 1933, "All women

180

are equal in this" was introduced as the new slogan. This implied that, even if one had to scrimp and save to buy one of these expensive machines, ownership put one in the same class as royalty and the well-to-do.

⋙

The simple act of driving a car gave one a good amount of exercise, since none of the equipment was automatic. A driver continually pulled out throttle and choke rods mounted on the dashboard. The choke was pulled when starting the engine, and the throttle was used to keep the car going at a set speed. In a way, it was a precursor to present-day cruise controls. It took muscle power to shift the floor-mounted gearshift, pull or release the floor-mounted emergency brake, move the tight steering wheel or roll windows up or down with a stiff crank.

Car windows were left down during warm months, since cars of the '30s and '40s had no air conditioning. Turn and stop signals were made by sticking one's arm out of the window.

"I'm about to turn left": the arm was pointed straight. "Turn right": the arm was bent at the elbow, and the forearm pointed up. "I'm going to stop": the arm was bent at the elbow and pointed down. Feet and legs were exercised by constantly moving back and forth to operate the clutch, gas pedal and foot brake.

These cars were not equipped with heat for the colder months, but since the windows still had to be lowered constantly to signal the driver's intention they likely wouldn't have been of much help anyway. Small heaters that could be installed in the front of a car came out in the late '30s. The heat they generated was extremely minimal, so passengers used heavy blankets wrapped around their legs and lower body to stay sufficiently warm.

It was to be hoped that multiple drivers of the same car were all of the same height. Moving a driver's seat back and forth was a major operation, and one that was usually not performed. I'll never forget my mother's anger when she got into our Ford V-8 after it had been delivered by a repair shop employee. Both of my parents were short, so the driver's seat was normally never moved. The delivery man was tall and had been unable to operate the vehicle with the seat pushed forward in its usual position. After he delivered our car, he forgot to return the seat to its original position.

Mother entered the car, preparing to drive to town and pick up my father from work. Her feet could not reach the gas, brake or clutch pedals, and she did not have the physical strength it took to alter the position of the driver's seat.

She stomped back into the house in a fury, grabbed the telephone and dialed the mechanic's shop. The person on the other end of the line was totally mystified when she blurted, "Your man pushed my seat back, and I want you to send him out here immediately to put it back in place!" In answer to a question, she continued, "My seat! My seat! He pushed it back! I want him to come fix it!"

My grandmother and I stood nearby in awe of my normally tranquil mother. We were both suppressing laughter, because my mother had not identified herself nor had there been any mention of a car.

⁂

Any form of lawn work, landscaping or gardening offered the worker a great deal of physical exercise. There were no power tools with which to do the job, so lawn mowers were pushed purely by muscle power. Stiff hand clippers were used for edging, and large hedge clippers were also operated by the strength of the user. Shovels, hoes and rakes were used to do jobs handled easily by power tools today.

Every household owned a wheelbarrow and used it with great regularity. Maintaining a pretty yard was a lengthy process, generating a lot of honest sweat and burning more calories than one would likely burn during a gym workout.

Walking was not done as a form of exercise but as a way to reach one's destination. Many families of the '30s had neither car nor money for buses. When I accompanied my relatives into the downtown area, once we located a parallel parking spot, we left the car and walked all over town from there.

If we rode a bus to town, we covered a lot of blocks on foot prior to returning to our bus stop for the return trip. In the meantime, we were able to do some serious window shopping along our route.

These trips were considered enjoyable, and people captured by the sidewalk photographers of that day were usually strolling rather than taking fast strides as if they were stressed to make a deadline. Such men, carrying a camera and snapping shots of passing pedestrians, were plentiful on San Antonio's downtown streets. People were handed a receipt, with which they could later order copies of the developed picture.

Donna Hooks Fletcher married the Rebel Private's son Clyde. She later became a divorced gringo pioneer in the Rio Grande Valley.

The prettiest girl in Beaumont: my mother in front of her family's home. I've tried to figure if she has a goat in front of her—her brother raised all kinds of critters.

My family's Ford V-8. This was the car we had at the beginning of WW II. Like others we were stuck with it all through the war and for a year or so later as car manufacturers converted factories to the production of war materiel.

Me, 1932. Doctors then considered a fat baby a healthy one. I aimed to please.

Playing with Jimmy Tom, the neighbor boy who spoke in a special way. I had no trouble understanding him, though no one else could. This was taken after a rare San Antonio snowstorm.

Betty Brent Schaeffler, who was the reason my mother made me "Catholic sandwiches" on Fridays.

The "home of my heart"—our ranch home on Karankawa Bay. It was finished in 1861 and built of cyprus timbers barged from Florida. I'm standing by the front door. A few years ago, the new owner had the house bulldozed to build his wife "something more modern."

My class at Highland Park Elementary; I was the head something-or-other in the dark costume (second row, fourth from right). Everyone is ducking their head or squinting because photographers of that day made you face the bright sunlight.

My beloved college roommate and lifelong friend Blanche Levy of Beaumont. I learned from knowing her that anti-semitism was alive and well on the University of Houston campus when the sororities that clamored for me to join ignored her.

L to R: "Nannan" and "Aunt Sister," my maternal grandmother, Lavinia Parker Haynes, and aunt, Norine Haynes Land. Nannan hated the way her dentures made her look, so most of the snapshots we had were eventually hunted down and defaced by the little lady.

Sometimes, our family took advantage of this custom. I still enjoy old pictures of my father and his brother deep in conversation and wearing the old-style three-piece business suits. I see myself holding my grandmother's hand and looking back over my shoulder at some fascinating sight. Since that photo shows just the two of us, I know that we had taken a bus downtown. Grandmother, like most of the women of her generation, did not drive.

When I visited a friend who lived in another neighborhood, I normally chose to walk. Unless there was some major thoroughfare that had to be crossed, that plan met with my parents' approval. Certainly, today's world, with its freeways and fast cars, offers a danger that my age never knew.

World War II gave my classmates and me a great deal of experience in walking around town as we fulfilled our patriotic duty by collecting scrap metal. There were times when San Antonio schools were dismissed for a half-day while children pulling their red Radio Flyer wagons canvassed neighborhoods for donations. Each neighborhood family had been alerted to the drive, so in most cases our house-to-house quest was successful.

When a child's wagon was totally filled, it was pulled back to the school campus and the contents added to a huge scrap pile on the lawn. Then the young scrap-metal hunter would once again go on his or her quest.

Girl and Boy Scout organizations conducted their own scrap drives, so we received much experience in covering portions of our city on foot. The war years also introduced a new style of shoe to women and girls. Huaraches, traditional Mexican footwear, turned into a national US fashion-craze.

Occasionally, members of my Girl Scout troop gave our huaraches a workout by marching in parades. The event I remember the clearest was the year we were invited to join the Battle of Flowers Parade during San Antonio's famous Fiesta Week.

Our family had always gone downtown to watch this parade from the bleachers on Alamo Plaza and marveled at the beautiful floral arrangements. Our scout leader, Mrs. X, asked us to bring fresh flowers to carry as we marched. When Mother learned that I was going to march in the parade, she began to design a large floral wreath that I could carry.

She finished her work of art on the morning of our afternoon appearance, and it was obvious she had really outdone herself. I felt proud as I visualized myself carrying her spectacular creation.

Just as the parade was about to start, Mrs. X walked back to where I stood and snatched the wreath out of my hands as she mumbled something about it being too pretty to be in the back of our group. I was standing at the end of a line where it could have been easily viewed by onlookers as we passed. By the time I realized I had been wreath-napped, Mrs. X had disappeared up front, and the signal to begin marching was given. What had happened was Mrs. X had placed her own daughter, who had not been provided with a floral arrangement, in the front line of marchers. Confronted with the fact that she had not done what she had asked all troop mothers to do, she looked around to find the prettiest arrangement in sight for Carol Joy to carry. Once she spied mine, she grabbed it and ran before I could object.

What Mrs. X did not bargain for was my mother being in the crowd of onlookers. Mother had been a constant helper for Mrs. X in all of our scout activities up until this parade. She also was aware of Mrs. X's ego and proclivities. When Mother recognized her wreath advancing down the street in the arms of Carol Joy, she knew exactly what had happened. She was furious and, after the parade, let Mrs. X know that she had worked long and hard creating a fresh floral wreath to be carried by *her* daughter and not the daughter of anyone else. Of course, her angry words were spoken after the fact.

Mrs. X and her daughter were the two people I can identify who were extremely rotund in an era where everyone else was slim and trim. Carol Joy was an absolute replica of her mother, who often announced to our troop, "I was pretty and slim when I was young and not fat like Carol Joy." We all cringed each time we heard her say this, for Carol Joy was a sweet girl who did not need to be humiliated by hearing this refrain over and over.

Mrs. X also told us tales about being on her way to stardom as an opera singer when, alas, she met and married Mr. X when she was far too young. She was called "Frenchie" by the World War I soldiers, she informed us, because they loved to hear her sing the French national anthem.

While other troops were mastering folk tunes and rounds, our troop members had to memorize the French lyrics of this anthem. Mrs. X frequently had us stand and perform "La Marseillaise" at Scout events or when our troop had visitors. None of us doubted this musical debacle was planned so that our leader's voice could be heard by everyone within earshot.

Mrs. X did have a good strong voice. I can only hope that no true citizen of France ever got close enough to hear verse after verse of that anthem rendered by a sea of green-clad young singers with thick Texas accents.

Just as marching in parades exercised our bodies, singing in French gave our brains and vocal chords a workout. In reminiscing about our rather unique Girl Scout troop meetings, I cannot help thinking of the old saying, "It ain't over till the fat lady sings."

CHAPTER TEN

EAST TEXAS WOMEN WHO KEPT
A FAMILY SECRET

Along with diapers and receiving blankets, each newborn child should receive a genealogical syllabus listing major traumatic events in the lives of those relatives who will serve as their elders.

I addressed a lot of women as "aunt" when I was young. Most of them were great-aunts; others were more distant relatives who were old enough to accept this catch-all term, and a few were simply friends of the family. Perhaps the most confusing moniker I used was directed at my mother's elder sister Norine. I called her "Aunt Sister."

Every good cook knows when you add an extra ingredient to a dish being prepared, and then stir the pot, a decidedly different taste can be achieved. Using that analogy, both actions and interactions of individuals one or two generations before my time kept ancient emotions, old animosities and a bitter secret stirred to a point where my life was affected by events of which I was totally unaware.

It took years of maturity for me to appreciate the role played by a number of strong East Texas women to whom I was somehow related. These intrepid women entered my father's life at different times and dramatically played a variety of roles in an ongoing saga. Each was resolute and displayed courage, determination and a will of iron.

Because of their place in, or connection to, the Fletcher family, these women eventually learned a family secret that created a rift so wide that it took a number of other powerful women, in distant locations and with differing lifestyles, to put the family back together. These women acted as an emotional support system for my father and the keeper of the secret.

Beaumont, Texas, when I was a small child, was the place where our family went to wear black, hug others wearing black and cry. It was sitting in a funeral home and then a slow drive in a big, black limousine that ended at Magnolia Cemetery. After leaving the cemetery, it was being the only child in someone's musty parlor while adults with somber expressions visited one another.

I knew that both my parents grew up in this town and most of their relatives still lived here. Little did I realize how much the actions of one of them would affect my life.

⊰❊⊱

If a writer were limited to the use of only one adjective to describe my great-aunt-by-marriage Gladys Fletcher, the choice would have to be "elegant." Tall and stately, she married into a family of short women.

A classic hooked nose, which might send a woman of today in search of a plastic surgeon, only added to Gladys's individuality and regal stance. A Native American friend insisted that such a nose bespoke Indian ancestry. Whether or not that was true, Gladys knew it did not detract one iota from her beauty.

When Gladys Fletcher, with her majestic posture, swept into a room filled with the cream of East Texas society matrons, all eyes were focused on her. A native of Mobile, Alabama, she later moved with her family to Opelousas, Louisiana.

I'm not sure where Gladys met my great-uncle Emmett, but the records show that Emmett Fletcher married Gladys Randall in New Orleans July 17, 1912. She was 28, and he was 43.

Emmett had been married before—for just a few minutes, it seems. He could not have been easy to live with, but he and Gladys adored one another. With her Alabama accent, she pronounced his name, "Ah-yum-mat."

Gladys's best friend throughout her life in Beaumont was my tiny but equally enchanting great-aunt Vallie Fletcher. It was through Gladys's sheer determination and intervention over a number of years that Vallie finally began to speak to her older brother, Emmett, again.

In my great-uncle's defense, it must have been difficult growing up as the eldest son of a man thought, written and spoken about as being one of the world's most perfect individuals. Bill Fletcher, his father, was so beloved by those who knew him that Emmett must have often suffered by comparison.

Bill, the Rebel Private, believed in moderation in all things, and Emmett was not one to be moderate. Bill did not trust preachers or politicians. Inevitably, then, and not being particularly religious, Emmett turned to politics and served the City of Beaumont as both alderman and mayor for several terms. Bill cared nothing about joining clubs or social standing. Emmett was a joiner and liked to hob-nob with the rich and famous.

During my childhood, I was allowed to visit Uncle Emmett and Aunt Gladys whenever invited. Staying with them in Beaumont, or at their country home, Twin Lakes, near Woodville, was always a delight.

Josephine, who lived with them and served as their housekeeper throughout their years together, would check the bedroom where I lay asleep each morning. The minute I opened my eyes, she brought me a tray filled with glorious breakfast delicacies. I had never before been pampered by breakfast in bed while enjoying excellent health.

As a child, I never questioned the fact that my great-uncle's visits to us meant having his chauffeur park the limousine in front of our San Antonio home. He, or he and Gladys, would remain in the car while my mother, grandmother and I went out and stood on the curb to visit. My father remained inside the house. If Aunt Gladys came to San Antonio alone, she joined our family inside for a visit.

My grandfather, Harvey Davis Fletcher, was two years younger than his brother Emmett. Like many gentlemen of Beaumont, he enjoyed a professional shave every morning. A rusty razor in the hands of his barber caused the up-to-then healthy Harvey's sudden death of blood poisoning at age 50.

Foolishly, Harvey had made no will to protect his estate. An important bequest had been left by his father, Bill Fletcher, for Harvey to administer until the elder Bill's grandson and namesake, Bill Fletcher II, came of age and could begin the ranching plans the two Bills had made together.

My father, Bill II, was the only one of the old Rebel Private's sons or grandsons to have inherited his love for ranching and understanding of agricultural pursuits. From the time my father could walk, he stayed by his grandfather's side as much as possible and became a sponge, soaking up lessons and stories his grandfather passed on. Throughout his childhood and teens, young Bill developed the inclination and work ethic to devote his life to caring for the land and animals his grandfather had acquired throughout East Texas.

Only two of Bill and Julian Long Fletcher's five children, Harvey and Marion, had children of their own. Like all four of the old Rebel's sons, two of his three grandsons valued social life and indoor luxury and were not too keen about making the effort necessary to learn how to work on a ranch. So, prior to Bill Fletcher's death, and with clear understanding of the entire Fletcher family, he and Bill II rode many a mile horseback and made plans for the future. Together, they decided where Bill II would attend college and the courses he should pursue in order for him to later maintain Park Farm and other East Texas lands he would one day partially own and over which he would serve as ranching administrator for the extended family.

The old Rebel did not want his Neches River home, the 2,658-acre Park Farm, cut up and sold after his death.

Young Bill majored in animal husbandry at Texas A & M after his grandfather's death. Unfortunately, he was prevented from putting the rest of their joint plans into action.

My father would have been about six months shy of turning 21 at the time of his father Harvey's death. He understood financial matters, so with the help of a lawyer, he could have handled the estate himself.

It probably seemed natural, however, for Harvey's older brother Emmett to step in and take over management of financial affairs for Harvey's widow temporarily. Indeed, he made sure that my grandmother Florence signed a large number of blank checks so that he could "take care of any outstanding debts." Most of these were minor and involved paying local tradesmen.

After the cleaner, the grocer, the butcher and others were reimbursed, Emmett "took care of things" in a most creative fashion. He loved to gamble in private card games with cronies who were also prominent in Beaumont. As the games progressed, most of the players became well lubricated and rather careless with their bets. Emmett put aside a certain amount for my grandmother and Nick, my father's younger brother, and told Grandmother, "Don't worry about Bill. He can take care of himself."

No one bothered to tell young Bill what was going on.

Emmett may have experienced jealousy and resentment over his father's love for his young namesake. Aunt Vallie always told stories enumerating the many ways that the two Bills were just alike. She felt that no one, with the exception of her mother, had been as close to her father as Bill II.

After Harvey's death, my grandmother took Nick and moved temporarily to Colorado, where Nick was treated for tuberculosis. Grandmother always denied that he had TB because of what she considered the social stigma of that disease. She remained most secretive about their Colorado venture and always insisted the treatment Nick received was for pneumonia.

Aunt Vallie, who had undergone treatment for tuberculosis in the same sanitarium, called a spade a spade and told my parents the truth. Nick did not learn the truth himself until x-rays were taken while he was in the service during World War II. An army physician showed him an x-ray of his TB scar.

In the meantime, when either my father or Aunt Vallie quizzed my grandmother about Harvey's estate and a potential date of settlement, she gave a series of extremely vague answers. This went on for years, while both cash and real estate, designated as my father's inheritance and for which he had been made responsible for keeping intact for the extended Fletcher family, quietly disappeared.

My parents married June 12, 1922, in the Methodist Church parlor in Beaumont. Neither the bride nor groom had any money, so "the prettiest girl in Beaumont" married without a traditional wedding gown or any of the usual bridal attire. No announcements, invitations, music or flowers were involved. Both mothers showed up at the last minute for the ceremony. Each had gathered a few friends and relatives to bring along, but no planned reception was held. The bride received an inexpensive wedding band as she married into a family whose women were adorned with valuable jewelry.

Since Bill II had been told he would not receive his inheritance "until the estate is settled," he put off his ranching plans and took a job with the Uvalde Rock Asphalt Company. After their wedding, he and my mother moved to Houston and rented the lower portion of a duplex at 1111 Leland.

Within the year, Dad was transferred to San Antonio, where his old nurse, Polly Fairbanks, owned a one-story duplex. Miraculously, one side had just become available for rent. She lived in the other side, so my parents became neighbors of the nurse who had made sure Dad would never become a cripple.

My grandmother continued her subterfuge for years when she was pressed for an answer as to when the estate would be settled.

When Mother and Dad began looking for a home to buy, Grandmother and Nick decided to come live with them in San Antonio. An agreement made among the future housemates was for Grandmother to pay half of each house payment and my parents the other half.

The Highland Park area in San Antonio was then in development, and they all liked the bungalow at 736 Kayton Avenue. Nick would occupy the front bedroom, Grandmother the back bedroom and my parents the bedroom on the east side of the house.

After the first few months of living together, Grandmother informed Mother that she would not be putting in her part of the house payment anymore. So, my father took over the support of his mother and younger brother. Though my grandmother made a show of having no money, Nick was voted "the best-dressed male student at Brackenridge High School." That was quite a title to hold during the Depression.

After graduation from high school, Nick attended John Tarleton Agricultural College (now Tarleton State University) in Stephenville. When he finished there, he returned to San Antonio to live with my parents, who expected him to start job-hunting. Instead, he showed no desire to apply for a job. My father loved him dearly but could not understand why he seemed to have no ambition. Nick slept late, went out to play tennis most days and appeared totally content with the status quo.

At one point, Nick came home and announced that he had taken a job as a car salesman. But, he told my grandmother, to do this job right he would have to own a car himself. Money magically materialized from Grandmother to purchase a new Buick. Once the car was in our driveway, Nick bid the salesman's job farewell because it interfered with his time on the tennis court.

Mother would laugh when she remembered my grandmother's constant consternation over an impending visit from Aunt Vallie or Aunt Lulu. Like my father, they did not understand why an able-bodied young man did not seek employment. So, my grandmother would awaken Nick, who was in the habit of sleeping very late, tell him to get up, get dressed and pretend that he was going to work.

191

It was Aunt Vallie who finally backed my grandmother into a corner and demanded to know what had happened to her brother's estate. Grandmother blurted out, "It's all gone! Emmett told me just to take care of myself and Nick. Bill can take care of himself."

Having been a witness to the many conversations her father had held with his grandson, Aunt Vallie was infuriated. Dad went into a depression, realizing his ranching plans could not be financed, Grandmother became secretive and defensive once more, and Mother had to deal with each of them and their conflicting emotions while trying to keep the household on an even keel. Nick had been too young when most of this transpired to understand the significance of the lengthy deception.

Aunt Vallie caught the next train for Beaumont and, upon arrival, confronted her eldest brother. She demanded an explanation as to why he had interfered with their father's carefully made plans and the funds he had left to finance them. She was horrified to learn that farmlands the old Rebel Private had intended for Bill II and the Fletcher family to keep had been sold off in sections. Other funds were simply unaccounted for. The written instructions she had personally watched her father draw up had disappeared.

No one ever knew everything that was said during Vallie's meeting with Emmett. She later reported reminding him that the old Rebel had provided well for all of his children, and that his desires should have been honored where his grandson was concerned. She also accused him of taking the actions he had because of long-held jealousy of his nephew.

For years, she would have nothing whatsoever to do with her oldest brother. My father never spoke to his uncle again, unless it was in the form of a nod at a family funeral. He also avoided going to Beaumont, where this state of affairs was carefully kept under wraps.

This all occurred prior to my birth, and I did not learn the details from Aunt Vallie and my mother until I was an adult. I wondered why Dad had not been more aggressive in pursuing legal action, but assumed it was the result of his own mother's foolish decisions and duplicity in the cover-up.

I realized as a child that our family lived much more modestly than my paternal relatives, but children accept such things without question; and I was perfectly content with our neighborhood. To his credit, my father never made a single unkind statement about his uncle Emmett within my hearing.

My mother later told me that one of the most difficult things for my father to accept were remarks made by some of his old Beaumont friends. He was often kidded by individuals who assumed our family was living way below our means because Dad was tight with money. No one was more generous than my father.

Strangely enough, Dad remained the source of solace and stability to whom the Beaumont Fletchers ran during any emergency or crisis. He was the one who, with a cool head and calm demeanor, took care of unexpected crises and distraught individuals while everyone else was falling apart.

Since Nick had been tremendously pampered by his mother, based on what she perceived as his frail state of health, my father served as a substitute parent to his younger brother and tried to guide him in finding employment in a suitable field. Dad remembered that Nick had enjoyed being a member of the ROTC in high school and when he served as first lieutenant in the Videttes Corps ROTC at John Tarleton Agricultural College from 1927 to 1929. So, my father suggested that he look into the Civilian Conservation Corps. Nick loved anything military, and this government program was designed to put Depression-era young men to work building roads and other public facilities. Members of the CCC wore uniforms and lived in army-style camps.

Nick followed his brother's advice, enlisted in the CCC and soon found that being away from his mother was a liberating experience. Grandmother tended to hover around him and warn him against doing almost everything of a physical nature.

He was soon sent to Oregon, where being on his own with responsibilities to fulfill allowed his delayed maturity to surface.

When Nick left our home, I was heartbroken. He had been more like an older brother than an uncle. Seated next to him during family meals, I enjoyed his constant attention and teasing.

When Christmas came around, Nick traditionally gave me a duplicate of whatever he gave his girlfriend of the moment. This amused the rest of the family and caused me to feel quite grown up as I opened packages containing beaded evening bags or sterling silver toiletry sets.

Probably Nick's most memorable gift to me, at age eight, was a matched set of luggage. I had no plans for a trip, but opening and closing those luxurious suitcases allowed me to take many an imaginary journey.

Nick was eventually transferred back to Texas, where he met and fell in love with a young woman named Ima Bean. Her childhood could not have been more different than his. She had learned supreme self-confidence during a very free and relaxed rural life in which she and her siblings were able to jump into the Angelina River whenever the mood struck. Nick had been raised, joined at the hip to his mother, in a luxurious city home. He was constantly encouraged to stay indoors and keep his feet dry so he would not succumb to some disastrous physical malady.

When Nick and Ima met, he was stationed near Woodville, where she taught second grade. He left the CCC and joined the regular army, with the rank of captain, at the beginning of World War II. An assignment to the Intelligence Corps provided him with a job he loved and at which he excelled.

Nick and Ima married in Newton on February 19, 1942, but our family had to remain in San Antonio thanks to a set of old tires and wartime gas rationing. Rubber and petroleum products went to war alongside our servicemen, so they were unavailable, or at the very least extremely scarce, for members of the civilian population.

From his marriage, Nick gained the love and support of an East Texas woman of great strength who would be a source of encouragement rather than the voice of caution and dire prophecy with which he had been raised. He eventually entered the retail field and opened Fletcher's Gift Shop in the Pines. Seeing Nick happy and successful, my father was able to relax and release the tremendous sense of responsibility for his brother's welfare he had carried for so long.

James Monroe Long, a hard-working entrepreneur from Georgia and pioneer Beaumont lumberman, left behind a good deal of money and a spoiled-rotten daughter called Lulu (pronounced Lou-lah). James was my great-grandmother Julian Long Fletcher's brother and my great-grandfather's business partner when he first entered the lumber business in Beaumont.

Lulu's five older siblings, as well as her many relatives in the Fletcher, Long, Carroll and Keith families, inherited the job of looking after Lulu after James died in 1873 when she was just a year old. This large clan of solicitous relatives contributed so much love that they lit a flame of self-realization that eventually blazed out of control. Gradually, friends and relatives alike learned to beat a hasty retreat when they saw Lulu headed in their direction.

Haughty and demanding as an adult, Lulu hired a companion to do her bidding at home and when she traveled. Tall, physically attractive and always impeccably attired, she surrounded herself with fine paintings and works of sculpture wherever she lived.

Friends and family members were not surprised that she never married; they found it impossible to visualize a man who could be attracted to someone so blatantly outspoken and assured of her own superiority.

My father was once ordered by his overbearing relative to drive her and her salaried companion from Beaumont to Houston. Bill was a young teen at the time. Since his grandfather owned one of Beaumont's first horseless carriages, he had learned to drive early when a driver's license was not a necessity.

Automobiles were still a rarity owned by wealthy individuals, and roads were sand, shell or dirt in dry weather; muddy, rutted and often impassible if it had recently rained.

Young Bill's parents should have taken Lulu's self-involvement into consideration before allowing their son to leave Beaumont with her. Obviously, they mistakenly assumed she would act like a responsible adult.

The Official Log Book For Texas, 1914-1915, was published by the Bexar County Highway League in San Antonio in an effort to give aid and solace to travelers who were brave enough to leave their horse at home and attempt to negotiate undependable, and sometimes non-existent, roads in an effort to reach a specific location. Only a thousand copies were printed, so its buyers made up a lucky group of individuals with access to a confusing list of step-by-step directions to follow while traveling between various Texas towns.

There were no instructions guiding a driver from Beaumont to Houston, so Bill was forced to read the "Houston to Beaumont" route and proceed in reverse from finish to start.

The writer of this log book was rather geographically confused when he wrote that Beaumont "is a thriving city of 26,000 located in southwest Texas next to the Louisiana border." Several other statements place the town in southwest Texas. Another sentence proclaims, "Good roads in East Texas are a rarity...but Beaumont boasts of excellent shell and macadam roads and travel by automobile and vehicle is a pleasure within the county limits. This however is not true of neighboring counties where most roads are in a deplorable condition."

The directions my father found in the log book were as follows:

Houston to Beaumont:

Start at Hawkins-Haiff Co. garage, Main and Dallas, north on Main to Texas

Right on Texas two blocks, turn left on San Jacinto

Cross Buffalo Bayou Bridge onto Willow St.

Follow brick pavement past S.P. freight house and turn left on McKee Ave.

Go two blocks, turn right on Odin Ave. Follow brick pavement within one block of end

2.6 Turn left on gravel street, turn right at two story grocery store, follow Shell road across railroad track

6.4 Cross Houston Belt and Terminal R.R.

7.7 East Houston, turn right across R.R., then left

10.4 Green's Bayou St. bridge

13.6 FAUNA station

18.0 SHELDON station

19.5 San Jacinto River bridge

21.5 Cross roads, take left hand road, right hand goes to Lynchburg

23.4 Take right hand, cross bridge, old church on left

23.8 Turn right, drug store on left hand corner, go one block, turn left, keep Straight to the railroad track

24.1 Turn right, following shell road on right hand side of railroad

25.1 Leave this shell road on to the dirt road

29.6 Enter into woods

30.3 Cross old bridge on new graded road, very rough

31.3 Valley switch on left

35.1 Keep center road on right side of railroad

35.3 STILSON station on left

35.4 Stilson Hotel

35.6 Turn left into sandy road

35.9 Turn right along railroad track

38.0 Turn left, then right

38.6 Turn left, old church on right hand side of road

38.8 DAYTON depot, turn right, go one block, turn left and cross railroad tracks, then right along railroad into very sandy road

39.8 Keep right hand road along railroad

40.2 Cross steel bridge, keep right hand road

41.0 You will enter Dayton flats and roads are very bad in wet weather

42.0 Cross wooden bridge

42.3 Cross wooden bridge

43.0 Turn right and cross two wooden bridges

43.8 Turn right and under railroad track, turn left

43.9 Turn right and follow the road to ferry

44.0 Trinity River, ferry across, pay ferryman 50 cents

44.2 Cross two railroad switches, road very sandy

44.5 Keep straight road

44.8 Turn left, cross railroad track, go one block, turn right at school house on left hand corner

45.4 Liberty County Court House, keep straight road

45.5 Take the center road to left, passing jail on left (painted red at present time)

45.6 Turn right on new graded road, red clay

46.2 Keep straight road

47.3 Cross steel bridge

48.7 Ames Switch on right, road follows alongside of railroad track

50.3 Turn right and cross railroad, turn left, follow graded road which is the new county road, but on account of bridge being out on this road, instead of crossing track keep left hand road alongside railroad track.

53.4 RAYWOOD station on right, keep straight road

56.1 Turn right, cross railroad track, follow graded road

56.4 Turn left and follow grade

58.1 Turn left

58.3 Turn right and cross steel bridge

58.4 Turn right, Devers hotel on right hand corner, go one block and turn left, church on left hand corner of second block, enter woods at this point, yellow graded road through woods which is very rough and has many turns

62.1 Turn left and rail fence on right

62.5 Leave the woods

68.9 Turn left

69.3 Turn right

69.7 Turn left

70.0 Turn right and follow graded road, several turns

71.4 Turn right, NOME station depot on left, keep straight road right hand side of track, road sandy but good

72.4 Turn left, cross railroad track, turn right

76.1 Cross wooden bridge over canal

76.8 Strike shell road, very good

76.9 CHINA station

77.1 Turn right, cross railroad, turn left and follow shell road

81.2 PINE ISLAND station

86.1 Turn left across railroad track, GULF PIPELINE station on right

86.7 Turn left, school house on left hand side

91.9 Santa Fe station, cross railroad track
92.8 Turn right, go one block

The trip was undertaken at a time when automobile tires were very thin and, with the horrendous road conditions, often did not survive a trip. As Bill was reading the book of directions in a hind-part-before manner, he was horrified to realize that one of the tires on Lulu's car had gone flat.

Trying to use the car-jack to fix the flat, he found that the weight of Lulu's extremely obese companion was making it impossible to pump up the tire. When he asked the ladies to please get out of the car, however, his request was met with a howl of protest from his horrified cousin.

"Certainly not! Ladies do not get out of cars on roads like these. Please hurry up and fix the tire so we can get on with our trip," was her adamant reply.

There were no other cars on the road in that location and no such thing as a service station. Then, while Bill was struggling with the jack, to no avail, another car came into view. By the time the driver reached their car, he had assessed the situation. He stopped to help Bill and immediately stuck his head into the car and shouted, "You women get out of this car. It can't be fixed until you do."

The women obeyed his command, but Lulu was seething. How dare that man tell her what to do?

The kind stranger helped Bill change the tire, then everyone got back into their cars and continued their journey.

In Houston, Lulu Long checked her party into a hotel for the night. Exhausted by the day's events, Bill slept a little late the next morning. After he dressed and went downstairs, he was more than ready for a hearty breakfast.

Bill did not see his cousin or her companion in the lobby of the hotel. He was unable to locate them in the dining room or their hotel rooms. Asking the desk clerk if he knew where they were, he was informed that they had checked out and left about an hour before. The desk clerk added that Miss Long had not paid for his room.

Bill had no money with him, since his expenses were to have been paid by Lulu. He realized that this was her retribution for what she considered the indignity of being ordered out of her car. Evidently, she had found a driver for hire and gone about her business, abandoning him in a strange city where he had no friends or relatives. To make matters worse, he was in debt to the hotel management.

Puzzled over what action he should take, he remembered overhearing a conversation about a Beaumont acquaintance who had moved to Houston and taken a job at a bank. Hoping that he remembered the bank's name correctly, he asked the desk clerk for directions.

Promising to return with the money owed, Bill left the hotel and walked in the direction indicated by the clerk. As he tried to locate the bank, he kept a fervent hope that the family friend was still an employee. Luck was with him. He found both the bank and the friend, and received a loan to pay his hotel bill and buy a train ticket back to Beaumont.

Once he arrived in Beaumont, Bill wanted nothing more to do with his thoughtless relative. This was the case for many years, but he finally relented and stopped leaving family gatherings when Lulu entered.

※

During my childhood, Aunt Lulu (a name I was taught to call her, though she was actually a cousin several times removed) was a constant presence in our home. After my parents moved to San Antonio, she followed and moved into a luxurious residence hotel. Later, she purchased a home in what was then called "a very ritzy neighborhood."

Aunt Lulu turned to the much-younger cousin she had once abandoned for advice on a large assortment of subjects. Possibly to repay him for all his help, she often took our family and Aunt Vallie to dinners at noon at San Antonio's most elegant restaurants. My favorite was the Anacacho Room at the St. Anthony Hotel. Several times, she hosted birthday luncheons for me there with an orchestra that was always ready to play whatever tunes my school friends and I might request.

It was not unusual for Lulu to embarrass any group she was with by her bizarre and demanding behavior. While dining with her at the St. Anthony one Sunday, she suddenly screamed out, "Oh! Take it away! Take it away! Take it away!"

The other diners, and certainly our totally innocent waiter, had no clue what had caused her to become so upset. The waiter had just placed her order in front of her and was about to leave the table prior to her outburst.

It turned out that the food on her plate did not look exactly as she had pictured it when ordering. Totally oblivious that she was creating a scene and humiliating the waiter, she reacted in her usual inconsiderate manner.

Aunt Lulu loved the gourmet food served at the Junior League tearoom called The Bright Shawl. The atmosphere was a little too trendy for my father, who preferred meals that were simple and menus more suited to the masculine palate. He accompanied her whenever she asked, but would usually leave mumbling something like "Who on earth would broil a perfectly good grapefruit?"

Lulu Long continued to enjoy an active social life in Beaumont even after her move to Central Texas. East Texas friends let her know about soirees in advance, so she would travel by train and be met at the Beaumont station. In the midst of some of these gatherings, Lulu ran into Emmett Fletcher.

No woman of that era could express scorn and disdain as skillfully as our unique relative. Once she learned of Emmett's mishandling of the Rebel Private's carefully made plans, and the disappearance of my father's inheritance, many Beaumont socialites were astounded by the verbal assaults launched at their mayor with utmost contempt by his first cousin. True to her nature, Lulu offered no explanation to listeners. But then, it's quite possible that none who overheard her remarks were brave enough to approach her and inquire as to the basis for her animosity.

Two years younger than her first cousin Lulu, my great-aunt Vallie Fletcher was totally opposite in nature. Aunt Vallie was petite, beautiful, humble and considerate of everyone. People who met her often inquired why she had never married.

The truth was she had been engaged to a physician who was about to finish his residency in New Orleans. In going about his duties, he contacted pneumonia and died prior to their planned wedding. Vallie and her suitor had been profoundly in love, so after his death she simply never found anyone who could compete with his memory. Thoughts of the young doctor never left her, and at times, she seemed pensive and far away in another world, perhaps lost in memories.

In the manner of unmarried women of her day, she continued to live at home with her parents until after their deaths. Because she considered my father to be exactly like her own father, she later followed my parents to San Antonio and stayed to make that city her home.

Aunt Vallie had a ready sense of humor and, unlike many in her generation, the courage to act extemporaneously. Embarrassed by Lulu on many social occasions, she would just laugh, say, "Oh, Lulu, for goodness sake," and shrug off whatever social atrocity her cousin had just committed.

Vallie Fletcher was blessed with an ability to paint, which she expanded upon by traveling to Europe and studying art with some dynamic Parisian art teachers. After the death of her fiance, art became her healer and canvas the surface onto which she poured her distress and sorrow.

When Vallie was still young, she was invited to give showings in New York City, Boston and other areas that were considered bastions of culture. As she traveled and presented her work, she realized that she was far more interested in the process of painting than she was in financial success and acclaim in commercial areas of the art world. Like her father, the Rebel Private, she was generous to a fault, and gave most of her paintings away to family and friends after having them framed.

Because of her quiet beauty, gentle nature and sweet disposition, Vallie was admired by all who knew her. I was one of several children named for her in later years. Actually, we were named for her nickname. The only daughter of William and Julian Fletcher was born on February 14, 1874, and promptly named Valentine. She was so small that the name "Vallie" was soon substituted as a diminutive.

After my great-aunt's move to San Antonio, she derived a great deal of joy from painting scenes of the Texas Hill Country. My mother, who served as her driver, would load the car with a picnic lunch, a thermos of lemonade and a stack of magazines to which she subscribed. Once Aunt Vallie found her desired vista, she would place her canvas, sketch her subject and later mix oil colors on her palette. Mother sat in a folding chair next to a stack of *Ladies Home Journal, McCalls, Life, Time, Colliers* and *The Saturday Evening Post*. The two women would repeat this routine each day until the painting was completed.

Though my aunt was well-known for landscapes and still life paintings, my favorites have always been the portraits of lovely women she executed so well. Above my desk hangs a portrait that was painted by one of Aunt Vallie's art instructors. He asked if he could paint her, and as she sat quietly for him wearing a simple brown dress and a long double strand of pearls, her thoughts must have turned toward the young man she had loved so completely.

I never wonder what she was thinking about as I pause and look up at that moment in time when she was the model instead of the artist. I saw that same wistful expression often when I was young. Her painting teacher so perfectly captured the moment when she tuned out reality and sent her thoughts to find the young doctor.

⧫

Noteworthy birthdays ran in our family. Sallie Aleen Haynes, my mother, was born April 1, 1900. Naturally, throughout her life she was teased about being an April Fool.

Just as visits to East Texas showed my father's relatives were financially blessed, most everyone in my mother's family appeared to be struggling to make ends meet. Aleen's father, most of her uncles and her grandfather were all doctors, so throughout her life she retained an abundant interest in the field of medicine. This was a time when only a minority of the men who called themselves doctors had actually received any formal training. My grandfather earned two separate degrees from the Kentucky School of Medicine in Louisville.

Today, we would say that his degrees were in general medicine and surgery. Thomas Benjamin Haynes earned his first degree in "Chemistry and Microscopy" on June 20, 1889. On June 17, 1890, he was awarded a degree in "Operations and Bandaging."

Livinia Parker Haynes, Aleen's mother, was a small fireball who had an attribute usually found only in works of romantic fiction—blazing turquoise-blue eyes. The daughter of Judge R. L. Parker, who founded Center and for whom the historic courthouse with the secret staircase was built, met Dr. Ben Haynes of Jasper when he came to her little town for a visit. The young doctor's father, Dr. Jeptha Phelps Haynes, was a well-known physician in Jasper and a 1870 graduate of Tulane when it was called Universitas Republicae Louisianae, the Latin version of University of the State of Louisiana.

The meeting resulted in the love-at-first-sight scenario of legends. However, their sudden romance was complicated by the fact they were both engaged to others at the time. Nevertheless, a short time and two broken engagements later, they were married.

Their first home was in Colmesneil, where Dr. Haynes began his medical practice. Several years later, he moved his practice and his family to Beaumont.

"Livie" Haynes sometimes left their children with the household help and accompanied her husband on medical visits he knew would be difficult. Though she acted as a physician's assistant to the best of her ability, her true calling was to perform at social events and sometimes teach elocution at home.

In that day, when families and friends provided their own entertainment, reciting long rhyming poems that related a story was the popular fashion. These sagas were quite dramatic and most often ended sadly. A series of rehearsed hand gestures always accompanied recitations of these memorized narratives. Ladies who were adept at performing them were extremely valued within society, so many socially prominent young women came to Livie for elocution lessons.

The Haynes household was often filled with extended family members performing on various musical instruments—musical talent was an attribute my mother and her two older siblings shared. An unusual circumstance occurred, however, that changed the life of each member of that family and prevented Aleen from receiving a musical education.

One day, her three-year-old younger sister joined the family at the dinner table and just continued to sit and look at her food.

"Pick up your spoon and eat, honey," her father instructed.

"I can't," Ella Victoria responded.

Their father realized soon enough that Ella V's arms were paralyzed. Later that evening, she began to run a high fever and could not be awakened. As her worried parents watched over her, she was hit by severe and frequent seizures throughout the night.

Dr. Haynes was totally puzzled by Ella V's combination of symptoms. Though the fever abated and the paralysis proved to be temporary, the seizures continued.

Prior to this, life for the Haynes children had been idyllic. Horse-and-buggy doctors were sometimes paid with the gift of kittens or puppies from families who had no cash. Their father often returned from attending a patient and asked, "Who would like to see what they can find in my coat pocket?"

At other times, payment materialized in the form of a pie, cake or candy made by a grateful relative of the patient. So, the Haynes children had enjoyed a sweet-and-pleasure-filled existence until the entire family found itself with a new, and rather terrifying, focus.

Ben and Lavinia Haynes began to travel, leaving their older children at home as they took their youngest child to famous clinics in the northeastern United States. They found that prominent doctors in that part of the country were just as puzzled about Ella V's condition as my grandfather, Dr. Ben. The seizures resembled epilepsy, but the family was told that they were not. They were also told to keep Ella V calm and quiet, since it appeared that anything that caused her stress sent her into a violent seizure.

These instructions had a profound influence upon my mother's life as a child. Less than two years older than her sister, Aleen was expected to be her constant companion and to keep her entertained. None of the children were allowed to cross Ella V in case controversy might result in a seizure.

As time passed, with a devoted family catering to her every whim, Ella V became used to her position of power. Smart enough to know the mandates her siblings must obey, she ruled the roost as a tyrant.

Aleen's required companionship made her feel as if she had been cast in the role of indentured servant. She missed having the freedom to choose her own pursuits and yearned to receive the parental attention she had previously enjoyed

When Ella V reached her late teens, the seizures stopped as suddenly as they had started. Of course, by then she was an extremely headstrong young lady. In later years, an interesting series of husbands found that they were unable to handle their role as her mate.

Unfortunately, when Ella V was in her mid-thirties, a raging fever combined with another period of unconsciousness struck again. The seizures returned with a vengeance and plagued her for the rest of her life.

My grandparents did the best they could to give all of their children love and attention. Their youngest child's illness meant they were faced with a series of emergency situations that continued to remain a mystery to medical science.

When my mother was only ten years old, her father died of what was listed as dysentery in his obituary. In later years, family members felt sure it was cancer, but doctors in 1911 knew very little about that condition.

Mother's older brother, JP, had planned to go to medical school when he graduated from high school. Suddenly, he was the man of the family. He felt the weight of responsibility so strongly that he dropped out of high school, took a job to support the family and abandoned all hope for a medical career.

Each of these events influenced my mother strongly. She was also imprinted by a strange series of shocking events witnessed in the home of her favorite aunt, who had become a sort of substitute mother during Ella V's illness.

Aleen's father's sister, Ava Haynes Patterson, married a Methodist minister when she was a very young woman living in Jasper. Reverend Patterson was a superlative orator and revered in the Beaumont area. What his congregation failed to realize was that their esteemed cleric was an extremely cruel husband and father. Today, he would be labeled abusive and emotionally disturbed.

During Aleen's frequent visits to the Patterson home, she witnessed this man mistreat family members and watched as he displayed even more bizarre behavior. Reverend Patterson began to take items like sacks of flour, sugar and other baking ingredients from the kitchen. He then hid them away somewhere in his locked study. Later, when these ingredients were needed for meal preparation, he stormed angrily at his family and denied that he had taken anything.

One day, Aleen was visiting when the reverend suddenly charged into the living room and flew at her aunt Ava in a rage. He wrapped his hands around her neck and began to strangle her. Aleen screamed for help, and two of her cousins ran in from the yard to pull him away from their mother.

Shortly after this incident, Ava Patterson and her children moved to another home. No legal separation or divorce was initiated, so as to spare the reverend embarrassment.

The terror my mother felt as a child witnessing violent outbursts in the Patterson home remained with her and colored her perception of all ministers in future years. She developed an intense dislike and cynical attitude toward anyone who claimed to speak for God. No one could have been a more gracious hostess to people who visited our home when I was a child. That is, unless the visitor happened to be a man of the cloth. Any time a preacher stopped by for any reason, one could see Mother's cheeks turn red with anger and hostility. Her facial expression mirrored distaste, and her words dripped sarcasm.

I'm sure these clergymen wondered what on earth they had done or said to be met with such cold antagonism. The unvarnished truth is she treated all ministers rudely, and seldom did they stay longer than a few minutes. I'm not certain she ever recognized the transparency of her feelings.

Mother's older sister, Norine, remained a staunch Methodist and often served as church pianist. However, Mother could not be prevailed upon to renew her early childhood connection to organized religion.

⚜

Aleen blossomed during her high school years and enjoyed serving as the captain of her tennis team and becoming an honor student in Latin. The achievement of which she was most proud, however, had to do with her physical appearance. She loved being called "the prettiest girl in Beaumont," as well as the caption under her yearbook picture, which read "A thing of beauty is a joy forever."

Certainly, my father believed those words during each of their sixty-three years together. To be around the two of them was to realize that they were deeply in love. Dad eagerly provided all of the love and security she so desperately needed. Sallie—he always called her by her first name—was happiest in his presence, dysfunctional in his absence and totally dependent upon his constant attention.

In their affectionate personal relationship, my mother lost the shyness she had been used to display in public. She was the centerpost of his support system, and he totally relied upon her unwavering devotion. As he faced the shocking disappointment of his purloined inheritance, he was able to find strength in the fact that, though she shared his disappointment, her total devotion was to him and not to any inherited funds or real estate.

My grandmother Haynes, called Nannan by her grandchildren, could have enjoyed a far easier existence if she had accepted my parents' invitation, often re-extended, to live with us. She insisted that she had to remain in Beaumont to look after Ella V and make sure that she always had money for her medicine.

My father cocked an eyebrow each time Mother read aloud another letter from her younger sister. The not-so-subtle subtexts of Ella V's letters always asked for money "for medicine." Dad firmly believed that she purchased her medical supplies at local liquor stores and used her physical condition to shamelessly take advantage of both her mother and mine. I could not be that cynical where Ella V was concerned, and felt any substance, whether from a drug or liquor store, that offered her momentary peace of mind would be justified.

I once accompanied my mother, Ella V and Nannan on a trip to Center. Mother and I took a train to Beaumont, where the four of us boarded a Greyhound bus to venture into the piney woods. Our destination was a vintage Victorian home owned by Nannan's sister Ella. During the week of our visit, I witnessed her namesake, Ella V, suffer a constant stream of seizures, and wondered how anyone could stand such a life.

Ella V usually sat in an overstuffed chair drinking coffee and smoking while the rest of us remained on alert. We all knew that, in addition to the many cuts, bruises and broken bones she had sustained from falls, there had been even more burns and scald-type injuries. So, as we visited in that Victorian parlor, we each stayed ready to jump out of our chair to grab a cup or lighted cigarette the minute her body began to twist and her limbs flew in all directions as if she were caught up in a tornado.

I regret that the time spent with Nannan was limited during my childhood. Both her father and father-in-law were legends in East Texas, and I would have liked to have heard more of the stories she liked to tell at bedtime while she scratched my back. This was her time-tested method of putting young children to sleep—"scratch their backs and tell them a story."

Nannan was kept informed about the situation within the Fletcher family but did not share her knowledge with others in Beaumont.

❦

The East Texas town of Jasper was the destination and meeting place for a number of people who left behind written records that elucidated my heritage. My great-grandmother, with the unlikely name of Alabama Eglantine Keith, did not leave a written record of her life. However, one of her brothers, K. D. (Kosciuszko DeWitt) Keith, wrote a memoir that has been a tremendous gift to me in appreciating the survival skills of my ancestors.

Their mother, Adeline Eliza Lawson Reviere, was a direct descendent of Simon Reviere, Paul Revere's uncle. Both Appollas, Paul's father, and Simon retained the original French spelling of that name while future generations used mainly Reviere, Revere or Riviere.

On the Keith side, the original settler was shot by hooligans who resented the fact he had commanded a regiment of Scottish-English cavalry troops when the colonies were at war with England.

K.D. wrote: "When the war of 1812 came, he had settled in South Carolina and become a prosperous farmer with a large family. This prejudice ran high since he was firm in any stand he took, and resulted finally in his death and the utter destruction of every kind of property, leaving his family entirely homeless and destitute."

The baby of this family was named John Williamson in honor of a peddler who helped find temporary homes for the children and later moved the entire family to Georgia.

When John W. grew up, he married a woman whose ancestor came to this country as a private soldier of our French allies commanded by Lafayette. It was this military heritage, I must assume, that inspired John and Adeline to name their sons after famous generals from around the world.

Alabama and K.D.'s parents, John Williamson Keith and Adeline Reviere Keith, moved their growing family through several Southern states and managed to get past all variety of adversity somehow, until they settled in Alabama. While some of the children were still young, both parents died, only one day apart, in a yellow fever epidemic near Mobile. It was after their parents' estate was settled that the older children decided they should all come to Texas and settle in Jasper County.

Alabama met her future husband, Archibald Nicholas Vaughan, in 1867 when she left Jasper to visit her brother John in Beaumont. A.N. Vaughan was the owner, publisher and writer of the first newspaper in that part of East Texas prior to the Civil War, when he closed his business and joined the Confederacy. At the end of the war, he returned to Beaumont planning to resume publication of *The Beaumont Banner*. To add to his anguish over the Southern defeat, he found the Federal occupation troops had wrecked his newspaper office and smashed all of his printing equipment.

This former mayor of Beaumont started over by beginning a private school in which he served as both principal and teacher. He was also elected as tax assessor and collector of Jefferson County in 1866 and served in that capacity until Reconstruction laws were passed that prohibited anyone who had served the Confederacy from holding public office.

A.N. and Alabama married January 1, 1868. In another fresh start, he joined his industrious brother-in-law, K.D. Keith, and moved to Sabine Pass, "the metropolis of Jefferson County." A.N. owned land there, which he had purchased prior to the outbreak of war.

Because of the deep water channel through the pass, and the Neches River being navigable by steamboat, their grocery, mercantile and cotton commission business thrived. Both families built new homes, and their warehouse and stores were filled with inventory which their ship, the *New Orleans*, forwarded to many ports. My grandmother, her older brother and two younger sisters were all born at Sabine Pass during the 1870s.

The family situation remained happy and stable until a mighty Gulf Coast hurricane wiped out that little town and destroyed their stores, warehouse, both family homes and sank their ship. So, these two Confederate veterans were once more in a position of having to start over. Vaughan was offered employment by Bill Fletcher the elder in the prosperous East Texas lumber business. K.D. eventually settled in Luling, where he became a successful merchant.

The Vaughans moved to Cairo, in Jasper County, where A.N. became an employee of Texas Tram and Lumber Company. In his new capacity, he ran the commissary and scouted for and acquired new timberlands.

Alabama and her children moved back to Beaumont after A.N.'s death in 1882. While living at the site of Bill Fletcher's Village Mills sawmill, Florence Vaughan met Bill's son Harvey, who would one day become her husband.

Florence and her siblings were all educated at home by private tutors. Her younger sisters, May and Addie, never married. Though they became reclusive after their mother's death in 1910, they kept in touch with the outside world through numerous handwritten notes and letters.

I doubt if my great-uncle Emmett Fletcher received any pressed flowers within the multiple letters he received from these zany sisters. Their letters expressed their shock and intense displeasure over his actions in dealing with their nephew Bill's inheritance. Eccentric as they were, my two great-aunts inherited their father's literary talent and could skillfully excoriate others with their intentional use of the written word. I hope no mail personnel received burns from the envelopes they delivered to Beaumont's City Hall.

Contents of these many missives were reported regularly to Aunt Vallie, who shared them with my parents. Though his aunts still called my father Billy-Boy, their words left no doubt in anyone's mind as to where their loyalties lay.

Totally overlooking their own sister's deceitful silence, these two United Daughters of the Confederacy stood ever-ready to fire their cursive cannons at the Mayor of Beaumont.

CHAPTER ELEVEN

BIRDS AND BEES

I think this is something you might be interested in," said my mother as she tossed a small pamphlet onto my bed, twirled around and literally raced from my bedroom.

Gosh, I thought, *I've never seen her move so fast.*

Lifting the pamphlet, I read the title: "Marjorie May's Twelfth Birthday." I had just turned eleven and was curious about Mother's desire for me to read about being twelve. I also wondered why she appeared extremely anxious to put distance between the two of us prior to my reading about Marjorie May.

It only took a few minutes to read the pamphlet and realize that it was a feeble attempt to explain the onset of menstruation. Introducing the subject with tremendously vague statements and oblique allusions, it switched to lyrical descriptions of the lives of young girls who would soon be learning all sorts of new things. I fervently hoped so, because I surely didn't learn one thing from Marjorie May.

I never forgot Marjorie May, nor her twelfth birthday. Between the covers of that skinny pamphlet lay the sum total of anything faintly resembling sex education that I ever received at home, public school or college.

My friends were in the same boat as I, though we often shared our horror tales of misinformation gleaned from distant cousins or self-described sophisticates at school. Being in the only-child category put me at a distinct disadvantage compared to those able to eavesdrop on older siblings and their friends.

I once read "What Every Young Boy Should Know" from cover to cover. This 1910 edition, which I found collecting dust on our bookshelf, was complete with date and an inscription announcing that it was a gift to my father from his loving parents. If this was his pre-pubescent sex education, it was even more saccharine-sweet, vague and rambling than Marjorie May. However, his tome was longer and contained many poems, Bible verses and philosophical thoughts for the day.

Parents taught the names of all body parts except for "down there." I did know I had a bottom, which was for sitting on and occasionally a place to be spanked.

Our assertive neighbor, Mrs. M, conceived and put into action some sort of '30s-era pre-school sex education plan when her son Harry Jr. began to walk. She began calling me "Vallie Girl" and him "Harry Boy" (Not to be confused with Valley Girl and Hairy Boy), pointing to each of us as she emphatically pronounced these names. She normally repeated the process of name-calling and pointing several times in a row for her disinterested toddler. Not only did she call us by these names, she insisted that my family and the neighbors follow suit. My father just snorted at the idea, and Mother used those ridiculous monikers only when Mrs. M was present.

Our neighbor's constant and repetitive attempts at naming and pointing at "Vallie Girl" were designed to insure that "Harry Boy" would learn to recognize the difference between boys and girls.

In later years, we moved from San Antonio and lost track of the M family. I always wondered if Harry Boy grew up thinking a gigantic hair-bow atop one's head indicated that person was female.

⁂

As far as Marjorie May and her subject matter were concerned, children of the '30s had no visual knowledge of, thus learned nothing from, media advertising of personal products. I remember the tasteful ads for a feminine napkin called Modess. The company took out full-page magazine ads that used only the words "Modess...because..." on the page. There were no pictures or anything else to indicate what segment of the population their product served.

In drugstores, feminine products came in boxes wrapped in plain brown paper and were normally kept out of sight behind a counter. For many more decades, a man had to request condoms from the pharmacist who kept them behind his case.

These items were never the subjects of conversation in homes or in schools. Glenn Longino remembers the three-sentence sex education lecture delivered by a physical education teacher and coach at Lake Jackson Junior High School.

In Glenn's gym class, one boy from a group of thirteen-year-olds had very hairy legs and arms. Coach Scarborough pointed at him and addressed his class.

"Y'all see old Jim over there? Well, he's caught the puberty. All of y'all are going to be catchin' the puberty real soon."

I once asked my mother point-blank, "How do women have babies?" Instead of giving me a short explanation of the normal manner, she described something close to a Caesarian section.

"The doctor cuts the woman's side open and takes the baby out."

Mother did not have a Caesarian, but I assume she felt that her description was "tidier." My question did not cover conception, so I never had the opportunity, then or in later years, to hear what her explanation would have been. There's a good chance it would have involved the Tooth Fairy.

I remember many warnings I received about never opening the door to, or getting into a car with, a stranger. I assume that these were warnings to protect me from potential sexual predators. However, Mother used the term *kidnapper*.

According to her, kidnappers constantly lurked nearby, ready to take a careless child away from her parents. In those days, I did not realize that a kidnapper seeking ransom would not choose the Highland Park neighborhood. They would operate in one of San Antonio's silk-stocking areas.

In elementary school, we had infrequent classes designated *hygiene*. The subjects covered were things that all children should have been taught at home when they were very young. Included were lessons on how to brush your teeth, take baths, shampoo your hair, clean your fingernails and other subjects within the field of personal grooming.

By the time we arrived in junior high school, hygiene classes were lumped into the general field of physical education. For the most part, the subject matter was a repetition of what was taught in elementary school.

If vigorous games were to be played during physical education class, and a girl was having her period, she could whisper into the gym teacher's ear and receive an excuse. This enabled her to skip the normal routine of changing into gym clothes and taking part in physical activity.

Many girls referred to the time of their period with "I'm sick" or "I've got the curse." Boys were kept in the dark concerning menstruation unless they received instruction at home.

The shower scene in Stephen King's book and the feature film *Carrie* may have seemed far-fetched to the generation of readers and viewers they first reached. However, in the '30s and '40s there were many girls who were terrified when they first began to bleed and had no idea what was happening. For whatever reason, many mothers waited to offer any explanation until after the fact.

Teenagers were expected to abstain from all forms of sex, and as far as I know, most of them did. The subject was joked about sometimes in general terms but never discussed on a personal basis. Though pregnancy was not a topic for polite conversation, sometimes we heard whispers that a certain girl had "gotten into trouble."

Teenage drinking and drug use were not an issue then, so that term always referred to a girl who had become pregnant. Risky condoms were the only form of birth control available, so girls of our generation equated premarital sex with becoming pregnant and disgracing one's family.

The girls who were the subject of those whispers usually disappeared for a long period of time. Their families told those who were brazen enough to ask that they were visiting an aunt or grandmother "up north." Wealthier families might say their daughter had an opportunity to tour Europe with her older cousin. When the girl returned to her community, she was alone and no questions were asked.

My parents had two perfect examples to cite if they had chosen to explain the difference between homosexual and heterosexual lifestyles to me. Two of our favorite relatives, both cousins of my father, were gay. As with other subjects regarding sex, however, they chose to ignore their opportunity.

King Ward grew up in Beaumont and, according to my father, "He was a big bully and the meanest little boy I knew. No one would have ever guessed that he would grow up to be a sissy."

My father's use of the word *sissy* did not allude to King's sexual preference. This was a frequently used word in the '30s and had more to do with someone's day-to-day activities. King preferred the company of women friends, with whom he enjoyed shopping trips, tearoom lunches and bridge games.

My father's cousin was flamboyant and usually sported a wicked grin to go with a wild sense of humor. Family members grew impatient when one of his visits was imminent because his style of telling stories kept all of us in stitches. Surely, he was destined to sound royal. In today's vernacular, King was a queen.

King's tales were true ones from his own experiences, related with an innate flair for drama and unique method of delivery. If timing is a comedian's most important tool, King's timing, combined with his every expression and form of body language, were absolutely perfect as he captured and enchanted his listeners.

A dramatic pause upon entering a room allowed this entertainer to survey his stage, select a likely spot to begin his narrative and slowly turn toward his audience. As he began his oratory, every shift of weight, gesture of hand, crook of brow, transfer of gaze or rearrangement of shirt-cuff were perfectly timed to create tension within his tale. He seemed to be a magnet for embarrassing situations which, when elaborated upon, became the fodder for uproarious family gatherings.

Family and friends often joked about how dangerous it was to share a meal with King. Formal dinners, in particular, seemed to bring out his inner naughty boy. As most of us were in the process of enjoying food or drink, he would deliver a punch line so outrageous that we were forced to clamp our hands over our mouth and try not to choke. It was for gatherings like this that the Heimlich maneuver was later invented.

Passenger trains were luxurious in the '30s and the preferred mode of travel for well-to-do people. My mother sometimes asked King to retell his story about returning to Beaumont after a lengthy vacation in the northeast.

As the train pursued its southerly route, he was enjoying a chat with a young woman who sat near him holding a baby. After giving the baby girl a bottle and getting her to sleep, the woman asked King if it would be alright for her to leave the baby on the seat beside him while she went into the dining car and ate lunch. Dealing with the baby and all of her paraphernalia, she explained, was very difficult on a train.

King was glad to help her out, so the baby was placed on the seat next to him while her mother headed off to the dining car. The baby slept soundly, allowing King to do some reading and ignore her while the young mother was away.

Suddenly, he realized that the porter was announcing the train would soon be arriving in Beaumont. Only then did it occur to him that the baby's mother had been absent a very long time.

King picked up the baby and began a car-to-car search. The mother was nowhere to be found. Enlisting the aid of porters and the conductor, it was finally discovered that the car she had been in at the time of the last stop had been switched off to another train.

This was where King would really begin to relive his frantic moments as the guardian of a strange infant. With much eye-rolling and arm-waving, he suddenly realized that the train was pulling into the station at Beaumont, where all his friends and family members would be gathered to greet him. What would they think when he stepped out onto the platform carrying a baby?

Eventually, the railroad took care of locating the mother and reuniting her with King and her baby. According to our favorite teller of tales, she was in worse shape than he.

Considering that King always dressed in the most formal and impeccable style, I'm sure that he managed his child-bearing exit from the passenger train in a manner befitting a royal head of state.

One of King's embarrassing moments occurred when he was in San Antonio visiting us and a few of the great-aunts. He enjoyed a large Sunday meal at our home then drove downtown to see a movie.

After the lights went out in the theatre, he took the opportunity to unzip his trousers because he had eaten too much and the waistband felt uncomfortably tight. An usher brought some late arrivals, a man and his wife, to sit in King's row. As he stood to let them pass, he surreptitiously re-zipped his trousers. As soon as the couple passed him, the woman began yelling, "Let go of me!" She was yelling at King, but he was not touching her.

Soon, her husband joined the chorus and was demanding that King turn his wife loose. Totally confused at first, King then realized that, as he zipped his pants while she passed, the sheer skirt of her dress had gotten caught in the zipper. Frantically, he tried to unzip his pants and release her. The zipper held fast and refused to move.

His attempts to explain were unheard due to the increasing volume of the woman's yells. Several ushers were by then holding flashlights on him, and he was instructed to come with them to the manager's office. As he attempted to comply, the woman was pulled along with him.

King had the unpleasant experience of ambulating crab-style up the stairs to the landing, then down the main stairs and through the lobby while his accuser, whose skirt was still caught in his zipper, followed conjoined-twin fashion. She glared at King and continued to protest loudly as her husband called King an imaginative series of pervert-oriented names.

During their slow journey to the manager's office, two policemen were somehow stirred into the mix. Spectators in the lobby seemed confused as to whether or not this bizarre parade was some sort of surprise live entertainment.

The manager listened to King's explanation while suppressing a smile and wielding a pair of pliers. Though the skirt looked sheer, the material proved to be tough, and the zipper refused to move up or down. To part the angered woman from King took a sharp pair of scissors and a promise that King would pay for the dress she was wearing and also buy her a new one.

⊱❧⊰

When not involved in one of his melodramas, King was totally happy with his life situation. He had a successful antique business and was the delight of his customers, mostly wealthy older women. He greatly admired my father, and often expressed a belief that Dad's deadpan dry wit was much funnier than his own retelling of experiences.

My father's cousin Katherine lived through some unpleasant situations prior to finding peace with her homosexuality. She later became one of the most respected cattle ranchers in the Texas coastal area where Dad and other cousins also ranched. "There's nothing a man can do that Katherine can't do just as well," Dad used to say with pride. He meant anything having to do with cattle-raising and ranch life.

Katherine was part of a large family raised in the Beaumont-Orange area. To her parent's distress, her body took on some obvious masculine characteristics after she entered her teens. Because of beliefs and attitudes in the early 20th century, she was forced to undergo a number of procedures to "cure" her.

By the time I was born, her face was terribly scarred from attempts '20s-era electrolysis hair removal. As a rancher, she had to buy and wear men's clothes because department stores carried only dresses for women.

Katherine owned a home in Palacious, where she lived in a committed relationship with a local schoolteacher. In an era when homosexuality was never openly discussed, this couple enjoyed the companionship and support of many friends and relatives throughout their long life together.

Whether or not my parents chose to discuss alternative lifestyles with me, I learned non-judgment during enjoyable times spent with both King and Katherine.

When my family moved to El Campo, I met two teenage boys who shared a similar problem. Each was an only child whose home life was dominated by an extremely strong-willed mother. Both of these women felt they were very socially prominent and were highly invested in the perceived social status of their sons. The boys' fathers appeared to be quiet men whose opinions were never openly expressed.

Both mothers seemed to be in total denial of their son's same-sex preference. I entered the picture only because these women, who lived in two different small towns, each decided that I was the perfect girl for her son to date and pressured him to take me out.

Finally, to get these boys off of the hook, I went to a prom with D in El Campo and a drive-in theatre with T in Victoria. Each was a perfect gentleman but no doubt had someone else in mind he would rather have been with.

During my first year of college at TSCW (now Texas Woman's University) in Denton, my roommate Catherine and I purchased a *Reader's Digest* issue with a large "Sex Education" blurb on the cover. Eager to see what we could learn inside, we soon discovered the entire story was devoted to the strong urge of male salmon to swim upstream and reach their mating grounds.

We struck out there, but were elated to hear our dynamic physical education instructor announce that she would soon begin teaching a unit on sex education that would last for several weeks. We were enrolled in her huge modern dance class and figured she was weary of watching as students awkwardly whirled and collided with one another in small groups. Our teacher deserved young Martha Grahams and had drawn eager and inexperienced small-town girls who collapsed into fits of laughter at the sight of their own clumsiness.

Anticipation was high on the first day of our sex education unit. Everyone in the class arrived at the substitute classroom a little early. Each girl carried pen and paper to record all of the new information we were sure would be fascinating.

Catherine and I headed for seats in the front row so we would not miss a word and would have a clear view of the displays, should there be any.

Our teacher arrived looking flustered and seemingly fascinated by the cement flooring. Her expression conveyed that she would really like to grab her briefcase and disappear through the nearest exit.

Finally, after a great deal of podium-area paper shuffling, she looked up at her class. The room became spookily quiet.

In a low and dramatic voice, she began reading to us about the strong urge of male salmon to swim upstream in order to mate. It was the *Reader's Digest* article verbatim.

Catherine and I looked at one another and realized, "This is it! There's not going to be any more." Our desire to learn, combined with the older generation's determination to keep us ignorant and innocent, suddenly seemed hilarious. Evidently, writers and academicians had reached a joint decision. Coeds who were conversant in lusty salmon lore would make excellent wives and lovers of the future.

Our teacher's rosy complexion signaled an advanced case of chagrin as she attempted to field questions asked during that one class. She ultimately decided she would rather deal with the awkwardness of neophyte modern dancers than inquiries into the subject of sex. Reversing her carefully outlined lesson plans, she announced that our next class meeting would be held in the gym and to be sure we wore our dancing attire.

CHAPTER TWELVE

READING AND WRITING
AND 'RITHMETIC

Reporters taking notes and photographers aiming cameras were not what I expected to find on my very first day of public school. Yet, these were pieces of the bizarre and puzzling scene encountered by a room filled with wide-eyed six-year-olds on the day we first entered our new pre-primer classroom.

Perhaps Mrs. Culpepper is a famous person and that's why cameras are clicking, I thought.

Hugh Philipus Jr., a fellow violinist, and I were lifted and placed on a tabletop to face the noisy melee with most serious expressions as a cameraman captured the moment. Somewhere in the midst of all the confusion, we learned that local newspapers had dispatched crews after learning three sets of twins were being enrolled in this one classroom. This offered editors a new twist in their quest for school news.

Sure enough, after Mrs. Culpepper managed to restore some form of order, Jack and Jacqueline, Jean and Joan and Lloyd and Floyd were posed at a small blackboard. By the time the story was in print, Gene and Dean were added to the mix.

I thought twins were fascinating, and immediately recognized that there was a dominant twin in each of our sets. Jacqueline was mature, while poor Jack was still a baby who slept through most of the day. When most of us passed into the first grade, he did not.

Jean was shy and sensitive with emotions always ready to give in to teary outbursts. Joan remained alert and aggressive as she balanced a good-sized chip on her shoulder.

These two sets were fraternal twins. The other two sets, both identical, also displayed a leader-follower pattern and distinct personality differences.

I had already learned everything that was taught in the first two grades at home with Mother. Yet, I was never disinterested because I was being re-exposed amidst a roomful of fascinating classmates.

One of my mother's teaching methods had been to inundate me with riddles to solve. I greatly enjoyed the process of trying to work out answers in my mind, so I thought perhaps our lessons in school would be in the form of riddles.

The only one of Mother's early riddles I can remember was:

> A house full
> A hole full
> But you cannot fill
> A bowl full

I was absolutely sure the answer was "children." It was easy to envision a house filled with children as well as children having a great time playing in a big hole.

"That's not correct," Mother said. "Keep on thinking."[1]

Merry Tom Blue, a friend from toddler-age dancing school days, was also in Mrs. Culpepper's class. Excitement filled me when I saw that she still wore her never-trimmed hair in two magnificent long blond braids.

Our group and the other first few grades were always served a "mid-morning lunch" of milk and gigantic sugar cookies. After lunch, we were allowed to put our heads down on the tables while the teacher read stories to us. Some of my classmates went to sleep, but that did not matter. They were gently awakened later.

Both our morning and afternoon recess periods were spent in free play and not regimented activities like most of today's young ones endure. A lengthy lunch break allowed us to walk home for a leisurely meal. If we chose to eat in the elementary school cafeteria, there was plenty of time left to go outside and play afterward.

---

[1] The answer is at the end of this chapter.

The schoolyard at Highland Park Elementary was filled with all varieties of playground equipment, which was constantly in use. If we fell off the seesaw or out of a swing and hurt ourselves, the school nurse repaired the damage. The nurse probably treated more stings from large red ants than any other schoolyard injury. Whatever their child's malady, parents never considered suing the school district.

Indeed, parents were the school's biggest supporters. They expected their children to conduct themselves well while away from home. With very few exceptions, their expectations were met. We had been taught to respect our teachers and classmates, take responsibility for our actions, pay attention and follow instructions, so that's how we behaved.

Normally, women did not take part in politics during the 1930s and '40s. School boards and other political bodies were governed by men. For that reason, young girls were supposed to wear dresses at all times and, even in the coldest weather, were prohibited from wearing trousers to school. No male school board member had experienced the chilling discomfort of enduring cold weather while walking to school with bare legs and short skirts.

During a period of frigid temperatures, my parents and others objected to this rule. It was decided that in very cold weather girls could wear long pants under their skirts during the walk to school. However, the minute they arrived at the school building, those offensive garments had to be removed. Dresses and skirts were considered the only proper and traditionally modest attire by the stuffed-shirts who governed school district policy.

If a school board member had chosen to visit any elementary school campus during recess, though he would likely have been shocked by the sight of numerous female students happily hanging upside-down from trapeze bars without any concern that their underwear was being prominently displayed to disinterested fellow students. True, children of either gender might recite one of the standard rhymes for that occasion as they passed by.

> I see London,
> I see France,
> I see someone's
> Underpants.

Or

I see Venus,
I see Mars,
I see someone's
Underdrawers.

These rhymes were offered in a teasing manner and were accepted in the same vein. None of the topsy-turvy females were offended or embarrassed when the verses were chanted.

The building that sits where my old school building once stood is probably three or four times larger than the original. Our building had a basement that housed the only restrooms. It was a long trip up and down those stairs, so the first few grades were lined up and taken en masse fairly often.

When I think of that basement and those stairs I always shudder with the memory of an impossible task I was once given.

My classroom was on the top floor of the school. Prominently displayed on a table was an absolutely huge, round fish bowl someone had donated.

One morning the teacher noticed that the water in the tank looked cloudy. I had finished my assignments, so she asked me to carry the fish bowl down to the basement, empty it and refill it with fresh water. Remember, children did not argue with, or talk back to, teachers then.

I could barely lift the bowl, but tried my best to do what she requested. The only person in that entire building who was actually capable of filling her request, as specified, was our hulking school janitor.

I walked very slowly and felt my way down, stair by stair, because I could not see my feet over the container. Leaning back and straining to hold onto the tank, which resembled a punch bowl on steroids, I could feel the contents sloshing and shifting. The poor fish were trying to survive a tsunami.

I made it around corners and down staircase after staircase, much to my own surprise. When there was only one flight of stairs left between me and the basement, the inevitable happened.

Enough water had sloshed out of the tank to make the outside wet and slippery. The tank slid right out of my grasp, bounced down several stairs and then exploded on the cement basement floor with a huge *crash-boom*!

The cavernous basement caused the sound of the crash to echo all the way to the top of the stairs and throughout each floor. I looked up and saw what seemed to be a thousand faces looking down at me as students and teachers hung over every stair rail and each landing. Spying the face of Mrs. Crain, our principal, among the onlookers I thought, "Oh, no! I'm in trouble."

Actually, help suddenly arrived from everywhere. The fish were quickly rescued and plopped into a smaller bowl as a crew with brooms and mops dispensed with the broken glass and water. The physical evidence of my catastrophe disappeared, but I still had to return to my classroom and face whatever music was to be played.

To my surprise, everyone was glad to see me. I had provided a welcome entertainment break and opportunity for the students to escape their routine for a few moments. My teacher expressed joy that I had not fallen along with the tank. She had already been lectured by Mrs. Crain and asked by several other teachers how she could have expected me to lift and carry that heavy tank. So, I was saved from possible punishment by her guilt trip.

As my elementary school experiences progressed, I became concerned that some of the children in my classes had rather pitiful-looking clothes and shoes. Mother and I discussed this and decided that San Antonio's parochial schools had the right idea.

Children who attended these private schools wore uniforms, so it was impossible to tell at a glance which ones came from well-to-do families and which attended on scholarships. This system seemed far more equitable because it avoided the artificial peer caste system based on a child's garments.

⁂

Classroom visual aids that would appear in schools several decades later were not available to '30s- and '40s-era teachers. They could not flip a switch and show us pictures, so they did a lot of explaining. Flash cards were used in almost every subject.

Students were encouraged to ask questions, and were guided into experiences requiring a great deal of verbal exchange. Ideas, opinions and feelings were freely expressed, and we eventually grew into a generation of conversationalists. We read constantly and exercised our imaginations by forming images and concepts that students of today are spoon-fed via modern technology.

Through the elementary grades, our report cards carried the letters

S for *Satisfactory*, I for *Improvement Desired* or U for *Unsatisfactory*. So, the grading system in use was lenient compared to some used today.

One of our most important grades was the one we received on the attitude we displayed during our time in class—comportment. Did we follow the teacher's instructions? Were we polite and considerate of other students? Did we comport ourselves in the manner of a good citizen?

There was no such thing as "social promotion" from grade to grade. Most students were competent to pass on to the next grade level at the end of the school year. Those few who were not were retained until they mastered whatever subjects had held them back. Unfortunately, the word used both verbally and stamped on report cards at that time was *Failed!*

So, students who eventually graduated from high schools were proficient in all of the skills that educators and society of that day demanded. College professors did not have to deal with freshman who could not read, spell or write essays.

❧

All of my teachers were pleasant women. There were no male faculty members until we reached junior high age and the boys were required to have a coach.

Mrs. Forester, my first-grade teacher, went to England the summer after I finished her class. Knowing that I collected dolls from various countries, she returned from her trip with a small Princess Elizabeth doll made in the image of the little girl who one day would be Queen of England.

Second-grade teacher, Mrs. Josea, was hard of hearing, and I often complained to Mother that she failed to make her students stop talking. I preferred a quiet classroom, and she could probably not hear the undercurrent of incessant murmurs.

Red-haired Mrs. Cain was our third-grade teacher, and she saw to it that we received a great deal of practice in singing. World War II had just begun, and Mrs. Cain's son had enlisted in the Marine Corps. Every morning, after repeating the Lord's Prayer, Pledge of Allegiance and singing our National Anthem, we continued to stand as we sang the official theme song of each individual branch of the US military. Mrs. Cain worked with us until we memorized every verse of all of these songs. Most of them had quite a few verses!

We also received daily updates on Dewey Cain and the activities of his squadron. After this, we were taught new patriotic songs. Mrs. Cain also initiated an afternoon "request program" where individual students could ask another student to go to the front of the room and sing. If a student was too shy to sing alone, she or he could enlist a friend and belt out a duo.

Our teacher preferred that we limit performances to patriotic songs, but we soon tired of those and began to request other tunes. Merry Tom's older sister was married to a real prankster who was stationed at one of our local air force bases. When I visited the Blues' home, George would call Merry Tom and me out to the back yard and teach us songs we had never heard. He called me "Rudy," referring to the crooner Rudy Vallee.

What George taught us were songs with risque lyrics, but we were too naive to catch on to his devious plan. Overhearing Merry Tom describe our request programs, he concocted a plan to set us up and took obvious delight in performing the role of singing instructor.

The other students loved hearing us sing a song called "I Must be Respected." I'm sure that particular song must have had some totally innocent verses, but those were not the ones George taught us. I'd heard the cliche "banned in Boston," but Merry Tom and I became the only act I knew to be "outlawed in the third grade."

The fourth-grade teacher, Mrs. Gilbert, was rumored to be extremely strict, so we were all a little nervous when assigned to her class. She turned out to be one of my favorites because she sailed a tight ship, allowed no nonsense and transferred an incredible amount of knowledge into our young brains. Though she *was* strict, she was always fair and, to my joy, insisted upon a quiet class atmosphere.

I inadvertently started a fad in that class that became quite a joke between Mrs. Gilbert, my parents and me.

I had developed a large and feverish boil in the center of one of my buttocks. For several days, I lay in bed on my stomach while Mother spread a black sticky substance on top of the boil. Our doctor did not believe in lancing, so he prescribed this smelly remedy to bring the boil to a head.

Mother was informed that I should take a pillow to use when I returned to school. I argued against this because of the embarrassing location of my malady. My mother insisted upon following the doctor's directions but let me know she would alert Mrs. Gilbert to the situation so no one would know why I was using a pillow.

As Mother promised, nothing was mentioned about the addition to my chair. Over the next few days, several other students arrived in class carrying pillows. Mrs. Gilbert never acknowledged that she noticed.

Within a week, almost every student in class had a pillow beneath his or her derriere. So, a popular classroom craze was precipitated by the condition of my tender behind.

A fashion craze that I did not start but certainly took part in was the wearing of sterling silver charm bracelets. Girls started out with a simple silver chain, which her friends were expected to garnish with the gift of a heart bearing the donor's name. Popular girls soon wore a wrist full of hearts engraved with various names and designs.

These adornments, also called friendship bracelets, tended to jingle and create distraction in the classroom. So, teachers sometimes had to admonish students to either take off the noisy bracelets or keep their arms still.

During one year this type of jewelry was in vogue, Aunt Lulu gifted me with a most exquisite and totally impractical solid gold charm bracelet. The bracelet contained not only a tiny gold heart bearing the name "Lulu" but other beautiful and skillfully crafted charms. A violin, a treble clef and a piano were among charms relating to my musical pursuits. New ones were added with great regularity and, no doubt, also at great expense.

This tremendously delicate gift was enchanting, so I wore it almost all of the time. Aunt Lulu spent a great deal of time with my family and took pleasure in seeing her gift on my wrist, so I assume that was why my mother allowed this impractical habit.

The extreme softness and pliability of links and charms made of solid gold allowed my charms to disappear with great regularity. Constant physical activity on my part rendered this lovely piece of jewelry most inappropriate. Perhaps dedicated tree climbers on Kayton Avenue, or treasure hunters on the old playground of Highland Park Elementary, may one day discover a tiny heart bearing the name "Lulu."

Our fifth-grade teacher, Miss Mims, was a memorable female role model. She was probably one of the sweetest individuals I met in any classroom.

I remember being upset one day because I thought I might have hurt the feelings of a friend by a remark I'd made. I continued doing my assigned work and, as far as I know, said or did nothing to display my feelings. Yet, with the intuition of a dedicated teacher, Miss Mims caught on. She quietly called me up to her desk and asked what was bothering me.

I explained the whole scenario, and instead of giving me some glib words of advice, she sent for my friend, who was in another class. When Jessie arrived, Miss Mims asked me to tell her why I had been worrying.

Jesse expressed surprise that I had been concerned and declared that she felt neither hurt nor angry. Her statement totally relieved my anxiety. If the situation had been different, it would have afforded me an opportunity to apologize.

Our school soon lost an exceptional teacher when Miss Mims enlisted in the SPARS, the woman's branch of the US Coast Guard.

Sixth-grade teacher Mrs. Bartlett suffered by comparison with Miss Mims. She was typical of a few others I have known who went into teaching because it was one of the few fields where women could be fairly confident of finding employment. Intuition told me that she would have rather been almost anywhere than a classroom.

In her defense, Mrs. Bartlett was challenged by a room filled with students who were just beginning to "catch the puberty."

I remember being asked to memorize the Twenty-third Psalm in this class. Our whole class often stood and repeated it. Perhaps the words of this beautiful psalm provided our teacher with a degree of calmness and comfort in the midst of a pre-adolescence-charged environment. Nobody at all felt there was anything wrong with the inclusion of Bible verses among our many other subjects.

During the weeks before Christmas, many of our classroom activities were devoted to celebrating the season. Our Jewish classmates shared the fun, the songs, the stories, the parties and always took part in an exchange of gifts. If Jewish parents resented this and thought the rest of us were insensitive clods, it was not mentioned. As children, we respected their religious beliefs and did not expect anyone to suddenly convert to Christianity. We simply wanted all of our young friends included in the school festivities.

When a Jewish holiday was imminent, our Jewish classmates explained the religious custom to the rest of our class in their own fashion. They were allowed to skip school and take part in the celebration of the actual events. I believe we all benefited from these presentations, as basic as they were. Thank goodness, the political-correctness egg had not yet hatched.

~～豢～

Mother did not lack for anything to do while I was at school. Each of my teachers heard of her skill creating decorations so asked her to be room mother. She took the job most seriously and came up with a series of classroom transformations using ornamentation made at home. Surprising and delighting our class on every conceivable occasion, her reputation grew to the point that other classes were allowed to take a special tour to view our spectacular themes. I always felt sorry for those classes, and realized it must have seemed unfair to teachers who lacked a genius at classroom garnishment as room mother.

My mother was also often asked to plan field trips to some of the fascinating places in and around San Antonio. This was an easy job for her because our family had visited most of these places many times. Her work involved making arrangements with sites and recruiting other drivers. There was an ample supply of stay-at-home moms, but many women did not drive and quite a number of my friend's families did not own a car.

Schools did not have their own buses then. There were not many rules about going on field trips nor was there a mountain of paperwork involved with leaving the campus. One simple permission slip requiring a parent's signature was the only red tape involved with these enjoyable journeys.

Mother's reward for time spent organizing these trips was watching expressions of joy and amazement on faces of children who had never had the opportunity to venture forth into the greater community.

Another task assigned my mother was not at all suited to her skills or personality, but she did her very best. At a time when there were no social workers available for such things, PTA members took it upon themselves to identify families who required help with finances required for medical or dental treatment or some other basic need. It was easy for teachers to spot needy children within their classrooms. It was another matter for a PTA member to suddenly appear at the front door of their homes and start asking questions.

My mother was a shy woman, and undertaking this job must have been torture. She remained a victim of her own rigid routine, and flexibility was not among her talents. Yet, Mother did her best to see that children with green teeth were taken to a dentist, children with no shoes and few clothes were provided with these things and families with little food were inundated with sacks and boxes of groceries.

Mother soon learned which families were so filled with pride that they were willing to see their children do without rather than accept any type of aid. She also saw which family was headed by a father so lazy that he preferred to sit in a porch rocker and recite a list of all of the things he expected the PTA to provide for his family. Of course, the children were the victims of his lack of industry, so distaste for the man himself could not allow a blind eye to be turned toward needs of the rest of the family.

One of this man's children, Wilbur, was a member of my class. Wilbur always had a terrible cold and never had a handkerchief. An offensive body odor, which caused other students to shun him, resulted from his home's lack of sanitary facilities.

My only terrible visual memory that lingers from elementary school is the image of an extremely cold morning when Wilbur entered our second-grade classroom long after school had started. San Antonio and its surrounding area seldom experienced the type of severe cold we were then having. I knew Wilbur was late arriving because he had walked several miles from his home.

Wilbur was crying, and I saw that he was barefoot. His feet looked purple, and his entire body was shaking uncontrollably. I felt sure that Mrs. Josea would send him to the school nurse and let her wrap him in blankets and give him shoes and socks to wear. Instead, she seemed absolutely unaware of his pitiful chilled condition.

The image of a child experiencing physical suffering combined with the realization that no figure of authority was going to offer any sort of help hit me like a storm surge. I worried from first grade on about the cruel ways some children and teachers had when dealing with one in their midst who had absolutely nothing.

Wilbur, who obviously lacked self-esteem, was always the last to be chosen for any activity. The traditional way of dividing into teams for schoolyard or classroom activities was for the teacher to appoint team captains and ask them to select their team members. All of the students knew exactly what was going to happen. The captains took turns selecting team members until Wilbur was the last child left at his desk. Only then did the captain whose turn it was call his name.

I wondered why teachers did not enact a policy of drawing numbers or some other method of dividing up children that would not always end in humiliation for the same child.

I have never forgotten Wilbur. Part of my memory can only be labeled guilt, for I did nothing at all to change his sad situation. The woebegone child with whom I once shared a classroom still haunts me as a revenant of missed opportunity.

⁂

In our elementary classrooms, we were taught in the manner that had been used for years. We learned phonics, memorized the spelling and meaning of words and held old-fashioned spelling bees frequently. Numbers were dealt with in a similar manner as we progressed in math skills.

Divided into teams, we lined up against the walls on both sides of the room. A word to spell or problem to solve would be given to each child one after the other. The teacher turned her attention back and forth, challenging members of both teams. When a student gave an incorrect answer, he returned to his desk. At some point, there would be just a few students standing. The competition would then become really hot.

Our teachers used a lot of flash card drills, so we were usually very well prepared for these math or spelling bees. I loved them because I had a good memory and often got to be the last child standing.

The only subject to which I had an aversion was penmanship. We were taught to emulate specific model-letters, and it was hoped that our cursive style would soon resemble the slant and swirls of the idyllic examples.

Despite my intense focus, my fingers could not produce the desired outcome. My slant varied, and my swirls were anything but artistic in nature. Of course, in those days, everything was written by hand. We used pencils and Big Chief tablets in the early grades, and later switched to composition books and fountain pens that required frequent dips into an ink bottle.

We were not allowed any marked-out words, smudges, inkspots or misspelled words. The bladder-type fountain pens in use could be tricky to maneuver without smudges or drops of ink spoiling an otherwise pristine paper. Teachers expected good penmanship throughout, or points were deducted from our grade. When we were assigned lengthy papers to write in high school, I often copied mine over five or six times so that it would look neat. This process could take hours at night or over the weekend.

Students who exhibited proficiency in writing were given the opportunity to write for the school newspaper. Evidently, my enthusiasm for this activity made up for my lack of exemplary penmanship. My first forays into journalism, both poems and stories, were published by the *Highland Park Elementary School Newspaper.*

An avid reader who enjoyed expressing thoughts with pen and paper, I considered book reports more of a pleasure than a task.

Our generation grew into prolific letter writers who kept up with family members, friends and sweethearts in this manner. Many stacks of letters were kept tied with ribbon by proud mothers or servicemen's wives. History has gleaned much from such treasures through the centuries.

~❈~

Learning experiences continued each summer break during my elementary school years. Cousins whose families were more affluent than mine were sent to Camp Waldemar near Hunt. My friends and I attended Girl Scout camps that were also located in the Hill Country but had far more primitive facilities.

We carried canvas army cots and bedding to camp and placed them in shelters with screens for walls. Each group of shelters had one path that ended in front of a three-seat latrine and another path leading to an open-air shower.

Every girl had chores to do at the shelter site and also in the dining hall. Jobs were distributed fairly by frequent lotteries. Food and drink were served by "hoppers." Tables were cleaned and dishes washed and dried after the meal by girls who had drawn those chores. The last ones out of the dining hall were those responsible for putting away dishes, glasses and silverware.

I remember writing home and conveying the message that it was my turn to clean the latrines. This meant simply sweeping out the insides of the wooden structures and trying to get rid of all the granddaddy longlegs who claimed them as their turf.

My mother had no idea what a latrine was, so she assumed that I had misspelled the word *lantern.* Dad had to explain that *latrine* was simply another word for *outhouse.*

~❈~

Walking to school was a social occasion in those days. Everyone had groups of friends who joined them along the route. Most of us could have gotten a ride, but we preferred to walk and share ideas, interests and plans for the future.

I remember a day when I walked home from elementary school by myself, which was unusual. As I headed down Rigsby Avenue, a boy of about eighteen walked from his porch and asked, "Hey, do you want to be raped? Come on inside with me. I'll give you a quarter." I didn't have a clue what he meant, but knew better than to stop and talk to him or go into his house.

When I arrived home, I saw that my father had come home early. As I described the incident to him, his face turned red; and he told me to come with him and show him where the young man lived. Identifying the house was no problem, since I passed it twice each day. Dad knocked on the door, and the same young man answered his knock. A heated conversation, most of which I could not hear, followed.

We soon left and returned home, where my father called the police. After two policemen arrived, I was asked to retell my story. The officers asked my father to file charges, and I was asked if I would be willing to tell what happened in court. My father agreed to file on the boy, and I volunteered to talk to a judge.

My parents soon learned that this young man had gotten into trouble in his high school and had been skipping school without his mother's knowledge. She was employed, so did not realize her son had been staying at home. He had not touched me, but there was consternation among the adults that at some point he might harm another child.

Later, my parents received a series of calls from both the boy and his mother begging them to drop the charges. The distraught mother promised to get her son counseling, so eventually they agreed. I believe they were more concerned about me having to testify than they were about any consequences to her son.

On the afternoon the incident occurred, I asked my father what the word *rape* meant. His response was "He wanted to hurt you." Avoiding a court case assured my parents that no further explanation would be necessary.

Upon graduation from elementary school, children in my neighborhood were offered a selection of junior high schools to attend. We were equidistant from schools called Page and Poe, so I was eligible to enroll in either. After conversations with good friends Rosemary Duke and Betty Brent Schaeffler, I decided to cast my lot with Edgar Allen Poe. After all, Poe had long been one of my favorite authors.

Many of my classmates who considered attending Poe were forbidden by their parents to make that choice due to an ethnic situation.

233

In San Antonio, there were Anglo, Hispanic and Black neighborhoods. In those years, neighbors all shared the same shade of skin.

Page Junior High, like Highland Park Elementary, was totally surrounded by Caucasians. Poe Junior High served both Anglo and Hispanic neighborhoods. This meant that those of us who chose to attend Poe would, for the very first time, have Hispanic classmates and friends. This situation suited everyone in my family and the families of some of my friends. However, it meant parting with other valued classmates whose parents must have forgotten that Texas had once been a part of both Spain and Mexico.

I totally enjoyed the years I spent in elementary school, years in which I excelled in the classroom and gained self-confidence. During my time in Poe Junior High, the pendulum swung in the opposite direction and diminished my faith in some of my abilities.

In another chapter, I related my unpleasant memories of my physical education coach, Mrs. F. There was an orchestra teacher at Poe who was aware of my reputation as a violinist. Memory has been kind in blotting out her name. However, when she learned that I had enrolled at Poe, she immediately sent for me.

I had not signed up for her orchestra class, and she put a great deal of pressure on me to do so. Since I was unwilling to change my elective, she absolutely insisted that I come to school an hour early every morning and attend practice sessions with her orchestra.

I did not want to do this, but she had an ace up her sleeve. She reminded me that I was in her math class and used this as a not very subtle form of blackmail. For years, I had been performing professionally in the area, and her orchestra comprised students who were handling instruments for the very first time and could not read music. The cacophony of ear-splitting discordant vibrations this group was capable of producing would send any music lover racing in the opposite direction.

This teacher received only a negative reaction to early-morning practice sessions from me, so she called my mother; and the two of them conspired to apply more pressure.

As a typical pre-teen, time spent with my peer group was extremely important to me. The period after our arrival on campus and prior to the bell signifying it was time for our first class was a social occasion. We were able to visit with friends that would not be around later in the day.

When my mother began to put pressure on me to help the orchestra teacher, who did have a totally impossible job, I tried to explain to her that I would miss out on the most enjoyable time of my school day. Her edict was that I should try it for a few months and then we could see how I felt about it. As the dutiful daughter of a strong-willed mother, I understood this issue was not negotiable.

I began carrying my violin to school and showing up early for orchestra practice. The audible sensations were pure torture. I remained the polite student and did what I was asked but resented the pressures exerted to place me in a situation I hated. After all, I spent many hours every week practicing the violin and performing with professionals.

After several months, I rebelled. I told both my mother and the teacher that I would not be attending early-morning orchestra practice any more. Mother actually honored our agreement. The teacher, however, glared at me and informed me that she planned to make things tough on me because of this decision.

Math had always been fun for me and was one of the subjects at which I excelled. This was about to come to a screeching halt. Suddenly, my teacher began taking out her frustration with me in a most humiliating manner. In her math class, I became the target of numerous sarcastic remarks.

I realized that I was being sent to the blackboard far more frequently than my classmates. Once I stood before the class with chalk in hand, I would be given problems in forms of math that we had not yet studied. If I hesitated, or remarked that I was not familiar with the process, our teacher informed me and the rest of the class that I was "extremely stupid."

I hoped that once this teacher got over her anger at me for dropping out of orchestra practice she would cease this method of revenge. However, her manner of inflicting retribution never wavered, so I received verbal attacks for the rest of the school year. I soon lost my enjoyment of working with numbers along with confidence in my mathematic ability. Those feelings unfortunately became permanent, and did not change in future years.

Another disagreeable experience, though not one with far-reaching consequences, occurred in a social studies class. From first grade on, schools used several different methods to make students aware of current events. Not every home contained a radio, subscribed to a newspaper or had money to take children to movies where they could view a newsreel. For that reason, classes read *My Weekly Reader*, a newspaper designed for different age levels, and each social studies class spent a great deal of time discussing events that were transpiring throughout the world.

It was 1944, the year of a national election. At that time in Texas, the only political party was the Democratic Party. The opportunity to vote for a Republican came about only in presidential elections. Of course, teens at junior-high level normally root for the candidate they know their parents support.

President Franklin Delano Roosevelt was running for his fourth term on the Democratic ticket. My father thought it was time for a change, so he planned to vote for Republican candidate, Thomas E. Dewey of New York. Several of my classmates had parents who felt the same way.

In an orchestrated political discussion as part of our social studies class, each student was asked to select a candidate and give a short talk listing reasons for supporting him. I was one of the first to volunteer. When I finished enumerating the reasons why I supported Dewey's candidacy, I sat down.

My teacher immediately leaped out of her chair and, with eyes blazing, screeched, "How dare you!"

I will not try to paraphrase the rest of her scathing remarks, although they included the fact that I should feel great shame for supporting a Republican. She continued to scream at me until I understood that she had not really wanted an objective discussion. Roosevelt was her candidate and hero. She had expected everyone in her class to praise him and recite reasons for his reelection. Exchanging glances with other Dewey supporters, I knew that they would either change candidates in midstream or just not volunteer to speak.

In junior high, for the first time in a school situation, I encountered lab classes in two separate fields of study in which I was a total disaster, if not a danger to my classmates. These situations introduced me to the idea that there would be some subjects for which I had absolutely no aptitude. Failure to thrive in a classroom setting was, for me, a new experience.

Fortunately, when I awakened to this insight, I was under the instruction of two marvelous teachers. I was further blessed by the fact that both women possessed an active sense of humor, which allowed them to observe my constant blunders without losing their cool.

Miss Carson, my beloved homeroom teacher, was given the impossible task of guiding me through a series of seventh-grade general science lab experiments. Pairing me with a Bunsen burner resulted in a succession of endless errors on my part and provided Miss Carson with comedic relief along with a certain amount of fear that I might blow up our building. As in the case of Dr. Frankenstein, each of my experiments was fatally flawed.

I looked up on several occasions to observe Miss Carson holding her head and laughing so hard that tears ran down her cheeks. Her facial expression seemed to say *Oh, no! I can't believe what I am seeing.*

Each student was given a list of experiments to perform, ingredients were available to select and mix and we were expected to record our outcomes. If whatever I mixed erupted into fizzes or bubbles, my heart began to pound and I leaped as far as I could away from the frightening concoction. My malodorous mixtures created absolutely horrendous atmospheric fogs. Like a novice witch struggling to learn proper cauldron procedure, ghastly olfactory sensations rose from my volcanic combinations as I stood by shaking with fear.

This situation kept me in a constant state of anxiety and caused my classmates to hold their noses and move farther and farther toward the opposite side of the room. My usual curiosity, interest and desire for further exploration into a subject deserted me as soon as I walked through the door of the science lab. I dreaded entering that room and had total distaste for the subject matter, taught in a hands-off style by my favorite and most admired teacher.

While taking general science, I was also enrolled in a sewing class under the heading of home economics. The teacher of this class thought that I had tremendous potential after I completed our first few assignments. We were asked to hand-hem cup towels and cut out and sew an apron completely by hand. I found these assignments repetitious but simple. My instructor bragged about my tight, even and invisible stitches.

Then, we were introduced to sewing machines. My classmates were delighted, whereas I found operating anything of a mechanical nature absolutely petrifying. Reminiscent of my Bunsen burner debacles was the sequence of unrecognizable garments I managed to produce while gritting my teeth and attempting to comprehend the operation of that dreadful machine.

I confronted the machine as an arch-enemy. We were engaged in a struggle for control in which only one of us could claim victory. At the end of each battle, I raised the white flag.

The only saving grace of science and home economics, as far as my grades were concerned, stemmed from the inclusion of written work and tests on theory in both classes. I was able to absorb theoretical ideas and garner perfect scores on all exams. This puzzled both of my teachers, who no doubt wondered how a student with the ability to grasp textbook material could be so totally inept at translating intellectual assumptions into practical physical manifestation.

No males were enrolled in home economics, even though half of the year was devoted to cooking classes. That idea was never even considered. Boys took shop classes where they were instructed in woodwork and basic mechanical drawing.

My favorite class at Poe was Spanish. The teacher instructed us almost entirely in that language and seldom resorted to English. With constant repetition, and the use of songs included in her curriculum, we gringos soon became fairly proficient in expressing ourselves.

Several weeks after the semester began, a new student was escorted into our classroom. This boy wore an obviously expensive dress suit and tie and displayed both military bearing and impeccable manners. Everyone in the class listened as he and our teacher greeted one another in Spanish. After assigning him a place to sit, she turned to the class and explained in English that this was the son of an ambassador from Mexico. He would attend our class so that he could learn English as we learned his language.

Our new classmate had been so schooled in gracious manners that it was impossible for him to remain seated when a woman was standing. Thus, when the teacher entered our classroom, he leaped up from his chair. When she got up from her chair to write on the blackboard, he immediately stood and remained standing until she once more took her seat.

Used to more informal classroom behavior, his Jack-in-the-Box style of leaping up out of his chair seemed humorous to the rest of us. Our teacher, who needed to be able to move about without disruptions, finally had to explain to him that, though she appreciated his respectful attitude, she would like him to remain in his chair during our class

238

period.

Everyone liked our new class member and enjoyed conversing with him in Spanish. His serious demeanor gradually diminished to the point where he appeared to enjoy our more relaxed classroom structure along with our teacher's bilingual jokes.

The conversational Spanish I learned in this classroom was far more valuable to me than any Spanish classes, taught by disinterested professors, I encountered in high school or college. Years later, as I welcomed tiny students into my own first-grade class and found they did not know English, I could smile at them and calm their fears with words and phrases learned at Poe Junior High.

My best friends and I ate lunch in the chaotically noisy Poe cafeteria on our first day of junior high school. After that, we chose to extend our lives by never again repeating that experience.

Laughing at our vivid descriptions of cuisine and colorful culinary complaints, our mothers agreed to fix lunches for us in the future. The contents of our tin lunch boxes were carried outside at noon and eaten on the school grounds from then on.

My friend Betty Brent Schaeffler came from a family in which the mother was a devout Catholic and the father a protestant. Each Friday morning, Mrs. Schaeffler fixed two Catholic (fish or cheese) lunches for her daughters and one Protestant (meat) lunch for her husband. The problem was, she very often mixed them up. If Betty Brent unwrapped her sandwich on a Friday and found that it contained meat, she could not make herself eat it.

If my lunch contained a tuna or cheese sandwich, we would simply trade. Finally, Mother and I decided that Betty was receiving Protestant lunches so often that I had better always take a Catholic lunch on Fridays...just in case.

The desire of our elders to witness a crop of junior high school students blossom into proficient ballroom dancers suddenly surfaced sometime during my year in the eighth grade. Before my friends and I realized what was happening, a combined group of parent and teacher wranglers lassoed us and herded us into a small local community center.

The night before this surprise soiree was scheduled, my mother broke her vow of silence and informed me she was prepared to teach me to dance. She led me into the dining room, where a small stack of Grandmother's records had been placed upon the dining table. Mother selected one of these records, placed it on the turntable and began to wind the old Victrola's crank. Wondering how dance instruction could possibly take place in a room filled with massive antiques, I took my dancing partner's extended hand and began a two-hour session of waltzing and twirling around the table.

As my perspiring parent finally agreed to halt instruction for the evening, I realized that I had become a passable dancer of the waltz and a champion avoider of protruding furniture.

I did not have the heart to tell Mother that my generation was committed to the jitterbug rather than the far more elegant waltz of her youth. Of course, she witnessed that lamentable fact while serving as a chaperone the following evening.

However, I tried to make her proud by executing some of the intricate waltz steps I had learned to the wild beat of the jitterbug. None of the sullen eighth-grade boys, who made it clear they were agreeing to this embarrassment with great reluctance, knew the difference.

The elders appeared to be satisfied when, sometime during the middle of this contrived ballroom fiasco, a few young people agreed to touch a member of the opposite sex and allowed themselves to be pushed, pulled or argued onto the dance floor as a couple. Prior to that, the girls remained in an immobile clump on one side of the dance floor talking, just as the boys were doing on the other side. Members of both genders were both secretly hoping, and icily fearing, that eventually they would be asked to dance.

I never attended this type of gathering again, since our family moved to El Campo within a month. My new home town, at the intersection of state highways 59 and 71, offered a much more informal style of country dances. Many of my new friends had been dancing, held in the arms of their grandparents, since infancy.

✤

During high school, our generation never gave a thought to holding a prom at an expensive hotel ballroom or combining that experience with dinner in an elegant dining establishment. Our proms were all held in the high school gym, which students were in charge of decorating. My junior year, I headed the decoration committee, which decided upon "A Spanish Garden" as a theme.

Actually, "A Czech Kolache" would have been more ethnically

accurate.

Plans were carefully drawn to help accomplish the impossible task of making a gym look like something it was not. In order to compete with the basketball goals on either end, we decided to place a garden, complete with wishing well, in the center of the gym floor.

As our begged, borrowed and created decorations were put into place, it became obvious that we needed a grassy area to surround that well. Our problem was solved by a student who worked for the local mortician and did some earnest negotiating on behalf of his classmates. The funeral home's large patch of fake grass was exactly the size we needed. As we stood back in awe to admire our last-minute completed Spanish patio, however, we were all aware that this entire scene could be suddenly scuttled by the death of a local resident.

So, while most of my girl friends were hoping that they would look dreamy in their new formal and receive a beautiful corsage, I was praying for miraculous cures for the seriously sick and contagious cases of rejuvenation for the elderly.

Many families who lived in the area around El Campo, including parents of the dancers, sat in the bleachers and watched those spring-time dances. These long-before-television events were a source of local pride, and a happy form of cheap entertainment for a generation of adults who were still in the process of emerging from total involvement in the seriousness of World War II.

No one had to worry about us getting drunk after the prom or speeding down highways. Very few teenagers of that day had access to anything but the family car, or farm truck—on loan. The ability to borrow it more than once depended upon the vehicle's being put safely back in the garage or barn by an agreed-upon time.

Our tastes were simple, our purses and pockets held change but few bills, and credit cards were unheard-of. So, this state of affairs allowed us to feel pleased with our efforts as interior decorators, and ecstatic over a borrowed patch of fake funeral grass.

※

I was mystified by my mother's reactions to her new surroundings after we moved to El Campo. She seemed to have gone into a form of social shock over the fact that she was living in a home she did not own and lacked domestic help.

Our two-story duplex seemed totally acceptable to me, and it certainly was in one of El Campo's nicest neighborhoods. We were living a scaled-down existence, furniture-wise, but Mother had artfully arranged the pieces she had been able to fit in.

Wondering why Mother turned down every social invitation she received, my father and I were informed that she was no longer in a situation where she could reciprocate, so she would accept no invitations. She was adamant that she would never entertain or invite friends into a home she did not own.

It was true that we had far less floor space than in our San Antonio home, but her objections seemed to be based more upon insecure feelings than a lack of square footage.

Missing our "social center" home life, I soon found a wonderful substitute in the country near El Campo. The first time my new friends Liz and her first-cousin Jeannie invited me to visit the Cs' farm, I found a home away from home for the remainder of my high school years.

Jeannie's mother, and the home in which her family lived, were totally opposite from my own mother and the surroundings she had always created. The Cs' two-story farm home was basic, utilitarian and totally devoid of decorative enhancement. Though Mrs. C had lovely features, and I always felt she could have been a knock-out, she dressed in a manner that ignored feminine attire and accoutrements altogether.

I remember this delightful woman wearing one dress, over and over. The buttons had disappeared long before I met her. In their place, the front was held together with large diaper pins.

Mrs. C's hair was untrimmed and worn in a single braid that hung down her back. She used no makeup, nor did she shave her legs. This was ever-apparent due to the fact that, unlike other women of this era, she did not wear stockings. Her wearing apparel was completed by a pair of men's work shoes.

The C family was financially well-off, and Mrs. C usually carried an inordinate amount of cash tucked into her purse. The fact that she appreciated pretty feminine attire was apparent when I accompanied her to shop for her daughters, Marie and Jeannie. She simply chose to dress herself as if she were headed out into the fields to work.

In the case of Mrs. C, "the fields" were political. She was the first political activist mover and shaker I had ever met. However, my involvement with her was limited to being allowed to hang out in the midst of her large and intriguing family. I felt as if I had suddenly been cast in a soap opera without first being handed a script.

I had never heard a single heated argument or harsh words spoken in my home. So, when voices were raised and shouts of disagreement reverberated from every corner of that farmhouse, my instinct was to run for cover and assume "the end is near." The realization that each sudden outburst would soon be over and promptly forgotten took a long time to still my swiftly beating heart.

I was surrounded by the interaction of siblings, along with their parents and cousins, each of whom held strong opinions and did not hesitate to express them. This was a total contrast to the quiet and reserved home life of an only child.

I owe this extended family thanks for many life-lessons. I also appreciate the fact that they introduced me to one of their Victoria cousins, Jimmy, who became my knight in shining armor.

Living in my new home town opened my eyes to the concept that, wherever I might move, I would find an assortment of fascinating and loving individuals offering friendship. This has been my experience in numerous subsequent relocations.

⟡

Speaking of scripts, I was offered an unusual opportunity during my junior year in high school that could have possibly led to a career. The fact that it did not was due to society's views on gender in general and my own thinking in particular.

On Friday, February 20, 1948, our state senator "Culp" Krueger and three other local investors made it possible for station KULP to sign on the air at 1390 on the AM radio dial. There was evidently a lot of empty airtime to fill up, so someone thought of asking high school students to host a program called *Junior Jamboree* and act as their own disk jockeys.

When I was asked, I chose three other students to co-host, wrote a script for the four of us and rehearsed the show. It seems that I was the only student host to act as producer, show up with a script in hand and a list of songs for the paid DJ to play on cue.

I recently found one old script, which began "Hello, everyone. It's time for your Saturday session of the *Junior Jamboree*." On this particular show, we played Spike Jones "Hotcha-Cornia," Perry Como's "Two Loves Have I," Guy Lombardo's "Frankie and Johnnie," Floyd Tilman's "Houston Waltz," Bing Crosby's "You Don't Have to Know the Language," "Indian Love Call" by Fred Lowery, Wayne King's

"Melody of Love," "Chloe" by Johnny Mercer and "Now is the Hour" by an artist who was left out of the script.

The rest of our time segment was taken up by sporadically reading names of fellow students I had previously interviewed in order to have song requests. It was the habit of listeners to call in and request a certain song to be played and "dedicated to" a specific individual. So, we encouraged our "fans" to "keep those cards and letters coming."

The people at KULP liked my script-writing and continued to call on me for more (volunteer) scripts until they had completed their professional staff. I found that chore both easy and entertaining. Yet, it never once occurred to me that this type of job could some day offer me gainful employment. Like most other jobs of that time, radio was a male dominated field.

Listening to KULP was a habit my friends and I immediately picked up. I had been accustomed to hearing Spanish language programs on WOAI and KTSA in San Antonio. In this area of Texas, programs in which Czech was spoken were broadcast frequently, and a variety of polka bands suddenly became well-known once their talents could be appreciated via KULP.

I had the opportunity to learn what a strong connection we form with our individual names during my senior year in high school. I was elected to represent our school, as well as the city of El Campo, by serving as duchess for the Texas College of Arts and Industries' Lantana Coronation in Kingsville.

When we arrived in the Rio Grande Valley, my escort Walter and I were presented with a shiny new convertible, complete with driver, to be our chariot on campus and in their big parade. I was mystified when I read signs on each side of the car which proclaimed "Duchess Jane Fletcher representing El Campo."

At my birth, feeling a one-syllable middle name was in order, my parents borrowed the name of a good friend's daughter. So, "Jane" was placed in the proper location on the birth certificate. After that, it was promptly erased from our family's consciousness and never again used except for filling out legal documents.

I met the original Jane on several occasions and found her to be a disagreeable, whiny little girl who was subject to frequent temper tantrums. Jane asserted the power she held over her mother by dropping to the floor and lying on her stomach. This put her in a good position to repeatedly kick her feet while holding her breath. Mildred, her mother, inevitably turned ashen-white in panic as she leaned over her daughter wringing her hands and pleading, "Jane, breathe! Please breathe!" It was a curious sight to behold, but these mini-dramas no doubt created even more subconscious distance between me and that middle name.

I assumed that "Vallie," my first name, must have appeared to be a mistake to the powers that be at the Lantana Festival. Rather than picking up a phone to inquire about the spelling, they simply substituted the next name on the official forms. So, during each ensuing event I felt and functioned like a statistic. They might as well have substituted "March 25" or "Five Feet Tall" on the signs.

People with cameras along the parade route called out, "Look this way Jane...smile!" My enjoyment of this festive weekend was greatly diminished because I saw myself as some sort of an impostor who operated in a state of confusion and never knew when she was being addressed.

Wearing the same aqua ball gown I had worn at our Junior-Senior prom, I smiled and bowed deeply to the assembled audience for Jane when the Royal Court was presented. However, I felt like Val had been left behind in El Campo.

Immediately after returning home, Walter and I shed our royal identities and joined members of our class in a big moneymaking venture called a "Slave Auction."

The idea of selling our services to the highest bidder having been decided upon, each of my classmates took his or her turn on stage while the rest of the high school population competed to bid for them. Winners were assured that they would have a servant to do their bidding when "Slave Day" rolled around.

Houston newspapers picked up on our moneymaking scheme and sent reporters. Articles were headed "Duchess Gets Top Bid at Slave Auction." The hook, or big surprise, was that I had been sold for twenty-five cents more than the captain of the football team. After all, this is Texas, where football reigns supreme and team members are traditionally considered the royalty of each high school. Even so, I sold for $11.50, whereas Charles's price was $11.25. Students of today could easily handle that, yet it was a major cash outlay for a public school student in the 1940s.

During high school, one of my most enjoyable experiences was being given an opportunity to work in the counselor's office. Unpleasant memories of physical education classes under Coach F at Poe in San Antonio, combined with the dank and musty dressing rooms in the El Campo High School gym, convinced me to opt out of that class. I took part in gym classes the first semester after our move to El Campo. At the beginning of the second semester, I walked into the principal's office and inquired if there was any other class I could take instead of PE.

The principal asked if I had any injuries or was ill in any manner. I informed him that I was very healthy but did have some back pain as a result of getting thrown from a horse. He instructed me to go to a physician, get an examination and, if the doctor concurred, bring an excuse back to school. I followed those instructions and soon returned with a doctor's note which was my ticket out of PE class.

The counselor at our high school had been complaining of overwork, so I was given the opportunity to work in his office since I had extra academic credits and really did not need another class.

After my first week at this enjoyable job, I was the only one working in his office. He would greet me, ask if everything was okay and then say, "I'm going to go down and have some coffee. If so-and-so comes in, give him (or her) this test." Or "Explain the results of the aptitude tests you gave last week." Or "Tell him about colleges that offer the best choices for the major he is interested in." Then, my boss would take off, and I would not see him again until the next day.

Fortunately for El Campo High School, I was extremely conscientious. If there was any test to be administered that I needed to take also, I insisted my boss stay in the room until I had finished taking it. Afterwards, I went through the whole procedure with the other students. I knew at the time that this was not standard procedure, but I also guessed that this kind gentleman might have a drinking habit that involved a beverage far stronger than coffee.

Directions for procedures to be followed during the administering and scoring of tests, or the advising of other students, were straightforward and simple. So, I continued to function in a counselor-like capacity and hoped that the absence of the one who held that position would not be discovered.

I had total confidence in what I was doing but continued to worry about what my boss was up to as I fulfilled tasks assigned to him. I loved the work and was grateful for the opportunity, rationalizing that what I lacked in credentials, I made up for in sobriety.

El Campo is in an agricultural area, and many of the people who live there make their living by ranching, farming or some type of agricultural service business. My father owned the agricultural implement business in town and a ranching operation in Jackson County.

One day, after I had taken a multiple choice IQ test, I saw my boss slap his forehead as he said, "Oh, No!" I asked what was wrong and he said, "Look how you answered this question."

The question was "Why do farmers rotate their crops?" I well knew it was for the benefit of the soil but had marked "To confuse the bugs." I erupted into laughter and impatiently awaited the end of the school day when I could hurry home and share that response with my dad.

My boss was upset and actually offered to change the answer for me, but I would not let him.

Dad and I laughed about that hand-eye foul-up for the rest of his life. From that day forward, each time I made a foolish decision, or a remark that was not too bright, Dad would ask, "Are you trying to confuse those bugs again?"

Oh, and the answer to the riddle? Smoke.

CHAPTER THIRTEEN

WAR AND OUR
CHANGING WORLD

"Our country is going to be sorry we allowed this type of cargo to be sent to Japan. There will come a time when it will be shot back at us in the form of bullets."

The one speaking prophetic words was my father. My parents and their friends the Burrs were enjoying a Sunday afternoon at the Houston Ship Channel when Dad spied Japanese cargo ships taking on loads of iron. Exotic foreign ships in port lured spectators, who enjoyed watching stevedores loading and unloading the vessels in the early 1920s..

My mother, along with just-married Mildred and Jimmy Burr, tried to tease Dad out of his somber mood. After all, the War to End All Wars, World War I, had ensured that there would be no more armed conflict. Had he forgotten that Armistice Day was celebrated each November eleventh?

My father's prophecies did not end with this one incident. An avid reader and researcher of books and articles pertaining to history and government, he often warned of events and dangerous liaisons that would result in another world war.

On September first of 1939, he rushed home from work and hurried straight over to my bedroom toy shelf. Grabbing up my Russian peasant doll, he angrily yanked the Soviet hammer-and-sickle flag out of her hand. His explanation that Russia and Germany had invaded Poland did not mean very much to me at age seven.

On Sunday, December 7, 1941, my Grandmother and I attended a show at the Majestic Theater in downtown San Antonio. Suddenly, the screen went black, and the houselights were turned on. A man who was clearly not an entertainer walked out onto the stage carrying a stand microphone.

It was the theater manager, who announced to the audience, "This morning the Japanese Air Force attacked our country's air force base at Pearl Harbor. Ladies and gentlemen, the United States is now in this war."

The movie was not over, but everyone left their seat and headed home. What was most noticeable as I watched the audience exit the theater was the total silence. Gasps and low moans sounded immediately following the announcement. After that moment, no one spoke.

Strangely, the movie audience had just viewed a newsreel that contained scenes of the Japanese ambassador and a colleague on a visit to Washington DC. Supposedly, they had been sent to the United States to conduct peaceful diplomatic negotiations.

Everyone moved from the theater enveloped in a cloud of their own contemplations. No doubt, each was entertaining the same thought: How will this affect my life and the lives of those I love?

I learned the answer to that question shortly after the Rigsby Avenue bus delivered my grandmother and me back to our neighborhood. By the time we reached home, my parents, who had heard the news as a radio bulletin, were in a heated discussion concerning my father's enlistment.

War would not be officially declared until the next day. Each classroom in Highland Park Elementary had suddenly been equipped with a radio, but the entire student body was taken to the cafeteria, where together we listened intently as President Roosevelt declared the Japanese sneak attack "a date which will live in infamy."

The president concluded his speech by asking Congress to declare that "since the unprovoked and dastardly attack" a state of war had existed between the United States and the Japanese Empire. Three days later, Germany and Italy declared war on the United States. So, suddenly, our country was a part of the Allied Powers along with Britain and the Soviet Union, who were warring against the Axis Powers: Japan, Germany and Italy.

For several years, movie audiences in the United States had watched newsreels featuring scenes from the war in Europe and the conflict between China and Japan. Our family often sat glued to the radio as Walter Winchell, Edward R. Murrow or Fulton Lewis Jr. gave us the latest news about the war overseas. Many young men from the United States had flown to England and enlisted in their Royal Air Force, since the United States government had continued to operate from an isolationist stance.

For the next week, my parents continued to argue over Dad's determination to enlist. Mother began using every ploy in her ample supply of manipulations to insure that he would stay home. To her dismay, none of them worked.

She felt that a forty-two-year-old man with a family should not be expected to go into the service. "Besides, you served in the navy in World War I. Let the younger men enlist."

Dad felt that fighting for his country was his patriotic duty, so he informed our family that he was going to re-join the navy. Immediately after we received his decision, something unexpected occurred to change things.

Dad worked for the Uvalde Rock Asphalt Company as a bookkeeper-revenue collector. This company was suddenly designated as strategic to the war effort, and all major employees were "frozen" to their jobs. Now, instead of being used to build roads and parking lots for the general public, asphalt was earmarked for airstrips and military supply roads.

With the question of his military enlistment settled, Dad offered to head a group of volunteer air raid wardens. Civilians were quickly organized to work within a certain area of their towns and cities dispensing information. Later, they returned to check up and see if families had outfitted their homes in compliance with the new blackout rules.

People in our country were used to watching newsreels that showed scenes of London and other European cities being bombed. The fear was that American cities might soon meet a similar fate. Homes were equipped with blackout curtains, and our cities held air raid drills, complete with warning sirens sounding the "air raid" and "all-clear" signals. Dad and his fellow wardens planned these drills and patrolled city neighborhoods while they were in progress.

Schools also held numerous air raid drills. In Highland Park Elementary, that meant getting everyone down into the basement in the fastest time possible. Officials from the school district always showed up with stopwatches to time our less-than-perfect descents.

I can remember arriving back at a third-story classroom and having the air raid signal ring again. The powers-that-be kept us going up and down those stairs with multiple drills until they were satisfied with our rate of speed.

Air raid wardens were also instructed in Red Cross first aid procedures. It was believed that they would be the first to reach victims if our cities were bombed.

⋙⋘

People in San Antonio were used to seeing men in uniform because of the military camps in and around our city. Soon, the population of these camps swelled almost beyond capacity, so a man who did not wear a uniform was in the minority.

Fort Sam Houston, within the city, was our famous old army training camp. Brooks, Randolph and Kelly fields trained fliers. Fort Normoyle, south of town, was a motor repair depot. Duncan Field took care of airplane repair. Recruits received rifle practice at Camp Bullis, and new recruits were inducted into the army at Dodd Field north of Fort Sam Houston.

Rationing and shortages, conditions Europeans had long been used to, suddenly materialized in the United States. Gasoline was one of the first products to be rationed, along with rubber, oil, automobiles and typewriters. An automobile owner registered his vehicle and was issued a window sticker indicating how the car was used. The individual's job category designated how much gas he or she was allowed to buy. Pleasure driving was prohibited.

Signs with slogans like "Don't travel unless your trip helps win the war" were seen posted in each neighborhood. Another warning slogan, "Loose lips sink ships," became a well-known and oft-repeated motto.

Because Dad's employer was an officially designated strategic industry, he was offered an "A" card for our old gray Ford-V8. In a fit of misplaced patriotism, he turned it down and took a "C" card, which was the one given to the average family.

Families with a "C" card did not make any out-of-town trips, and had to be very careful how much in-town driving they did. New tires were no longer available to civilian households, so a blow-out was a major disaster. Used tires sold at premium prices, and all tires were patched and patched again.

On the home front, housewives had to change their way of grocery shopping to comply with ration coupons. Each family was issued a War Ration Book according to its size. Ration coupons became a new form of currency. Sugar, meat and coffee were rationed, and butter was almost impossible to find. Stick oleomargarine, stark-white in color, was introduced as a replacement. Included in the package was a powdered yellow dye that could be mixed into the margarine if one's family rebelled against spreading the white stuff on their bread.

Juggling the price and point value of ration coupons, my mother purchased a package of this new oleomargarine. Though in later years the name of this new product was shortened to *margarine*, during the war years it was referred to as "oleo."

After dealing with its unappetizing appearance, Mother decided she would not allow her family's mealtime aesthetics to be poisoned. Using her wiles and powers of persuasion, she obtained butter from the same butcher who kept our family well supplied with meat. She had always been one of his best customers, so when strings could be pulled, he supplied her with items she did not have the ration coupons to purchase.

Every family was urged to plant a victory garden to supply their vegetable needs. My father dug a small garden in our back yard; however, I don't remember it being a significant source of food for our family.

For fashionable women, the biggest lack was silk and nylon stockings. Prior to the deterioration of U.S.-Japanese relations, our country imported its raw silk from Japan. Ninety percent of that silk went into stockings.

Nylon stockings, made from DuPont's new synthetic fiber yarns, were first commercially sold on May 13, 1940, at prices of $1.15, $1.25 and $1.35 a pair. Department stores were jammed with buyers. On March 8, 1942, the War Production Board issued regulation L-85, which regulated every aspect of clothing and commandeered nylon for use in the war effort—specifically, for parachutes and tires. By 1943, nylons had vanished from display counters in American department stores.

The stockings of that time were made with a dark seam at the back of the legs. Suddenly, leg makeup and a pencil with which to draw a faux seam appeared in drug and department stores. This attempt at deception became popular with young women, but the older ones did not have the aptitude or patience to deceive the public. Extremely wavy stocking seams resulted from a woman's attempt to draw a neat line on the back of her own leg. Bare legs could be darkened, but they could not be made to appear sheer.

The criminal element wasted no time in finding a way to subvert the rationing system and profit from the theft of hard-to-find items. People could purchase these items on the sly at sky-high black market prices.

A European black market had been in operation for years, dealing mostly in clothing and liquor. In the United States, marketers carved their niche of profiteering from sales of meat, sugar and gasoline. Stockings made from bootlegged fibers were a valued commodity on both continents.

Texan Stanley Marcus, of Dallas's Neiman Marcus Department Store, served as the apparel consultant to the War Production Board. He announced to the fashion industry that it was each designer's patriotic duty to design fashions that would remain stylish through multiple seasons, His appeal was answered by the creation of separates and coordinating components that would create an illusion that a woman owned more outfits than she actually did.

With leather and rubber going into the war effort, shoe designers switched to materials like reptile skin and mesh. Wood or cork-soled wedge-heeled soles became popular, and all of the imaginative shoe-adornments were kept at a minimum. Rationing rules limited the height of shoe heels to one inch and allowed for only six color choices.

One of the most conspicuous losses to the war effort for little girls of my age was the elastic used to hold up panties. As I grew, the only thing available to replace the pink silk panties I had always worn were bloomer-like garments made of white chintz and secured at the waist with a button. Girls quickly determined that these wartime substitutes were ugly, uncomfortable and poorly constructed.

My friend and neighbor, Georgia Lee, wore a pair of these chintz panties while accompanying her mother on a downtown shopping trip. Suddenly, the waist-button popped loose, causing Georgia Lee to panic as she walked down a busy city street. Fortunately, one of the old-style wooden phone booths stood on the sidewalk nearby. Georgia Lee grabbed her mother with one hand and her south-sliding undergarments with the other. Both females quickly dived into the phone booth, where Mrs. H. attempted to furtively anchor her daughter's drawers without passers-by becoming aware of what was taking place.

Young females soon learned that carrying a large safety pin for such an emergency was a necessary back-up device.

I began noticing women and girls wearing two new colors I'd first seen in films. To my eye, they looked good on practically no one. Because so many items of apparel were turned out in these colors, few women and girls were able to escape wearing fuchsia and/or chartreuse. No matter which direction I turned, one of these ultra-vibrant colors would soon glare into sight.

Televisions' classic movie channels are a great place to view the suit and dress styles designed by American designers working with new restrictions and limited materials. War-goods manufacturing monopolized the stock of natural fabrics, so domestic manufacturers had to search for substitute fabrics to use in their garments. Suddenly, rayon production was geared up, and an austere silhouette with narrow hips and padded shoulders was the style. One-piece dresses with peplums also came into vogue.

Women who sewed could obtain McCall's patterns that showed how to transform men's suits into ladies' suits and women's dresses into children's clothing. After all, the men were now in uniform, so it was patriotic to use what was left hanging in their closets.

Speaking of clothing, my family and I once listened to a frustrated young soldier who had joined the army with a strong desire to render much-needed medical services. His story was not an uncommon theme, illustrating the idiocy that sometimes ensued when incompetent military officers were put in charge of other men.

My mother had a distant cousin named Gladys, whom I thought was probably one of the most beautiful women on earth. The lyrical description "skin like alabaster" was one used by far too many writers of that day. Yet, Gladys truly had an alabaster-perfect complexion, along with large blue eyes and even features. Light auburn hair, cut short and surrounding her face with ringlets, served as the icing on the cake.

Gladys could have easily been a film star or artist's model. The role she actually played was the happy bride of a handsome young physician named Marcus. The couple lived in western Louisiana, where Marcus had a thriving medical practice.

Every film one attended at the beginning of World War II ran a short feature begging doctors to enlist. Magazine and newspaper articles told stories emphasizing our country's urgent need for physicians and other trained medical personnel. Signs were nailed onto utility poles and posted in railway terminals touting the patriotic duty of every able bodied young man of medicine to volunteer his services. Public service announcements on radio preached that same doctrine day and night.

Mother was elated when she received a call from Gladys informing her that Marcus had enlisted and was stationed in San Antonio. She and Gladys agreed upon a night for the couple to come to our home for a visit.

Of course, Marcus had expected to be assigned to the Medical Corps after completing basic training. Instead, he was assigned to the Quartermaster Corps and given a job counting shoes.

Though every branch of the service shared a need for good footgear, here was a highly trained physician and surgeon placed in a spot where his formidable medical skills were being wasted.

Marcus had certainly complained and asked for reassignment. He had tried to reason with those who gave him orders. No matter to whom he spoke, he was basically told to shut up and do his job. Totally frustrated, he continued to count shoes day after day.

One warm San Antonio morning, a buddy of his complained of a bad sore throat. Marcus examined him and swabbed his throat with a medicine used at that time. For that sympathetic gesture, he was placed under military arrest because he was not an army-trained medic.

Marcus's experience was not unlike similar tales related by others who had enlisted with a specialty to offer and been assigned to jobs where their education and specific skills were ignored. Karen Wright traces the history of the world's first Dr. Pepper bottling plant in her book *The Road to Dr. Pepper, Texas*. Citing events that occurred during World War II, she relates another ludicrous example of an assignment given to a young man who was drafted.

"One of the Dr. Pepper employees called to service was Tom Lewis Peacock. Much to his chagrin, he was assigned to the Medical Corps. When he inquired why, he was told, according to his work history, he had medical experience. Even explaining that Dr. Pepper was a soft drink, not a physician, Peacock was still unable to avoid assignment to the hemorroidectomy unit."

In another chapter, I mentioned schools dismissing students so we could pull our Radio Flyer wagons throughout our area to collect scrap metal for the war effort. There were other salvage and recycling efforts that came with rationing and stayed in effect for the duration.

How seriously we took our job can be seen by reading the October 1942 edition of our school *Highlander* newspaper. My fifth-grade classmate Anna Nell Wolter and I wrote the following;

SCRAP METAL DRIVE

"The boys and girls of America have always been willing to do their part for National Defense. The government gave them a big job to do when it asked them to collect scrap metal. Scrap metal is badly needed for war munitions. The children were asked to find it, bring it to school and stack it on the Hammond Street side of the school.

The children of Highland Park as well as those all over Texas were sworn in as Junior Texas Rangers. We did our part as could be seen by the huge pile of scrap.

Most of the articles in our elementary newspaper dealt with patriotism or the war effort. Anna Nell and I each had our own byline in the following issue. Mine was on the Armistice Assembly, and hers was titled "Scrap Metal Drive." It announced that our scrap metal was sold for $223.45, a formidable sum at that time.

Our stories were followed by one of the many Hitler jokes of the day. "Why doesn't Hitler have his teeth pulled?" ("He's afraid of the Yanks.")

Other stories related the fact that, every week, mothers sold defense stamps in front of Principal Crain's office, and listed the many activities of our Junior Red Cross.

Lard, rendered hog fat or bacon grease were the oils used to fry foods. Suddenly, each family was asked to save these cooking oils and turn them in during "Grease Drives." Children were asked to save and collect scraps of tinfoil like those used to wrap sticks of chewing gum. We squeezed out every last bit of toothpaste and then flattened the tube to be exchanged at a store before a new tube could be purchased.

In addition to grease, tin and metals, rubber and paper were saved and collected during specific drives.

The government urged civilians to help finance the war effort by purchasing war bonds. Even though these bonds offered a rate of return below market value, and the median income during this era was about $2,000 per year, people sacrificed to invest in these bonds.

My friends and I purchased defense stamps, starting at ten cents apiece, with our allowance. When the book that held these stamps was filled, it was saved and we began to fill up another book. Once a sufficient number of books filled with stamps had accumulated, we could trade them in for a $25 war bond. This procedure took a long time, because a child's average weekly allowance was between five and fifteen cents.

Movie stars, artists and composers were recruited by the government to push the sales of war bonds and stamps. Composer Irving Berlin wrote a song titled "Any Bonds Today?" that became the theme song of the Treasury Department's National Defense Savings Program. The song was recorded by Bing Crosby, the Andrews Sisters and other well-known singers. Disc jockeys were probably pressured to play it often because each time we dialed up a musical program on the radio, we heard it played repeatedly.

Artist Norman Rockwell created a series of illustrations that the *Saturday Evening Post* reproduced and circulated to promote bond buying. Bond rallies were held throughout the country, with Hollywood film stars appearing as a lure. This type of event created an emotional appeal and usually surpassed its quota of bonds sold.

Because there were suddenly so many young servicemen and their wives moving into San Antonio, housing for these couples became high in demand and short in supply. Our neighbor, Mrs. M, viewed this as a get-rich-quick opportunity. Surely, if a household had an extra room, renting it to a serviceman with a spouse, and often a baby, was a patriotic gesture. However, quick to take advantage of others when it put money in her pocket, Mrs. M went overboard.

The M home was similar to ours, with three bedrooms and one bath. Harry Jr. was moved into the master bedroom with his parents, and the two other bedrooms were quickly rented to young couples.

The extra money was so appealing that Mrs. M. did not stop there.

Another young family was installed in the living room, and still another paid for the privilege of living in her dining room. Several babies and toddlers were included in the mix.

With five couples and their children crammed into this one small house, Mrs. M assumed that the schedule she posted for use of the bath and kitchen facilities would suit everyone. My parents felt she was taking advantage of young families who were desperate to be together before the husbands received their overseas assignments.

As signs of the times, Burma-Shave began posting messages along the highways that read:

> We've made Grandpa
> Look so trim
> The local draft board's
> After him
> BURMA SHAVE

Hollywood changed its focus overnight. A number of famous actors joined the armed services, so new actors were drafted by the film industry. After sitting through the new films, we assumed that most of the talented screenwriters and directors must have also joined the service. War movies—combat films—with the same predictable formula were turned out in triplicate. Civilian actors like John Wayne received an opportunity to leave grade-C Westerns behind and act in films from the A-list.

Musical films featured patriotic songs, and the ever-present chorus lines were garbed in military-uniform-style costumes. Dance routines were choreographed into rhythmic marches rather than the more traditional dance steps. With a few notable exceptions, like *Casablanca*, most films of that day were what my father called "a sorry lot."

Films did add three distinct terms of approval to the vocabulary of young men and boys during World War II. The wolf whistle, "woo-woo" and "hubba-hubba" were first used by servicemen viewing pretty women in movies. Before long, the distinctive whistle and the expressions were adopted and used frequently by schoolboys in every grade.

Our family was very close to a young man from Brownwood, who suddenly arrived at our door wearing a newly issued Air Corps uniform.

Mother and Daddy had once planned to adopt Bobby Nevans, but things had not worked out.

After my parents settled on Kayton Avenue in the 1920s, their best friends were neighbors "Pop" and Nonie Nevans. The two couples spent a great deal of time together, along with the Nevans's son Bobby. Pop had served in World War I, as had my father. However, Pop's combat experiences ended when he was gassed in the trenches while fighting in France.

Pop spent several years in hospitals after World War I ended. Overcoming the aftereffects of poison gas was a lengthy process he had to endure before being released to resume life as a civilian. His other illness was a lifetime disability.

Doctors of the World War I era referred to Pop's condition as shell shock, a catch-all phrase relating to the aftereffects of war. Today, it's known to be an extremely rare condition known as a *disassociative fugue state*, and describes a person who experiences bouts of amnesia, forgetting who and where he is.

Pop was a traveling salesman who normally made excellent money on his sales trips. However, there were other occasions when he simply did not show up, send money or telephone Nonie. If his fugue state lasted for an extended period of time, Nonie had to obtain work to pay the household bills and feed herself and her son. Bobby lived with my parents during those times, and Nonie joined them for meals.

This was prior to my birth, so Bobby actually gave my parents their first experience at child-rearing, and they loved it. He seemed to be one of those magical children who brought joy to everyone.

Pop would eventually awaken to reality and return home, to the relief of his family and friends. The doctors had warned Nonie about his condition, so no one judged him to be lacking in character or a delinquent husband and father.

During a visit to her parents in Brownwood, Nonie caught a cold, which quickly advanced into pneumonia. This vibrant young woman suddenly succumbed to a disease that was often fatal during that time.

Nonie's death left her grieving husband faced with a huge decision. It was obvious that his medical disability, as well as the nature of his job, disqualified him to be a single parent. My parents asked to adopt Bobby, and Pop agreed that living with them would be in Bobby's best interest.

Then, two sets of grandparents in Brownwood threw a fit. Both sets wanted Bobby to live with them. Bobby wanted to stay with my parents. It was a heartbreaking and confusing time for everyone concerned.

Bobby was eventually sent to Brownwood, where he moved back and forth between the homes of his grandparents. I'm sure they treated him well, but he kept running away and returning to my parents' home.

His habit was to walk to the highway and hitchhike a circuitous route to San Antonio and the young couple who loved him as their own. Pop and his grandparents always knew where to find him.

Eventually, he adjusted to living in Brownwood, but he still took every opportunity to hitchhike to San Antonio and stay with my parents. Once I entered the picture, I loved him as much as they did.

So, I grew older looking forward to visits from this adorable "older brother" who never wanted to leave us when it was time to go home. Like my parents, I wanted to adopt him.

Now, with Bobby standing in our living room looking extremely handsome in his uniform, the war suddenly came into a more personal focus.

Bobby visited often while he was taking flight training near San Antonio. After he was sent overseas as a fighter pilot, we wrote him using an APO address and frequently received the tiny V-Mail letters that service personnel were allowed. He could not tell us exactly where he was, but the nature of his communiques indicated that the Air Corps was keeping him tremendously busy.

The last letter we received from him was dated April 3, 1944, and told us he was stationed in New Guinea. The return address was Lt. R.G. Nevans 0-750668, 36th Fighter Squadron. It read:

> Dear Bill, Aleen and Vallie, Here it is Easter Sunday and I've got a few minutes off, so thought I would drop you a line. Just wondered how everything is in San Antonio and how you guys are getting along.
>
> This New Guinea is not exactly a place where I'd like to spend a vacation. It's around 120 degrees in the shade most of the time and full of jungle and pot-bellied natives.
>
> It's not so bad though because we get plenty of flying. I'm in a P-38 squadron and they are really fine ships. Also we have the Nips beat down to their knees and that's good. Drop me a line and tell me about the USA. Love, Bob Nevans

Bobby was probably flying one of Lockheed's P-38J Lightnings. The company redesigned them in 1943 to improve their roll-rate and maneuverability at high speeds.

Throughout our city, service flags featuring a blue star in a field of white, framed with red material and fringed in gold, hung in the front windows of many homes. The star symbolized the family inside had a son in the service. Several stars announced that this family had given more than one child to the war effort.

When a blue star was changed to gold, observers realized a family's son had been killed while performing his duty. Sadly, the organization called Gold Star Mothers grew rapidly in number.

Mother had a habit of leaving notes on the dining room table for Dad and me to see after work and school. The notes usually contained bits of news she had gleaned from a telephone conversation or a reminder of a dental appointment. They concerned rather trivial matters she might forget to tell us otherwise.

One afternoon, I returned from school and saw a yellow piece of notepaper on the dining table. Hoping it was not a dental appointment for me, I picked it up and read "Bobby Nevans has been reported Missing-in-Action."

This was a shocking way for Dad and me to receive the news. I never understood why Mother used such an impersonal and rather brutal method to inform us. I can only assume she could not bring herself to say the words aloud. We learned later that his plane had been shot down during a combat mission.

Since we were not his official family, we had to rely upon secondhand news. It was difficult for our family to find real closure in dealing with the death of this beloved, yet unofficial, son and brother.

Bobby has always remained in my mind's-eye as we last saw him... standing in our living room looking proud and handsome in his new uniform. His Blue Star Flag had hung in our hearts instead of our front window. So, people on Kayton Avenue could not share our grief as we changed it to the dreaded, but honored, Star of Gold.

※

Women also enlisted in branches of the armed service; however, their talents were used as nurses, drivers or clerical workers instead of combat. A small number were trained as pilots who ferried planes. Certainly, some did find themselves in dangerous situations, but their branches of the service were kept separate from those of the men.

261

One of Aunt Vallie's good friends, Oveta Culp Hobby, became the director of the Women's Army Corps. The Fletcher family had been close to former Governor William Hobby during the years he published *The Beaumont Enterprise*.

My parents often joked, "Governor Hobby went on our honeymoon with us." After their simple wedding in Beaumont, June 12, 1922, my parents boarded a train bound for Galveston. Dad spied his friend, so he and Mother sat with Hobby until the train reached Galveston. Then, all three of them climbed down the steps of the train and headed for the Galvez Hotel.

Aunt Vallie had become close to Oveta after she married Will Hobby in 1931. After World War II began, I was often taken to Oveta's San Antonio home when our family went to visit. Today, I'm sorry that I missed hearing each and every word spoken by this wise, famous and multi-talented woman during these visits. I should have remained within earshot of the fascinating conversations I feel sure must have transpired in the living room.

Oveta, however, quickly discovered that I loved animals, so she led me to a particular clothes closet, where I remained for the rest of our visits. In it dwelled a mother cat with a new litter of kittens. So, although I learned little of Oveta Culp Hobby's legendary wisdom during our visits; as her feline family grew, I was able to observe the fascinating world of cats and kittens for the very first time.

I was never tempted to join the army in later years, but there are a number of good homes enjoying the progeny of mother cats who for years have shared my office space and used it as a birthing-room.

※

During the war, public school students were encouraged to correspond with children of our overseas allies. So many European young ones had been displaced and seen terrible scenes of destruction. We were asked to reach out to them and write letters of support.

I drew the name of a boy who was older than I and wrote lengthy letters. Derek John Masters lived at #9 St. Michael's Avenue, Yeovil, Somerset, England. We continued our correspondence for several years and, because of the differences in our forms of English, often had to ask one another for the meaning of words and phrases used in the other's letters.

Derek's family listened to the "wireless" and he drove his Mum wild when he practiced the "flutina." He wanted to know what kind of "youth movement" I was in. His mum and sisters were "often in chapel," and he was glad I was a Methodist "because they have such jolly times!"

At fifteen, Derek was the youngest of five children and worked as an apprentice upholsterer. One of his two older brothers had been killed in the British Navy at age nineteen. When we first began to correspond, Derek was worried about another brother who was then fighting in the thick of things. This brother later fought in the D-Day invasion, but made it through alive. After the war, he came home bearing gifts for all of his family. Derek and his dad received watches. The sisters and his brother's "young lady" received stockings (probably of the black market variety). Derek's mum received slippers and a box of Black Magic Chocolates. She had saved her ration coupons in order to obtain the ingredients to make a cake for her son's homecoming.

❧

Civilians in San Antonio were urged to invite servicemen into their homes on weekends and holidays. These young men were in an area where they knew no one and were eager to leave the barracks and share a meal and a visit with civilian families.

My memories of the servicemen we entertained are rather vague, but I still have vivid mental pictures of attending similar gatherings at our eccentric Aunt Lulu Long's.

Knowing how haughty she was, and how she was liable to blurt out just about anything that came to mind, we worried about the outcome of the Sunday meal we were driving to her home to share with her guests. Lulu felt she was doing her patriotic duty, though, and fortunately, she was wise enough to invite my informal and well-informed father to converse with her honored guests.

Lulu's home was decorated elaborately, since money was no object. However, comfort was sacrificed in the acquisition of furniture that was in the priceless-art-object category. Entering through a hall dominated by large statuary, her guests must have felt they were in a museum.

Lulu had absolutely no idea how to engage young servicemen in conversation, so my father really saved those occasions by steering us all down conversational trails. He also managed to save Aunt Lulu's paid companion, Marie, from total humiliation.

Marie was an extremely shy young woman from East Texas who served as Lulu's chauffeur and errand-runner. Lulu had decided that it was time she found a boyfriend, and made numerous pointed remarks to her young male guests, hinting broadly that it would be an excellent idea for them to take Marie out on a date. Miraculously, the young men were able to relax and enjoy these Sunday affairs—thanks to Daddy, Lulu's gourmet cook and their own good humor.

※

My grandmother Fletcher had always been a part of my life. When she visited her two younger sisters in Beaumont, we knew that she had to steel herself in preparation to be transported back into the past.

As the last, and only, descendant of the Vaughan family in my generation, I had been taken to the stately old Victorian house on Beaumont's Calder Avenue for numerous visits. Grandmother's sisters May, nick-named "Duck," and Addie were the embodiment of characters from an antebellum novel. They spoke baby talk to one another and the rest of our family. They never spoke to or "received" anyone who was not in the family. After their mother's death, they never again left the Vaughan house. There was an extended period of time when they refused to receive visits from close friends and even first cousins with whom they had grown up.

Both Aunt Vallie and Aunt Lulu, cousins and cradle-buddies of these peculiar siblings, had experienced being turned away at the front door of the Vaughan home due to some capricious whim of "the girls."

This bizarre behavior did not run in the family. Both of their parents had survived many varieties of hardship and periods of starting over. Still, my two great-aunts seemed dead set on continuing to live in the past as they reinvented the word *eccentric*.

I have vivid memories of Aunt Addie meeting us at the front door, catching sight of my father and calling out, "Oh, Duckie, Duckie, come quick! Here's our Billy Boy!"

Daddy once survived a miserable two-week visit with "the girls" while on a business trip to Beaumont. They had been delighted to have him stay with them, and their cook-housekeeper always had a delicious meal ready at the end of his business day. Feeling as if he needed to contribute something to their arrangement, Daddy visited a local grocery store and purchased several sacks of food. The sisters took this to mean he thought that they were charity cases and cried for the rest of his visit. They instructed their cook to fix two separate meals each night. Cuts of meat and vegetables Dad had purchased were served at one end of their extremely long dining room table.

Duck and Addie ate only the food they had paid for. Their dinner table conversation consisted of several versions of "Billy Boy thinks he has to give us charity" as they sobbed and dabbed their cheeks with handkerchiefs.

When Daddy returned home, he regaled our family and the San Antonio great-aunts with tales of these miserable evening meals. Of course, my father was advised by friends and family that he should have gifted his aunts with flowers and candy instead of groceries. In their own minds, they were still young Southern belles, so this would have been the courtly thing to do.

Aunt Duck and Aunt Addie often sent me letters and included pressed flowers between the pages. One time, I wrote them a thank-you note and left the second A out of their printed last name on the envelope.

Though I was less than school age at the time, I received a scathing rebuke by return mail. I was to always be mindful, they said, that the "better class Vaughans" spelled their name with two As. Those who omitted that second A were "very low class." Their words gave my family another laugh and a new addition to our collection of tales about "the girls."

We were both surprised and elated that Beaumont shops and grocery stores continued to deliver goods to the Vaughan house. This custom was long out of style, but it was what "the girls" expected.

It was October of 1944 when my grandmother decided to make an autumnal visit to her sisters and return home in time for Christmas. My mother and I helped her pack; then Daddy drove her to the railroad station.

Grandmother, with the exception of suffering some arthritis pain, had always been healthy. While in Beaumont, she caught a cold, which lingered on and turned into laryngitis.

Unlike her younger sisters, Grandmother loved social events and had made plans to meet with relatives and old friends during her visit. She was also the only one of our immediate family who was able to accept the invitation to attend the Beaumont wedding reception given for Faye Emerson and Elliot Roosevelt.

As Christmas grew closer, we received a letter dated December 17th complaining of the parties and receptions she had to miss due to her cold. She teased me about missing Cousin Faye's reception by writing, "Vallie, if I had had one of your gardenias for my hair, I would have been tempted to go anyway...even though my hair had Vicks in it."

"I just can't think of not getting home for Christmas, but my chances seem to grow dimmer..."

About the time we received this letter, we got a phone call saying she had been taken to the hospital. My father made several calls to her doctor and was told that her condition was not serious, but he felt she should stay in the hospital for a short time. Daddy asked if he should come to Beaumont and was told, "No. She'll be up and about in just a few days."

Dad made arrangements to leave anyway, and headed east on Highway 90. As he arrived at the hospital, he saw a doctor leaving his mother's room. Introducing himself, he was told, "I'm sorry to have to tell you this, but I have just pronounced your mother dead." Since he had been repeatedly assured that Grandmother's condition was not serious, this was a shock to all of us.

Sharing the sad news with our Kayton Avenue neighbors, we found that a family who lived down the block wanted to attend her funeral, so Mother and I were able to ride to Beaumont with them.

As my father made funeral arrangements, "the girls" were asked for a picture of Grandmother for the use of the hair stylist and makeup artist at the mortuary. They complied with the request and handed the emissary from the funeral home one of their favorite pictures.

After Mother and I arrived in Beaumont, the three of us drove to the funeral home for the viewing. My great-aunts Kate and Gladys had shopped for a dress for Grandmother and selected a gorgeous sheer lilac gown. As we approached the casket of my seventy-two-year-old grandmother, we saw an extremely beautiful young woman who appeared to be ready to attend a formal ball.

My mother immediately went into hysterics. "That's not Mother Fletcher! That's not Mother Fletcher," she cried out repeatedly. She could not stop sobbing. I looked at the vision before me and staggered back to sit in a chair before I fainted. I was totally stunned by the elegant young woman who lay in the casket. Daddy and I handled our overwhelming emotions by holding them inside.

After my senses stopped spinning out of control, I could deduce how this had happened. My grandmother had always worn a sunbonnet, or carried a parasol, when out-of-doors. This lifetime habit was probably what kept her skin totally flawless.

During my lifetime, she wore her hair pulled back from her face and knotted into a bun at the back of her head. When loose, it reached down past her waist. Its color was a vibrant dark brown without a single strand of gray. Grandmother brushed it daily, and had never subjected it to a permanent wave, so her tresses had retained a lustrous sheen.

Using the old photograph, made when Florence Vaughan Fletcher was a young woman, the hair stylist had duplicated her elegant up-do. The make-up artist used an extremely light touch, so the translucent beauty of her own skin was evident.

The woman in the lilac ball gown was a Cinderella awaiting the arrival of Prince Charming.

Attempting to calm my mother, Daddy told her, "The aunties have seen her, and they are very pleased. This is the way they have kept her in their minds, and they don't even realize that there is anything unusual about her appearance."

Certainly, others who attended Grandmother's visitation and funeral did not live in the past and reacted in various ways. Jack Fletcher, my Dad's first cousin, burst into tears and had to leave the funeral home. He later told us that she looked exactly the way she did when he had run to her for comfort as a little boy. His parents, Marion and Kate Fletcher, were extremely strict, and Jack had been a sensitive child. Aunt Florrie was the one he always ran to when upset, and she never failed to console him and make him feel better.

This experience made me cognizant of the total fallacy inherent in using chronological age as the measure of a person. Because my grandmother moved slowly and wore clothing designed for older women, I had always thought of her, and treated her, as an old woman. As I mustered the courage to approach the casket once more, I became aware of the person she had been all along. It broke my heart.

After taking care of matters in Beaumont, we returned to San Antonio for a non-celebration of Christmas 1944. We were totally unaware of events that would soon transpire and alter our lives greatly.

At the beginning of the war, when Dad and other Uvalde Rock Asphalt employees were frozen to their jobs, their wages had also been frozen. The cost of living had surged upward, and employees were having a hard time making ends meet.

In his job handling company finances, Dad was very much aware of this situation. He had been elated when the board of directors asked him to provide them with the paperwork necessary to apply to have more funds released for employees.

At this time, obtaining permission to alter any "frozen" situation required having political connections. Application forms and other entreaties went all the way to Washington D.C. Dad was sure that the wealthy owners of the company had sufficient political clout, so he looked forward to more realistic wages for himself and the other employees. He worked long hours gathering statistics and formulating a document that would convince the proper bureaucrats to grant the company's request.

In due time, permission to split a generous sum among employees was granted. My father assumed that he would be writing future enhanced paychecks to his fellow employees

In World War II, the entire American public supported the war effort. Patriotism was shown in a multitude of ways, which included working at very low wages in order to perform jobs deemed strategic. So, my father looked forward to being able to hand his coworkers a reward for past service.

The company president walked into his office and handed him a paper showing the amount of each check to be written and to whom it should be made out. As Dad read the paper, he realized that all of his hard work gathering statistics and filling out forms had been nothing but a ruse and cover-up. No employee would receive a larger paycheck. The entire sum of funds granted was to be split between the president of Uvalde Rock Asphalt and members of the board of directors—all very wealthy individuals.

Prior to leaving Dad's office, the president cautioned him, "Don't say anything about this to anyone."

Fuming inside, Dad wrote each check as he had been directed. He then typed out his letter of resignation and carried it, along with the completed checks, into the president's office.

Dad had not previously planned to quit his job, but he took the opportunity to look around for something he could do that would finance his lifelong desire to get into ranching.

⁂

Many changes in the American lifestyle occurred during the war years. Women and ethnic minorities were able to find good jobs in defense industries. Families began migrating from rural settings in order to live where these jobs were located. By moving into cities, countless rural families were able to enjoy living accommodations with electricity and indoor plumbing for the very first time. It was not unusual for heads of households to begin receiving paychecks larger than they had ever visualized. Images of things previously considered out of reach, like home ownership or college educations for their children, no longer seemed impossible to accomplish.

The slow-paced rhythm of 1930s life switched to an upbeat tempo. Servicemen were transferred to parts of the country they had never before seen. Families followed when they could and tried to adjust to a multitude of cultural changes. Wives, left behind when their husbands were sent overseas, took jobs in defense plants. National and regional companies began to transfer employees to other states in order to fill vacancies left by men who had been drafted.

Betty Brent, one of my best friends, and her family were typical examples of individuals who suddenly found themselves uprooted and sent to an unfamiliar environment. For generations, Betty's extended family lived in Lafayette, Louisiana. This was a town where many residents spoke only French and the ambiance hummed with Cajun culture.

"It was a closed society," she once remarked.

After the war began, the Southern Pacific Railroad transferred her father to San Antonio to be the Round House Foreman. Moving west before his wife and family, he discovered that there was no local housing available.

He eventually located one room for rent, so their family of four lived there for three months until a rental house became available.

"The bed was always warm," she said. "Daddy worked at night, so Mother, my sister and I slept in the same bed. When he came home, we got up.

"We cooked on a little gas hotplate and lived on soup and bread for those three months. None of us had ever been farther away from Lafayette than an occasional trip to Baton Rouge."

After leaving a multitude of friends and close relatives behind in Lafayette, Betty Brent and her immediate family were undergoing a similar type of culture shock felt by many uprooted families of that day.

After the beginning of the war, the parade of hungry men who had long beat a path to our front door gradually came to a stop. Opportunities to join a branch of the service or get a job in a defense plant were suddenly open to those who had been unable to find employment.

About the same time, I realized those bedraggled families who scavenged garbage cans on the other side of our back fence had disappeared. I visualized Vivian Jean and her parents living in a comfortable home, wearing clean clothes and sitting at a dining table where they were able to eat from china plates heaped with fresh food.

This was the first time in my life I did not feel deeply touched and saddened on a daily basis by the desperation reaching out from eyes in the alley.

⁕

Mother and I enjoyed having Dad home with us for awhile. Since he was no longer supporting his mother and brother, he had a little financial slack to work with after quitting his job. Traveling mostly by train or bus, he made trips to various parts of the state looking into businesses to buy.

Since Dad's schedule was now flexible, we decided to accept an invitation offered by one of Mother's cousins. "Teer" and Leonard Armour lived in a three-story historic home across from the beach at Rockport. Cousin Teer had often written letters inviting our family to come stay with them.

The Armours lived on the first floor of an impressive Victorian mansion. We were given the entire second floor, with stairs leading to a third floor ballroom from another era. The home's interior walls were covered with imported woven rattan.

In August of 1945, I had just entered my teens. My focus was on getting to wear the daring two-piece red bathing suit I had purchased for our trip to the beach. By today's standards, that suit would be considered extremely modest. Midriff suits, as they were called, had just come into fashion and were beginning to replace the familiar one-piece bathing suit. My new beach attire consisted of a bra-style top and a bottom trimmed with a frilly skirt that fell to mid-thigh.

Normally, the three of us would have been together at the beach, but Mother managed to step off of a curb and sprain her ankle the first hour we were in Rockport. Confined to a bed on the second floor, she endured her pain as we dealt with her extremely hostile mood. Dad diplomatically split his time between staying with her and going to the beach with me.

On August 6, as I collected shells on Rockport's lovely beach, something called "Little Boy" fell from a bomber, named *Enola Gay* for the pilot's mother. Later that day, total strangers gathered in small groups on the beach, asking one another if they had heard the radio reports about the atomic bomb the United States had dropped on Hiroshima, Japan. The bomb had been developed with such great secrecy that, at first, the public did not comprehend exactly what an atomic bomb was or how it differed from other weapons of warfare.

Three days later, August 9, "Fat Man" was dropped on Nagasaki. On August 15, Japan told the world that it would accept unconditional surrender. The rationale behind dropping those two bombs was to bring an immediate end to the war and save many lives on both sides.

However, when the civilian population learned of the true nature of the weapon by watching newsreels at their local theatres, there was a great deal of debate as to whether using such means of warfare could ever be justified. Pictures of the *Hibakusha*, or "bomb-affected people," who had survived the atomic explosions were on every magazine cover and featured in numerous articles. Most of them were civilians, and the ghastly photos were horrifying.

Suddenly, medical science was faced with the urgency of developing ways to treat severe radiation burns as well as other effects caused by radiation. The entire medical field recognized a need to reinvent itself and enter a new, and heretofore unforeseen, era.

Soon after our trip to Rockport, Dad located a Ford-Ferguson tractor and implement dealership that was for sale in El Campo. The town had about ten thousand residents and was not too far from the coastal ranch where he kept his cattle.

The reality my father faced was that American farmers might have to wait a long time for new tractors, since companies who normally manufactured them were at that time making tanks and other vehicles of war. Our country was still at war with Hitler and his European allies, so it could be years before my father received a new tractor to sell.

Another of Dad's predictions, which later came to pass, concerned what he expected the American government to do once the war ended and tractor production resumed. He felt laws would be passed that allowed major contractors to commandeer the new tractors from manufacturers and use them to rebuild Germany, Japan and the countries of our other former enemies. This is exactly what transpired as our American farmers and ranchers begged for tractors to replace their worn-out farm machinery. Newsreels showed pictures of tractors being loaded onto ships with overseas destinations. American tractor dealers, and men who had patriotically farmed with decrepit machinery and no complaints during the duration of the war, could only seethe with anger and remain on waiting lists.

Understanding what he might have to face, Dad located a well-known tractor mechanic and decided to rely on tractor repair and the sale of parts—when they were available. His long-range plan was to build the business until it continually showed a good profit. At that point, he would sell it and use the proceeds to become a full-time rancher.

Dad was already acquiring purebred American Grey Brahman and Hereford cattle to cross-breed for what he considered the perfect herd to thrive on the Texas coast. His herd would feature the beauty and meat quality of the Hereford along with the tick-resistant tough skin of the Brahman.

Dad traveled to Beaumont and took out a business loan from his cousin Jack Fletcher. That, along with his own savings, allowed him to settle into an agricultural area and the style of life he loved.

I was delighted for Dad but realized that Mother was despondent over having to leave her home and the familiar surroundings of southwest Texas. Dad moved into a rooming house in El Campo and, with his open-hearted personality, soon knew everyone in town.

Years of stress and frustration from holding an indoor office job soon melted away, along with the ulcers they had caused. Dad became a hands-on sponsor for FFA students raising farm animals and thrived on being back in an agricultural setting. He also enjoyed joining the Lion's Club and serving as an officer in the Interdenominational Men's Sunday school class. The camaraderie of small-town life was decidedly his cup of tea. I had never seen him so happy.

Mother and I stayed behind to sell the house and let me finish out the 1945-46 school year at Poe Junior High. From the time I was a very young child, Dad had always instructed me to "Take care of Mammy" when he left for work. After his move to El Campo, I learned soon enough that someone had to do just that.

On May 16, 1946, San Antonio had a severe hailstorm that threatened to become a repeat of the storm of March 1935. Once the sky began to get black and the wind howled, Mother totally panicked and "abandoned ship." She ran next door to ride out the storm with the M family while I stayed home to look after things and admire the dramatic weather events. I inherited my enjoyment of a good thunderstorm from my Grandmother Haynes. Obviously, this storm-enjoyment gene skipped a generation.

The hailstorm caused more than $5 million damage in San Antonio. Fortunately, none of that was in our neighborhood. However, Mother and I did have one very near miss during a series of spring storms.

As I sat reading near an open window in the living room, she stood at the kitchen sink, also next to an open window. A horizontal lightning flash suddenly zoomed through our home and narrowly missed both of us. We were stunned statue-like until the thunder that followed awakened us to what had just transpired.

～❈～

The real estate agent Dad had signed with brought over a charming Mexican couple soon after we put our home on the market. They obviously liked what they saw and left with the agent to talk about a possible offer.

As soon as their car pulled away from our curb, next-door neighbor Mrs. M rang our front doorbell. Mother was subjected to a tirade of admonishments for even letting a Mexican family *look* at our home. Didn't she know that having a Mexican family on our block would lower the property value of the M house as well as all of the other homes? How could she do such a thing to her long-time neighbors? How could she subject Harry-Boy to the taunts of his friends that were sure to come when they learned he lived next door to Mexicans?

It was too bad that my father was in another part of Texas. He would have listened politely to this irate woman and then let her know quite firmly, but without being offensive, that he did not share her ethnic values. In fact, I don't believe Mrs. M would have dared bring up the subject in my dad's presence.

Mother listened as her very aggressive and prejudiced neighbor ranted, long and loud, on the subject of class distinctions according to skin color. Finally, she gave in to Mrs. M's demands and promised that she would follow her specific instructions.

With a smug smile, our neighbor lingered on and listened as Mother called the realtor's office and left instructions for her to show our house only to potential buyers who were Caucasian.

Within the week, the real estate agent was back. This time, she brought along a tall, dark-haired woman whom she introduced as "a doctor's wife." The woman roamed around our home and raved about its beauty in an extremely giddy fashion. She sounded like she was describing the Taj Mahal, but her highly exaggerated praise pleased Mother. My parent was elated that her home might be sold to someone with an appreciation of its virtues.

When the two women left, I told Mother, "She's not ever going to move in here. She lives in a much fancier neighborhood. She's pulling your leg!"

A contract was soon offered, which my parents accepted, though it was for less than the Mexican family had been willing to pay. Mother quickly informed Mrs. M that she would soon be living next door to a Caucasian physician.

On the day the moving van arrived, Mrs. M was back at our front door. This time her request was of a very different nature. My grandmother's 19th-century Victrola, which had given me such joy as a small child, was probably one of our most valuable antiques. It was in perfect shape and still capable of playing records from Grandmother's very old collection.

"You will never know how much I have missed Mother Fletcher," Mrs. M told Mother. "Will you please give me that Victrola so I will have something to remember her by?"

I almost choked hearing her speak those words. One thing I was sure of, Mrs. M did not have a sentimental bone in her body. She was all business. On the other hand, family stories of my mother's gullibility were legion.

Our house contained many items that everyone associated with my grandmother. Why had our acquisitive neighbor not asked for an afghan she had crocheted or a footstool she had covered with needlepoint?

Expecting to hear Mother turn her down saying, "I'm sorry, that Victrola means too much for us to part with it," I was stunned when she agreed to give it to Mrs. M. *You're being conned*, I thought. This was another situation our brazen neighbor would not have initiated had my father been present.

Mrs. M commandeered our movers and had them immediately move our beloved musical antique over to her house. Knowing that we were heading for a two-story rental duplex in El Campo may have encouraged my mother to part with what was, after all, a rather large and heavy piece of furniture.

As the moving van pulled away from 736 Kayton Avenue, a group of neighbors gathered around to hug us goodbye before we got into our car and headed east. Some of these same neighbors called us within the next few days with a "Victrola report." It seemed that we had only been gone a few hours before a delivery truck with the name of one of San Antonio's prominent antique stores painted on its sides pulled up in front of the M.'s home. Two men went inside and soon emerged carrying Grandmother's Victrola. They lifted it into the back of the truck and carefully anchored it into place. As the truck drove away, Mrs. M was observed standing at the curb counting her money.

However, as the saying goes, "she got hers." The doctor and his wife never planned to move into our home, although the real estate agent had probably suggested it would be a good idea to pretend they would assume residence when conversing with Mother.

Mrs. Doctor had recognized our house as a profitable piece of rental property in perfect shape. Once the closing papers were signed, she rented it to a Mexican family with seven children.

⁂

The end of both The Great Depression and World War II brought about a multitude of changes, one of which was a rapid decrease in the number of people in our nation who thought and acted in the manner of our prejudiced neighbor, Mrs. M. Another major change was in what the average person expected to do with his or her life.

So many people had seen parts of the United States that they had never seen before, and met people whose ideas differed from their own, that portions of our population were no longer content to stay in an area where, or live in the same manner that, their family had lived for generations. Climate change, severe drought and loss of topsoil, along with high winds blowing black dust storms across the southern Great Plains, had caused a massive migration west, especially during the years 1934-37. After the war ended, servicemen returned and took advantage of their GI Bill of Rights to obtain college educations and buy homes for their families. Unlike the lean Depression years, jobs were plentiful and the economy was booming. A large number of both rural and inner-city dwellers entered into a different lifestyle by settling in newly designed suburbs.

Many servicemen, along with people who worked in the defense industry, became close to individuals who had a skin color different from their own. Their experiences, along with a better educated and more mobile population, pruned twigs, branches and roots from the Tree of

Bigotry. Though it took a long time, people with views like Mrs. M eventually became fewer and farther between. For that, I am thankful.

EPILOGUE

I lost track of most of my childhood friends in San Antonio after our move to El Campo. Still later, we moved to an 1861 plantation-style home on a coastal ranch in Jackson County.

Through mutual friends, I learned that I was a sure loser in the growth-spurt competition with Merry Tom Blue. I heard she grew to be a very tall woman, whereas I stopped growing at a little over five feet. I cannot think of her without wondering if she ever cut her magnificent long hair.

Losing track of Jimmy Tom robbed me of an excellent opportunity to become bilingual, and possibly fluent, in a mystery language. Georgia Lee's absence deprived me of an extremely talented musical collaborator in both classical and hammy performances.

By the time advertising executives invented the slogan "The wet head is dead," Hugh Philipus Jr. and I lived in different parts of our state. Hair products for men and boys changed drastically, and mothers stopped combing syrup-thick hair oil into their son's crowning glory. I never discovered Hugh's true hair color.

I hope my frustrated next door neighbor, Harry-Boy M, grew into an extremely happy and prosperous Harry-Man.

I still enjoy a friendship with Mary Gwen, who lives in Fredericksburg as the wife of a retired Episcopal Priest, and Betty Brent, who is a widow now and resides in her native town, Lafayette, Louisiana. I remember all of those young ones, and many others, with a fond appreciation of time spent together.

END

YESTERDAY'S YOUNG ONES

Those yesterday's young ones
we met on the stair
or trav'ling down back roads
that led everywhere.
Adventures called forth
shine in memories fleeting,
worn snapshots, nostalgic
spontaneous meetings.
First sweethearts and heartaches
were part of our growing.
The paths of our future
we'd no way of knowing.
Are we still those young ones,
still tied to the past
with bright colored heartstring-
connections that last?
Do yesterday's young ones
still live on inside
and whisper their secret?
"Our past has not died."

— Vallie Fletcher Taylor

ABOUT THE AUTHOR

By Vallie Fletcher Taylor

According to historians, I was born in one of the Great Depression's worst years—1932. I certainly recognized signs of poverty and lack when they came into focus, but at home, my family managed to create an ideal environment where reading and learning took top priority.

We were fortunate to live in San Antonio, where we could enjoy repeated visits to the wonderful old buildings erected during the Spanish and Mexican eras. That city whispers historic secrets from so many different cultures into your ear, no matter which direction you turn.

I believe that writing must have been genetically inherited in my case. So many of my ancestors took time to record important events from their lives and pass them on to future generations. I dictated my first stories and poems to my mother before I was introduced to the art of arranging alphabetical magic. Mrs. Niggli, who taught me to play classical music on the violin, begrudgingly put the music to some of my first songs on paper so I would quit playing them and turn to the music she planned for me to perform.

I was a great-grandmother before I ever spoke about what happened to me at age two. The term *near-death experience* was not coined until many decades later. But, that did not keep the aftereffects, which have been identified and studied for the past thirty years, from becoming a part of my life.

Shirley Temple made her first film the year I was born. Her fame convinced an entire generation of young mothers that their child was meant to star in the performing arts. My friends and I were coerced into taking a variety of dance and music classes and cast in strange types of amateur theatrics by the time we bid diapers adieu.

My family moved to the Texas coast when I was in my early teens, which afforded me the long-awaited escape from the life of being on stage as a child violinist. Attending high school in El Campo introduced me to small town life, and I loved it.

A later move gave me the opportunity to experience living in a plantation-style ranch home built in 1861. This place was built on a bluff overlooking Karankawa Bay and provided almost unimaginable pleasure, on a daily basis, for a young woman who loved history.

I am now the proud mother of four and grandmother of seven. At this time, I have two great-grandsons—both totally perfect, of course—and I eagerly await the addition of others.

I have enjoyed careers as a teacher, journalist, seminar producer, bed-and-breakfast operator and owner of a small ranch, where I have the opportunity, peace and quiet to sit and write. I enjoy the company of good friends, delicious food, fine wine and an ever-growing population of eccentric mother cats (whom I serve as midwife) and their kittens.

ABOUT THE ARTISTS

For nearly twenty years, FRANÇOIS THISDALE has worked as an award-winning freelance illustrator, creating images for children's books, news magazines, annual corporate reports, and book covers on behalf of North American and European clients. His trademark multi-textured images are the product of a unique blend of traditional drawing and painting techniques with digital imagery. An experienced musician, he has also composed soundtracks for short films and art exhibits.

CHRIS CARTWRIGHT is a computer artist who uses 3D programs and paint programs to create her works. Although she creates covers for any type of story, her favorites are fantasy, sci-fi and horror. She originally became interested in web design, which she went to school for, but after taking some art classes, found a new passion. Besides Zumaya, Chris has also created covers for *Apex Digest*, Outskirts Press, *Penwomanship*, *Whispers of Wickedness*, *Midnight Street*, *Insidious Reflections* and many other publishers and authors.

   If you are a writer or publisher and are in need of a cover artist or illustrator, you may contact Chris at digitellart@yahoo.com or visit her website at: http://www.digitelldesign.com

Printed in the United States
219317BV00001B/46/P